By Any Means Necessary

A Betrayal of Justice

Rebekah Thonginh Ross

The cases, events, and experiences are true. Though many of the individuals, including some of the child victims, are publicly identified in the media, court transcripts, and published opinions from both the 6th Court of Appeals and the Texas Court of Criminal Appeals, I have chosen to change their names. Others specifically asked to be revealed or gave permission to use their true names. Many of the conversations re-created come directly from court transcripts and other records, while others were re-created from my clear recollection and personal notes. I do not hold any ill will toward the professionals I continue to work with on a daily basis. My intention is to share this story in hopes it will empower others to keep pushing forward and never give up, no matter what it takes.

First Edition, 2019

ISBN-13: 978-1-7338951-0-1

To all those who work tirelessly protecting those who cannot protect themselves. May you continue to have the strength to press onward.

Acknowledgments

This journey and book wouldn't have been possible without the support of my family, friends, and colleagues. The list of those who have supported me in this journey is endless and I could include everyone.

But I must give a special thanks to my husband and children who began this journey with and have had to fend for themselves so I could write.

Thank you to Regina Saucier, Julia Laurence, and my mother for reading and re-reading the drafts.

Thank you to Natalie and Audrey Lauren for living through this with me.

Thank you to my editor, Cherise Papa, for helping a new author pull this book together in three short months.

Thank you to my trial attorney, Pete Schulte, for putting up with over 1000 emails while the case was pending, which later helped me write this book. I know you thought I was insane.

Thank you to Jessica McDonald (formally Jessica Edwards) for sticking with it to get the appeals all the way to the top and for sticking your neck out to hire me, knowing your reputation was on the line.

Thank you to Abigail Spain for not being scared to work with me.

And last but not least, a shout out to my professors, Libby and Robbie, for teaching me everything I needed to know to overturn my conviction.

Contents

Foreword

I am honored and privileged to be alive today and to be on a path that is worth living. This used to not always be the case for me. Rebekah is a lady I met in some of the darkest times of my life. Now looking back, I can see how she is a hero in the lives of my daughter and my own.

I did not always think this way, and for this reason I am speaking up today. While Rebekah's message should show how brave, courageous and strong she is to stand up and go to extreme measures to do what's right to save the lives of others, my message is how Rebekah and people like her, saved my life.

Rebekah and others like her are the reason why I realized I desperately needed to do something different or I was going to die and possibly harm others severely in the process. I made an important decision. One that was life altering. One that determined the course of my life today. Whether I was going to continue on a path of destruction or if I was going to choose a life that has peace and harmony. She helped me choose a better life.

It is this message of recovery that is why I'm alive today. Because of recovery I am no longer afraid of my past, I embrace my mistakes, and take ownership of them so that I might dare to do something different and grow from them. It is a privilege to be here now to send a message of hope. For those who may have had a doubt or been lost or know someone who is lost, don't give up. When you feel like you might not have any strength left, don't give in.

People like Rebekah didn't give up. It's unfortunate that she went through so much in an attempt to do the right thing. I am so thrilled Rebekah was able to come through on the other side. I'm so glad she was able to be the one who did whatever it took to save the lives of our precious children of the world. Glad she poured her heart and soul into saving lives in a world that is so broken. In an environment that was extremely dangerous. For whatever it's worth, I'm grateful for the impact that the ripple effect had on the lives of the parents of the children she had to intervene for. That ripple effect participated in the events that later gave me the life I live today.

Because Rebekah was determined to save my daughter, she ended up saving me. I'm glad to have an opportunity to gain some understanding of what I did to cause her to have to go to such great lengths to find my daughter and bring her to safety. Once I started to understand the depths of my wrongs, I hoped that I would have an opportunity to return the favor and one day maybe pay it forward.

While this might be silly, dangerous, or dumb, I am grateful and willing to utilize this unique opportunity to come forward with my identity in her book for the purpose to share the message of hope and recovery. If I can do it, anyone can do it.

The character in the book, C.J., is me. My real name is disclosed at the back of the book in a brief short story of my recovery and how it relates to this time of my life. I have my identity available for anyone who may have questions about this event or is struggling in recovery. You are not alone.

Chapter 1

December 16, 2011

The door swung open by a single hinge in the early morning darkness, broken down by the Sheriff's deputies. Thick, black plastic covered the windows and made it difficult to see inside. The deputies had already entered and conducted a cursory search of the home for safety reasons. After all, they were armed and protected with bullet proof vests. As an investigator for the Texas Department of Family and Protective Services, or CPS, I wasn't allowed to wear any type of protective gear and carry any type of weapon, even though I was a reserve police officer and carried a concealed handgun license.

"It's clear," Deputy Ridley stated as he exited the residence. I stood on the front porch, chilled by the early morning December air. The judge's court orders authorizing us to enter the residence were in my hand, ready to be executed.

"Okay, let's find out what happened and where they are," I said cautiously.

Deputy Ridley stood over six feet tall with a thick build. He would be a good bodyguard if something went wrong. He nodded in agreement and without another word, we walked into the home, together, to search for a missing, drug exposed, infant. The court orders said I could observe the premises and surroundings where

3

the abuse or neglect may have occurred, and we believed it had occurred in this home.

Adrenaline surged through my body. The house smelled the same as it had two days before when I first visited. I had been trying to find this baby for three days. The ammonia still burned my nose, but now it was mixed with something bitter, something sweet. It wasn't sweet in a good way.

A large barrel, approximately three feet tall and three feet wide, stood upright two feet in front of me, a large biohazard sticker plastered on the front. I had never seen anything like it inside a house. Where could they get something like this?

An old desktop computer sat on a table to the right of the room, with cords, keyboards, and other electronic devices scattered around it. They hung off the table and piled below. I had seen this in other meth houses. There was something about being on methamphetamine that made someone want to take apart everything in the house but never put it back together.

Seven propane torches lay scattered beneath the table, a few upside down. Seven seemed a bit extreme in a house only about 600 square feet. Maybe it wasn't unusual but keeping them and not throwing them away seemed odd. Like they didn't have time to gather them before running.

The table with the computer was the only piece of furniture in the room. There wasn't a single chair, cushion, or any sign there had ever been furniture. A pile of trash lined the left wall with various papers, water bottles, and beer bottles, as if someone had pushed everything into a pile and left it.

Deputy Ridley and I made our way through the front room, almost to the bedroom. Tiny shreds of the morning's first light helped us navigate the gloom. Passing a bathroom to the right, we made it to the middle of the home where the kitchen and bedroom connected. The layout made it impossible to walk through to any other part of the house without going through the kitchen. I considered it a kitchen because it had shelves, a sink, and a refrigerator. It didn't have a stove, something not unusual in small homes or those we investigated. There were no doors or drawers, leaving everything in the tiny kitchen exposed in plain view. I hated kitchens that couldn't close off the junk in the cupboards, but this one didn't have any junk in it. It appeared empty with a few forgotten dishes sitting on the shelves, but I didn't stay and look. My concern wasn't the kitchen. Nothing was in it.

My concern was the room next to the kitchen. It appeared to be the only other room, besides the bathroom, that had a wall separating it from the rest of the house. Two days ago, two individuals had refused to grant me permission to enter but said Mom and baby had possibly stayed in the bedroom, a room they said was always locked.

The door to this room wasn't locked though—it was wide opened. I started to enter the room but stopped short at the sight of the walls and ceiling. The rest of the house had been plain, bland, unappealing, but here it was fascinating, almost nauseating. Black lights hung from the ceiling, and the walls were painted lime green. I had never seen anything like it, and it made me dizzy and disoriented.

"I think this was the fun zone," I joked to Deputy Ridley, who stood with me at the door.

My sense of humor was something the deputies understood and enjoyed. We could banter back and forth with each other, even those of us who weren't friends. I couldn't banter with most of my coworkers. They thought I was cruel and called me Ice Queen. Some of them went as far as nicknaming me Hitler and Satan. I didn't appreciate it, but it wasn't a fight I felt worthy of my time. They thought no one should be able to laugh about the things we saw and had to deal with daily. They didn't understand what I found funny. It wasn't that anything was funny, but humor was the only way I could process what I saw, heard, and read. My coworkers dealt with this line of work by binging on alcohol, smoking cigarettes like chimneys, abusing prescription drugs, and rumors whispered a few used illegal drugs. I didn't do any of those, so I coped by laughing and burying any emotions I couldn't laugh off. My other vices were drinking Diet Mountain Dew and cussing like a sailor. Cussing always let off steam and relieved stress, but I never cussed in front of parents or children. In front of them, I remained professional.

"Yeah, I think I'm getting high just looking at this." Deputy Ridley rubbed his eyes and lowered his head to get his bearings, then laughed at himself and tried not to stumble. What made us sick to our stomachs probably was the ride of your life if you were high. I could only imagine what this room was like for someone stoned out of their mind.

I shook my head, trying to ignore the glowing walls, while I scanned the rest of the room. To my left, by the door, hung a large, metal spring scale, the kind you might see if someone wanted to weigh large quantities. To the right was a dresser with a bottle of prenatal vitamins on top. I walked in for a closer look. It was the clue we needed. If there were prenatals in the house, then we might be in the right place. The missing infant could be nearby.

I grabbed the bottle and spun to show Deputy Ridley, who still stood by the door. Excitement coursed through me. We were on to something. I held up the bottle to speak, but nothing came out of my mouth. The bottle fell from my hand, the rattling of pills echoed as they hit the ground. There in the other corner of the room was a bed. I hadn't seen it when I had first entered the room as my eyes had been affixed to the green walls. Yet when I turned around, there was no mistake. Covering the bed, the headboard, and the walls behind it was blood. Blood was splattered and sprayed; it had dried as it dripped down the walls and pooled on the headboard below.

"It looks like someone was killed in here," I whispered, mostly to myself. I stared in disbelief, partly in shock. Unable to say anything else, I pointed. Too many thoughts raced through my mind for me to articulate.

Deputy Ridley followed my gaze.

"I thought you said we were looking for a baby and its parents. Not a dead body. I didn't even see this when we were clearing the room," he said. His eyes were big. I didn't blame him—I had missed it, too, at first glance. Now we were both trying to comprehend what we saw, what we needed to do next. This was a joint investigation with CPS and law enforcement about a drug-endangered child. We both had our own roles to play in such investigations, but we weren't sure how to proceed. Neither of us had ever faced this before, in this exact scenario.

"I have the court orders," I said, not knowing what else to say. I held the copy out to him, but he shook his head at me. He had already read them and knew what they said. "It's a joint investigation."

I waited.

Fear paralyzed me. For the past three days, I had searched high and low trying to find this family, hoping and praying the baby was alive and well, scared it was already dead. I had only slept when I dozed off in the middle of working. I hadn't touched any of my other cases. I had barely eaten. This case had been everything for three days. My supervisor had helped me, another state employee who worked for a different department, Julia Laurence, had assisted for hours, and we had involved a District Judge, our CPS attorney, and the Sheriff's Department.

"It's a joint investigation," I repeated.

"You're right, it is. Let me call Captain Eve."

"Good idea. I'm calling my supervisor."

I called Natalie and laid out everything we had seen so far. She shared my concern, fearing something had happened to the baby.

Knowing the situation could quickly turn into a complicated legal case, she called Polly Patterson, our CPS attorney. Polly's job was to represent CPS and provide legal advice in our cases. We relied on her advice to ensure we were following proper procedures and not overstepping our authority. She would also advise us on any additional steps we needed to secure a legal case if we had to take parents to court. We relied on her heavily, often contacting her before Natalie's direct supervisor, Audrey Lauren. In this case, after being told about the blood in the room and the missing child, her advice was clear.

"I just got off the phone with Polly. She said do whatever it takes to find the baby. You have the court orders and law enforcement with you," Natalie said. It was the same thing Polly had told me the day before.

Polly had drafted the petition and order I held in my hand; she knew it was signed by a district judge, and she knew we had authority from the order but also exigent circumstances.

Deputy Ridley got off the phone with his captain and gave me a look. The look said it all. We didn't know what was about to happen. I still didn't know exactly what I could or couldn't do. Neither of us, even with all our training combined, had faced anything like this before.

Standing in the room, court orders in hand, blood splattered along the walls, and an infant nowhere to be found, we made a choice. The consequences of the choice we made together would cause me and my supervisor to endure a six-year legal battle with appeals that would reach the Texas Court of Criminal Appeals, the highest criminal court in Texas. But it was the only choice we could make. And it was the choice we believed the court orders, both of our supervisors, and our CPS attorney, fully authorized.

"We have to find the baby," I said. Deputy Ridley nodded.

"Let's get to it," he replied.

We would do whatever was necessary to find the baby.

Chapter 2

December 16, 2011

"Help me lift the mattress. Let me see what's under it," I said to Deputy Ridley. If someone wanted to hide something, they would put it under the mattress.

Worn papers were scattered beneath the mattress, some stained with blood around the edges. I hoped they contained the clues we needed to find the parents and baby. Even if the paperwork only confirmed who had actually lived at this house, it would help piece evidence together. I combed through receipts, pink forms with faded ink, and crumpled lined paper until I saw *Mary and John* on a folded hospital bill. These were the two individuals Natalie and I had spoken with two days before, the same ones who had told me they didn't live in the house, hadn't seen the baby, and the parents had *just left* right before we had arrived. This was proof they had lied and proof no one in the family would cooperate with the investigation. It was the epitome of interfering with an investigation, a criminal offense in Texas.

"You can set it down," I told Deputy Ridley as I backed out from under it. He lowered the massive mattress and wiped his hands on his pants. "Let's look in the dressers and see if there's any sign this baby was born and born alive. See if there's anything with names or addresses that will help us figure out where they went."

While we searched, Deputy Ridley called Captain Eve again, keeping her informed of the situation. I called Natalie back and told her about Mary and John. She relayed it to Polly, giving her a constant update in case this became an emergency removal.

"What are you guys doing in here?"

I snapped my head around, startled by Justine Jacobson's voice as she entered the room. I had completely forgotten she was with me. Even though she was in a different unit and under a different supervisor, she worked in the same building as me. I had asked her to help because she had worked a past case on the same mother and would recognize her if we found her. Justine had agreed to help with the one condition: she would drive. She wanted to claim mileage since the State made us use our personal vehicles for work. When Deputy Ridley and I had entered the residence, she had stayed outside, for whatever the reason, and was completely unaware of the situation until she finally joined us.

"Where have you been?" I asked, almost snapping at her. Now that I had remembered she was with me, I didn't care if she was just along for the ride or not, I needed real help. "Take pictures. Document everything. There's blood there, there, and there." I pointed to each thing I needed documented as if she couldn't see what we were seeing. "Get the headboard, the wall, the floor, get it all."

I still didn't know if we were looking at a crime scene or a terrible birth. The report I was assigned three days before alleged this baby had been born at home, without medical care, to drug-addicted parents. But I had never seen a birth this bloody. Besides having had three of my own children, I had helped deliver my younger brother and sister when I was a teenager, and I had training as a midwife. A natural, uncomplicated childbirth didn't leave behind this much blood.

Justine huffed and rolled her eyes. I gaped, shocked at her response. Deputy Ridley wasn't taking pictures—he was digging through drawers. If this was a crime scene, we were contaminating it as we trampled about, searching frantically. We were unprepared to handle a crime scene, but Deputy Ridley and I could search for evidence of the baby while Justine took pictures. It would preserve the evidence and clues. If the baby was dead, we would have pictures of the scene. If the baby was found alive, we would have pictures for court if this turned into a removal. We didn't know for certain if Mom and Dad were really using illegal drugs, as the report alleged. If they were, we would need to determine how the child was affected. Pictures were vital.

"I really don't see why we need to do this. It doesn't look like the baby is here to me. I think we just need to leave. And I'm hungry. This wasn't supposed to have taken this long," she said.

Somehow, in the five seconds of coming inside of the house, with blood sprayed everywhere in the room, and not trying to look, Justine had determined the baby wasn't here. Evidently, at no point in any of her training, was she ever taught to take pictures, look for evidence, or simply investigate a case. She knew we had court orders. She had seen them, and I read them aloud while she drove to the residence. She knew they said we were to observe the premises or immediate surroundings where the child was located or where the alleged abuse or neglect occurred, by any means necessary. She knew the deputies had authorization to break down the door if no one answered it. I didn't understand why she was now acting like we should just give up and leave.

"How do we know if the baby is or isn't here if we don't look for it?" I asked her.

I wanted to slap her in the face, maybe knock some sense into her. She had worked child deaths before. Deaths that occurred on her watch. Deaths that could have been prevented had she made timely contact with the family or worked a bit harder. Her supervisor, Rachel, had removed a child and never noted in the paperwork he was suicidal. He hanged himself immediately after being placed in foster care, something that could have been prevented had the foster placement known he had threatened suicide. She only received a slap on the wrist for leaving out critical documentation. It was the type of carelessness I didn't want to perpetuate. I didn't want a preventable death on my conscience.

"Look," I said, trying to gather my composure. "Get the camera and take pictures. Deputy Ridley and I will look and see if we can find the baby or any clue of where the baby might be. As of right now, I don't know which house we should even try next if we can't find it here."

She argued again and complained about hunger.

"Justine, do you remember the mom who cut off her baby's arms and legs? Or the mom who stashed her child under the washing machine? Or the one that stashed the body in a shoebox in the closet? Do you think that just happens in the big city and we couldn't possibly be standing in the same situation? You know the history in this case. You removed mom's last kid because of her inability to stop using drugs and the dangers it was to the child. There's too much blood for this to be a normal birth. I don't want to be the one who just walks away and doesn't look hard enough to find this baby." We had only been inside the house a couple of minutes. Explaining to her what I thought was common sense for a reasonable person was wasting precious time.

"Fine, I'll take pictures," she huffed while backing away from me. She fumbled with the camera, finally taking out her cell phone to use instead, and started snapping pictures.

I searched the taller dresser since Deputy Ridley had started with the longer one. The bottom drawer was already half way pulled out, allowing me to see the items inside before opening the drawer the rest of the way. A pack of unopened diapers waited in front. Diapers were a good thing to find with a new baby, but unopened diapers weren't common in newborn cases. I gritted my teeth, pulling out unopened socks, onesies, outfits with tags, and a couple of unused receiving blankets. I opened the next drawer. It was empty. The next one was empty, too. They were all empty. Why would they take everything except for the newborn clothes and diapers if this baby was still alive?

"Have you found anything?" I asked Deputy Ridley. He was still going through the other dresser, opening drawer after drawer.

"Nothing but some socks and a couple of undershirts." He held them up. Adult size. "It looks like someone left in a hurry, but here's a journal or something on top of the dresser." He picked it up, glancing through it. I joined him, interested. What he called a journal was a notebook with numbers written in columns. After twenty or so figures on each column was the word *bust*.

"Okay, I took pictures of everything… What is that?" Justine entered the bedroom again, walking up behind us. She pointed to the journal.

"I don't know. Take pictures of it though," I said. Deputy Ridley placed it back on the dresser and Justine paged through it before taking the pictures.

"What is this? Is it how much they were selling a day and when they got busted?" she asked.

I shrugged. I had other priorities on my mind and wasn't paying much attention to her.

"I've walked through the house, looked through everything, and took pictures of everything else," she said while I continued to scan the room, looking for anything we might have missed.

A small calendar hung across the room, nearly the same lime color as the wall next to it. I hadn't seen it before, probably because of the blood on the walls. I stepped closer for a better look.

Daisy. Baby girl born at home. 5:44 a.m.

The small note was barely legible, but it confirmed the baby was born at home and it was a little girl. It left us no other clues.

Nothing had ever prepared me for a case like this. I didn't know what I was in the middle of.

"Daisy," I whispered. "What happened to you?"

Chapter 3

December 16, 2011

Worry churned in my stomach. The evidence verified the baby girl's birth, but it didn't tell us where she was. The court orders authorized us to search seven houses, though we probably didn't have time to search all seven if she was dying. My gut told me the family was watching us from afar, bouncing from house to house, like a game of cat and mouse. They had always been one step ahead of me somehow. If we searched each individual home, one by one, the family could easily move from house to house with a simple phone call to each other informing them of where we had been.

"What do you want to do next?" Deputy Ridley asked me, still putting me in the lead.

"We need to figure out which house to hit next before the family figures it out. Otherwise, we'll just be chasing our tails in a game of cat and mouse."

Justine, Deputy Ridley, and I left the house and joined the other deputies. We needed to work together and come up with a plan.

"I think I've ruled out the other residences inside the county," came Captain Eve's voice. "I've put calls into dispatch to get service calls. The other residence in the county is probably the most unlikely place they would have gone. I think you need to call Greenville PD and have them assist you with the homes inside of the city limits first." Her cell rang interrupted her, and she left to take the call.

"So, I guess Greenville PD takes over from here," Deputy Ridley said.

Justine paged through the orders to pinpoint the other addresses.

"Yeah, I guess so," I said, preoccupied with formulating the next plan.

"You know, I just need to tell you something, Rebekah," Deputy Ridley said.

I eyed him, wondering what he was about to say. I realized for the first time he towered over me.

"You work under Natalie, right?"

I nodded.

"I just want you to know if you and Natalie ever need anything, anything at all, all you have to do is call. I trust you, and her, and anyone that works under her. You guys aren't like that other group at all."

I didn't understand what he meant by "that other group."

"Who's the supervisor in the other group?" he asked.

"You mean Rachel?" I asked.

"Yeah, Rachel. I went out with her and that other girl," he paused, thinking. "That other girl, she's got a loud mouth, bossy, I think her name starts with an E or something. Like Erin or something."

"Ester Franklin?" I asked.

"Yeah, her." Frustration and disgust pinched his face. "That's the one. I went out with her and Rachel the other day to a house. They told me they had all the paperwork they needed, and everything was on the up and up. They seemed fishy about something, but I didn't think much of it. We got into the middle of everything, they were trying to remove, and I find out they lied to me and didn't have court orders or permission to even enter the house. I could've lost my job over the whole mess. I won't ever help them again. You and Natalie have always had your ducks in a row and your investigation into this case is amazing. I read the affidavit you wrote. You really did your homework. Anything, anything at all you need, you call me. Any time. I mean that."

It was the nicest compliment I had heard in a long time. Smiling, I wanted to thank him and tell him to shut up. He must not have known Justine, who was right next to me, worked under Rachel. She glowered at him, irritated.

Before I could respond, Captain Eve returned, breathless and tense. Her urgency to move quickly matched my racing heart. We had spent far too long outside in the yard, trying to nail down the plan of where to search next.

"I just confirmed with someone who's been to the other residence outside the city limits out. They also think the residences inside of the city limits would be a much better bet." She waved at the other deputies, signaling for them to leave. "Call Greenville PD if you need to. We'll be available today if you have to come back here."

I trusted her judgment. The Sheriff's Department worked the county enough to know where to suspect something might occur and where it probably wouldn't. Everyone nodded, some parting with a few "see you at breakfasts," and then departed as Justine and I continued our search without them.

"Does he know I work for Rachel?" Justine asked as we drove to the next location, a house where I thought someone might tell the truth. I didn't answer and she continued, "Then again, Rachel pulls some really shady stuff. I remember when she wanted us to search a house just because it involved someone she knew, and she wanted to know if she could use something in some custody case she had. And Ester just plain lies. Ester was lying to a client the other day, right to her face. Rachel won't stand up to her and lets her get away with anything because she's scared of her. They give us all a bad name."

I didn't know how to respond, so I didn't say anything at all. This woman had just refused to take pictures and wanted to go eat breakfast rather than search for the baby. Now she was complaining about her supervisor and our bully coworker?

"I want to go Tracy Perez's house," I said, changing the subject. "She's the reporter in the case. Originally, she told me she didn't know where the family was staying, but I swear she's hiding something. She's the one who told me not to come out here alone, that the family wouldn't cooperate, and to bring law enforcement. Alison has an open case on her, and I think it's why Tracy won't speak. I think I can make her talk though if she knows we have court orders."

"Do we want to call Greenville PD for this one?" Justine asked.

"Not yet. Tracy will speak to me. If she doesn't know where the family is, I think she'll know who does. She's hiding something for sure. If I can convince her the information won't be used against her in her open case, then I think she'll talk."

The truth was, nothing she could spill about the missing baby had anything to do with the CPS case she had open with Alison Hayes. I had linked Tracy to a drug ring in town, and I knew she had lied to Alison about which boyfriend or husband was living with her. I also knew they were dealing cocaine. Alison didn't want to hear it and didn't follow Natalie's instructions to close the case, so she was just sitting on it. My concern was a missing infant. I didn't care about anything else at this point.

A tan truck was parked on the road in front of Tracy's house—someone was home. I gathered the orders as Justine parked behind the truck. As I climbed out of the car, she waved me on.

"I'm going to stay out here and smoke and call Rachel and tell her what we're doing," she said.

I didn't care. It would easier for me to get my point across with Tracy if I didn't have someone standing behind me questioning me. I banged on the front door while Justine made her phone call. She left the window down, and I heard the whole call as I waited for someone to answer the door.

"We didn't find the baby at the other house. Rebekah thinks this person knows where the baby hiding so she's going to see if she'll tell her." It was the fastest report I had heard her give.

"Can I help you?" An older woman opened the door, her voice tired. I had spoken to her the previous day, but I couldn't remember her name. She had been helpful, and I suspected she would be helpful today as well.

"Hi, I'm Rebekah. We spoke yesterday. Is Tracy home?"

"No, she's still at work."

Tracy worked nights, or at least she claimed she did.

"That's okay. I'll wait for her. Can I come in? I'll explain what's going on and maybe you can call her for me? We have these court orders to go into these seven other homes and she owns some of them. I'd like to talk to her first." I handed her a copy of the orders.

"Come in. Please excuse the mess. I'll call Tracy." She opened the door wider and let me in.

I chuckled at the *mess*. This house was the opposite of the others had I visited for work, especially the last one. It was kept neat and clean, everything in its place. The bedroom door to my left was cracked open, and a man crawled out of bed. He stumbled forward to close the door, making eye contact with me. It was the same man I had told Alison about: Tracy's boyfriend, the dealer, the one she stayed with when she and her husband had problems. He nodded in acknowledgment and I responded in turn as he closed the door. He knew I knew, and I didn't care.

"Your name is Rosa, right?" I asked the woman. She stayed with the family due to Tracy's schedule and helped clean the house and get the kids to and from school.

"Yes, it's Rosa. Have a seat. I'm calling Tracy," she said and started dialing as Justine entered.

She watched me wait on the couch, confused.

"She's calling Tracy," I explained. Rosa glanced at Justine. "She's with me, she just had to smoke outside."

"Oh, okay. I'm going to step into the hall," Rosa replied as she left. I waited patiently, trying to listen to the conversation.

"You need to get home. She's got a warrant in her hand. She's looking for the baby. I didn't have a choice, the warrant says she can come in. I know the baby's not here, I don't know where it is, but it says she gets to search the house. She's not going to believe me. You need to come home right now. Okay, okay, okay. Bye."

Rosa returned, attempting to look in control, but I could tell she was frazzled. It sounded like the baby really wasn't here, but Tracy knew where the baby was. Rosa didn't know, and she had referred to the baby as an *it*, which led me to believe she had never seen the baby. She sat in the rocking chair by us, remaining upright and stiff, her eyes darting between Justine and me.

"So, you're looking for C.J. and Nathan," she said.

"Yes, yes we are. Just like that order says we are," I replied. "Mostly, I'm scared the baby is hurt or injured or even dead. Have you ever seen her?" I hoped this would jog something in her.

She shook her head. "I don't know much about that side of the family. I just know that lady was pregnant, then I heard a rumor she wasn't pregnant anymore. I don't know what's going on."

We sat in an uncomfortable silence for several minutes until Tracy flew through the front door. All three of us jumped out of our seats, startled. Tracy grimaced.

"Hi again," she said. She stood about five inches taller than me and glared down her nose at me. "I told you everything I knew.

I'm not sure what else I can help you with." She heaved, sweat glistening on her brow and in the roots of her hair—she must have full on sprinted home.

"I know you did. And we went out to the house. Funny thing was, the house looked like it had been cleaned out in a hurry. Almost like someone told them we were coming," I said, trying to make her understand I thought she had warned them.

"I didn't tell them anything. I don't even know where they are or that you guys were coming. I didn't know you would be out there this early," she said. "I've never seen the baby. I have no idea where it is, how it's doing, or what they did with it."

"Okay, thank you for your time," Justine said. She stood next to me, close enough for me to elbow her in the arm. I wasn't finished with Tracy, but I was worried Justine thought we were finished and ready to walk away.

I knew Tracy was lying.

"Tracy, I don't have any intention of getting you in trouble. I understand you kicked your husband out after Alison investigated you," I said.

"I know. I did. He's not here anymore. Alison said she'd close the case if he left and he did. You can look around, he's not here," she quickly offered, her face expressionless.

I didn't have time to keep going back and forth. Time was ticking and we had wasted too much time waiting for her to get home and when we were formulating a plan with the deputies at the first house. It was time to get information.

"Tracy," I began in a calm but clear voice. "I'm done playing games. I know you kicked out your husband. Problem is, your boyfriend is in the room right there and he's a dealer. You know it, I know it, and half the town knows it. He's worse than your husband. And you know what? That's something you have to deal with between you and Alison and whatever happens in your case." Tracy kept quiet, thinking. "I just need to find the baby. I need to know she's okay and healthy. Or I need to know what happened to her. That's what I'm after. If you saw what I saw in that house this morning, you'd be scared to death something happened."

"I don't know where they are. I don't even know if they have the baby with them," Tracy started again. "Someone from CPS was supposed to adopt the baby. They had an attorney. I don't know if it happened. I don't know."

This was the first I had heard about someone in CPS adopting the baby.

"Someone works for CPS and has been telling us he'll adopt the baby and to just tell you so you wouldn't keep looking."

"Someone works for CPS and is telling you to say this? And they know where the baby is?" I couldn't believe what I was hearing. I glanced at Justine, complete shock and disbelief written all over her face.

Someone was getting into my case, reading the documentation, and feeding it back to the family, keeping them one step ahead of me. This was why it had been so hard to find them.

"Yes, he doesn't work here, not in this county, but he works for CPS in Texas. He knows everything you've done on the case. He keeps telling us what to tell you if you found us." Tracy didn't sound confident anymore, as if she realized she had said too much.

"We'll deal with whoever this worker is later. I will figure out who it is, but I won't mention you said anything. Right now, though, I need to find the baby. It's her life that could be in danger and I need to find her." I handed Tracy a new copy of the court orders. Thankfully, our previous CPS attorney had taught me to make at least ten copies in case I ran into multiple people when looking for someone.

"These orders authorize us to take the police with us to every single address listed on this page." I flipped to the second page and pointed to the paragraph with the multiple addresses listed. "The police can break down every single door at those addresses if they need to. We are authorized to enter every single one of them. In fact, I am ordered to do whatever is necessary to find the baby. Tracy, I know some of these residences are rent homes. I don't want to disturb your renters or ruin your business or make you repair the doors. They don't need to know your business. I just want to make sure the baby is okay. That's all. I need to find the baby." I waited, watching Tracy's face for any sign she was ready to tell me where the family was hiding or what happened to the baby. "I just need you to point to the right address. Just point. You don't even have to say anything.

She pointed to an address with her left hand. It was another one I had tried to contact before getting the orders, one that was listed on the tax records. No one had opened the door and the house had looked abandoned.

"Are you sure?" I asked her.

"Yes, that's where my husband is staying. They're with him. At least that's what he said right before I got here today," she mumbled. "I don't know if they're still there."

"Thank you. Tracy, please do not call anyone. Not the CPS worker helping hide them, not your husband, not anyone. No one. We need to find the baby. You're the only one who knows where we're headed. I'm not documenting it until after we're done so no one else can find out."

She nodded. "I swear I won't say anything, but please don't tell them I told you."

"I don't even have to tell them how I figured it out. The address is listed right here on the paperwork. It'll be like it just happened to be the next house we tried." I tried to reassure her, thankful for her help but still suspicious she wasn't being truthful.

Justine and I gathered our things and left immediately. I was afraid the family would run again, and Tracy didn't know if Daisy was with them. Plus, we had this CPS worker, someone related to this family, feeding them information. We would have to deal with that issue later. Right now, I needed to find Daisy.

Chapter 4

December 16, 2011

Justine didn't drive as slow as Alison, but my goodness, let's just get to the house. I tapped my fingers on the armrest, wishing I had drove, while she took her time on the road. Time stood still despite the subdivisions passing by and early morning commuters starting their day.

We approached the house and Justine slowed down. She asked, "Do you want me to stop?"

"No, just drive by slowly so I can get a good look of what's around."

There were too many unknowns to know if the house was safe. There could possibly be at least five adults ready to bolt if Mary and John, Tracy's husband, and C.J. and Nathan were all there. They could all be on drugs, higher than kites. There could be other visitors. Hopefully the baby was there in the middle of it all.

"The car's there. Look. That's the car that was at the house a couple days ago. It belongs to Mary and John. They're here. They lied to me at the other house." I pointed to a silver car parked in the yard next to the tiny, tan home. The broken windows and missing siding made the home look abandoned.

"Do you want to call Greenville PD?" she asked.

I glanced at the time. It was 6:45 a.m., just after shift change, which meant they wouldn't be ready to help for a while. Greenville PD, though always willing to help us, would need to be briefed and then organize a team to help us. We typically worked with the detectives and they weren't on shift yet, so any new officers would need additional explanations of how to work with CPS. The family could take off again as we waited. I didn't know how long Tracy could hold out from tipping them off.

"No, it's going to take too long."

"How about we call Kenderick," she suggested.

Surprised, I glanced at the clock again. Usually Kenderick Stinson never worked before 10:00 a.m. "Why is Kenderick working this early?"

"He's eating breakfast at Donna's."

Justine's attitude made sense. She wanted to leave to eat breakfast with Kenderick.

"Sure, let's see if he'll help," I said.

Kenderick had his moments when he wasn't lazy. He was a special investigator, an SI, which meant he had law enforcement background. SIs were specially trained in areas the other investigators might not be. I was regularly asked why I wasn't a special investigator since I also had a law enforcement background. The answer was always easy: there wasn't an opening. The position paid more than regular investigators, they didn't have to carry their own workload, and they rarely, if ever, worked past 5:00 p.m. Kenderick always said it was the best gig in town, which must have been true because there was never an open position to apply to.

Justine made the call. Kenderick complained we were interrupting his breakfast, but she talked him into helping anyway. He wanted us to pick him up at the office so we could take one car. Since the office was only a few blocks away, I agreed.

My stomach churned the entire drive—the family would surely leave while no one watched the house.

Kenderick jumped into the car as we pulled into the parking lot, and we darted back to the house. I felt like I was holding my breath the entire drive back, and I jumped out of the car as soon as Justine pulled up to the house. Justine and Kenderick hurried behind me. The silver car was still parked in the yard and nothing appeared disturbed outside.

I ran up the steps and banged on the front door. Stepping to the side, I made sure to allow enough room between me and door. I didn't need someone barreling out and knocking me over with the door. Nor did I want anyone reaching out to stab me or pull a gun on me. It had happened before, and I had no desire for it to happen again.

An eternity passed as I waited at the door. Without law enforcement, no one could legally break down the door. CPS wasn't allowed to do it on their own. Kenderick stepped to the left and watched the side of the house. I left the porch and checked the right side. If someone tried to run out the back door, we would see them. There wasn't a fence to jump or any type of shrubbery to use for cover. I asked Justine to take my place so I could bang on the door again. The door muffled movement from inside, but no one opened it.

This was taking too long. We needed law enforcement. As I pulled out my phone, a female opened the door just enough for her to squeeze through. She slammed it behind her and raced passed down the stairs.

"Hold on," I yelled as I tore after her. Kenderick was already briskly walking toward her.

She looked like she had just woken up. Her hair was messy and her makeup smeared, but she had a purse on her shoulder as if she was ready to leave and we hadn't just spooked her out of bed.

"Mary. Hey, stop. Remember me? We met the other day at the other house?" I asked as she raced to her car.

"Yeah, I remember you. No one is here. I was just leaving."

I caught up with her, stopping her from getting into the car and handed her a copy of the orders. "That's what you said before. We have court orders allowing us to enter the residence by any means necessary. Like I told you before, we have an open investigation and we need to see if the baby is okay. These orders authorize us to come in and search for the baby. It would be easier if you let us in, but we can call law enforcement if you prefer. They can break down the door."

I watched while she read the papers, flipping each page. Her eyes looked glossy, making it impossible to tell if she was reading them or not. Either way, I gave her time to review them.

"The baby isn't here. We already have someone in the system who's going to adopt it. The paperwork is already started."

Did everyone know about the CPS worker who was going to adopt? I asked, "Have you seen the baby?"

"Well, no, but I know it's going to be adopted. Our cousin works for CPS and he told us to tell you all that. He'll adopt the baby. That way you can just close the case and leave," she said as if that was all it would take.

"I'll find out more about this adoption thing after I see the baby. Are you going to open the door, or do we have to call law enforcement and have them break it down?"

She glared at me, at Kenderick, at Justine, and then back at me. I wasn't playing. I wasn't smiling. I knew the baby was in that house, in whatever condition she was in, and I was not going away until I knew if she was okay. She saw the look on my face, turned around, stomped up the stairs, and opened the door.

"They have a warrant to search the house for the baby and C.J. I told them Mr. Perez is in the bathroom taking a shower," she lied, yelling as loud as humanly possible as soon as the door was opened. Warning someone.

The three of us quickly entered the residence. It looked as abandoned on the inside as it did the outside. The only furniture in the living room was a toilet. The kitchen appeared to be on the right of us and rooms with closed doors to the left and in front of us.

Tracy's husband, Mr. Perez, must not have heard the announcement about him showering. He opened the door in front of us and walked out, fully clothed, and dry.

"They have a warrant to search for the baby," Mary said again, this time handing him the court orders.

He glanced at them and shrugged his shoulders. "Then do what you need to do."

I brushed past him, heading for the room he had just exited. I stopped short of the door frame, gawking at the ground about three feet beneath the house. There wasn't a floor in the room except for a small piece by the sink. I had no idea if he had crawled up from under the house or if he had balanced on the tiny floor's ledge. There wasn't anywhere else to be in there.

Had the family taken off through the floor under the house? It's what I would have done if I was on the run.

"The baby better not be under the house," I yelled to Mr. Perez. "And you better not have let them take off under it."

"The baby isn't under the house," he said.

For some reason, I believed him. He had responded too seriously and too quickly to have put much thought into it.

I opened the door to the left. John, Mary's husband, slept alone on a messy bed. The bed was nearly the size of the entire room, leaving me at the doorway.

"John, wake up," I shouted. He didn't flinch. "Wake up." I shook the bed with my foot, not wanting to get too close. If he was on drugs, he could react violently. "Where's the baby?"

"I don't know. I just moved here. I'm not involved in this. They have some family member adopting it," he said. He rolled over and passed out cold again.

I left him to sleep and walked toward the kitchen. Justine still stood in the middle of the living room, next to the toilet. Kenderick was in the kitchen, searching through a purse laying on the ground. I had no idea whose purse it was, but next to it was a pile of blankets, a pile of adult clothes, and a diaper bag. The kitchen was rather tight, with a small round table to the right to the pile of clothes and a crock pot on the counter to the left. Closed cupboards and drawers throughout kept smaller items and evidence hidden.

Rustling came from the back area of the kitchen. A half wall hid our view to whatever or whoever was back there. Kenderick popped his head up and we watched for movement.

"Come out of there," Kenderick yelled. The yell was enough to make anyone jump out of their skin. The rustling stopped. Justine joined us in the kitchen and started asking whose stuff was on the floor when Kenderick yelled again. "Come out of there right now."

"C.J.," I shouted. "We know it's you. Come out." I hoped saying it nicer might help her come out on her own.

A small door opened, having been hidden from us by the wall, revealing a small closet. Piles of junk, cardboard boxes, trash bags, empty bottles, and paper fell out of the closet onto the floor. The junk shifted around as if someone had hidden beneath it.

"C.J., come on," I called again.

A petite woman emerged, crawling over everything that had fallen. She wore a thin t-shirt, a pair of jeans, and had bright pink hair. As she crawled over the pile surrounding her, more boxes and trash bags were pushed out of the way, revealing an infant carrier. She pulled the carrier out from under the bags and boxes. Holding it next to her, she turned so we couldn't see inside. I wanted to snatch it out of her hand, wanted to see if the baby was inside, wanted to check if the baby was alive. She was too far away for me to reach the carrier, so I waited, agitation tingling along my skin.

As she fumbled her way through the pile of junk, a tiny white leg with a tiny, little foot stuck out from the bottom of the carrier.

"Is she alive?" I asked. The words were harsher and stronger than I had intended. They startled her.

"Oh yes, she's alive. She's just sleeping," C.J. said.

She finished climbing through the pile and approached us, crying. She knew it was over. I reached into the carrier and touched the baby girl's chest. She was warm, alive. Her body shifted when she felt my hand. She was the tiniest baby I had ever seen in person, clearly malnourished. She wore only a diaper and had a shoe string tied around her umbilical cord.

"My name is Rebekah. I've been looking for you." I tried to be kind—it is always hard, no matter the circumstances, for a parent to know CPS might take their child. Even for parents who hadn't done anything wrong and understood their child wouldn't be removed, it was nerve wracking to be questioned by CPS. I always wanted to follow the golden rule, to treat the parents the same as I wanted to be treated.

"I know. I heard. I really thought she'd be adopted by our cousin. He works for CPS. I thought he had taken care of this," she said. Tears were flowing down her cheeks.

"Do you remember Justine?" I asked, pointing to Justine. I needed C.J. to calm down so we could talk about what had happened. This wasn't a fun situation for anyone. I had spent the last three days looking for them and they had spent the last three days on the run. Everyone was tired and we had a lot of work ahead of us.

"Hey there, I remember you," C.J. said nodding toward Justine, who smiled back.

Her husband was still missing.

"Where's Nathan?" I asked.

C.J. called for him, telling him to come out. He was hiding in the same area C.J. had been, using the same trash bags and boxes to hide behind. He was infuriated. Where C.J. was trying to be kind, Nathan looked like he wanted to kill us. We needed to leave and go to the office where it would be safer.

"C.J., Nathan, we have court orders that authorize us to interview you guys and see the baby. Here's a copy. Do you mind if we go to the office and talk some more?" I asked.

"Yes, I'll come with you to the office," C.J. agreed.

"Like hell we will." Nathan jumped in. "We aren't going anywhere."

"You're going, whether you want to or not," Kenderick snapped. He wasn't going to play. I was glad he came. His six-foot-plus frame and large build was intimidating to most people, but Nathan wasn't backing down.

"Let's just go with them. We know this is over," C.J. coaxed her husband. "We can follow them to the office with the baby."

Bad idea. Even if C.J. was cooperative, her husband wasn't. Letting them drive themselves in their own car would be risking them taking off.

I quickly called Natalie, who got permission from Audrey to allow us to transport the baby in Justine's car. C.J. convinced Nathan to let the baby ride with us and gave me the infant seat. I buckled it in Justine's back seat, checking on Daisy. She wasn't moving much or responding. I placed my hand on her chest, startling her. Her breathing was rapid. C.J. stood next to me, watching in concern.

"I've got her buckled in," I told her. "We're only a couple of blocks from the office."

C.J. nodded and asked her husband to hurry along. Justine started the car, Kenderick jumping into the passenger side. I slid into the back, next to the car seat. Daisy started to cry, a small whimper at first. Within seconds she screamed the highest pitched, terrorizing scream I had ever heard. She tried to pull her legs up to chest and tighten down her body. It wasn't the scream of a regular infant. It was deafening.

The screaming meant only one thing. We arrived at the office and pulled into the parking lot the same time as C.J. and Nathan. C.J. scrambled out of her car as I was opening my door—she could hear her daughter's painful screams.

"C.J.," I asked, hoping she would tell me the truth. "Why is she screaming like this?"

I knew the answer, but I didn't want to hear it. The hairs on the back of my neck stood up as I tried to get the baby out of the car seat. Nothing was soothing her. "You hear the way she sounds, right?" I needed to know how C.J. would respond.

"Yes, I know. I've been breastfeeding her. She's about five days old. I've breastfed her from the start." Once again, tears streamed down her cheeks.

"And?"

"And I got high with cocaine while nursing her. This is the first time she won't have any. I used it all during my pregnancy. Meth, K2, alcohol, marijuana, and little bit of everything. Please help her. Please help my daughter."

Since conception and during her short five days since taking her first breath, all Daisy knew was addiction. The pain of withdrawal would have started sooner, but her mother had continued to feed her cocaine through breastmilk. Today would be the first time Daisy experienced the torture and unrelenting pain of withdrawing from the multitude of drugs forced into her system, by no choice of her own. Her tiny body would go through tremors, seizures, vomiting, deafening high-pitched screaming, uncontrollable crying, and muscle tension that would make it next to impossible to hold and console her. Whether or not she lived would depend on doctors and her ability to keep fighting.

Chapter 5

March 2012

Sgt. Watson sat on the couch in Natalie's office, waiting for us to finish typing an affidavit requesting a Writ of Attachment. A Writ was the order needed for law enforcement to take possession of a child. Natalie was on the phone with our attorney, as always, giving her a rundown of everything that had occurred over the past two days.

"Night Intake went out and put a safety plan in place. Dad promised to move out of the house and leave the children with Grandma. He was positive for methamphetamines. We went out there this morning to follow up and Grandma said Dad went back to the house and wouldn't leave. She can't get him out and he's refusing to follow the plan. He seems high, possibly tweaking… Yeah, we are working on the Writ… Yes, we've called the police. Sgt. Watson is on the couch in the office right now… Dad's girlfriend is supposed to be a dealer, but she's not anywhere to be found and doesn't live in the house. We're only worried about Dad right now. Mom died, and the family on her side are all in prison. Yeah, Grandma told us he can't do this alone and needs our help, otherwise he'd be an appropriate caregiver… Okay… Yeah, I'll tell them… Bye."

"Guess you heard all of that," Natalie acknowledged to Sgt. Watson.

"Yeah, I heard. We've been watching the house for a few weeks. We didn't know Dad was using. We were watching the girlfriend. She was staying there until you guys showed up. She's taken off and now we aren't sure where she went," Sgt. Watson said.

He was a nice-looking man, middle aged with a balding head. I had known him for years, but he was new to the detective role. His experience with CPS kept him cautious, concerned we wouldn't have everything we needed. Natalie had worked hard to repair CPS' relationship with other department, but his personal negative experiences with CPS kept him cautious. He was not above micromanaging us.

We finished the affidavits and sent them to Polly for review. She reviewed everything so she knew every detail on every case we worked. We didn't mind. After all, we relied on her to let us know if we were doing something wrong. Polly sent back the affidavits, saying they were fine and the legal liaison had drafted the petitions.

"We'll be ready to go in about forty-five minutes," Sgt. Watson told Natalie.

By "ready to go," he meant he had six officers that were coming with us. The plan was to meet at the police station and drive in a train to the house. A couple of squad cars would be ahead of my car, and then three more squad cars would follow behind.

As soon as Polly sent us the petition and order, we left for the police station. Pulling into the back, the gates to the yard opening in front of us, we joined the officers, ready to go pick up the kids.

One by one we followed in a close train down the road to the house listed on the orders. Natalie took the lead when we arrived. Despite having the Writ ordering us to take the children into our possession, we still needed permission to enter the residence and speak to everyone. Natalie was responsible for ensuring CPS didn't charge into the house without permission.

She knocked on the door. The door swung open immediately, revealing a surprised grandma. She hadn't expected to see six officers and two CPS investigators on her doorstep.

"Hi, Ms. Williamson, I'm Natalie and this is Rebekah. Can we come inside and speak to you?"

"Of course, come in," Grandma said as she opened the door wider.

"Can we come in, too?" Sgt. Watson asked.

"Sure, sorry, of course," she said.

"Are the boys home?" Natalie asked.

"I don't know," Grandma said. She eyed her son, who had just walked into the room. Tensions mounted as soon as he saw all of us standing in the house.

"What the hell are you doing here? Get out," he demanded.

"We have a Writ of Attachment to take possession of the children," Natalie said as she showed him the paperwork.

"I don't care. Get out. Leave. You don't have permission to be here," he screamed.

"We do actually. Your mother gave us permission, and she owns the home," Natalie replied. "Can we just talk about this and see what the misunderstanding is? You had agreed to leave the house and let your mother take care of your babies, but you came back."

"Sure, whatever, let's talk," he said as he sat down on the couch.

The officers were looking through the front of the house for the children. We didn't know if they were at school or in the house, and we couldn't leave without trying.

"Can I look in your room?" I asked Dad, interrupting Natalie's conversation.

"Sure, I'll show you where it is," he said while he got up. "I just want to get this over with."

He led the way down the hall to his room, opening the door for us. I stood next to him, at the doorway, and inspected the bedroom.

"What are those pills sitting there on the table next to the bed?" I asked. I couldn't believe he had opened the door for us while there were random pills laying on the floor, the table, and the bed. "Are they yours?"

"Well, fuck. Yeah, those are mine. Guess you've fucking seen it all now," he growled.

"I'm going to take pictures of everything, if that's okay," I told him.

"I don't give a shit what you do. I should've left that bitch a long time ago. She got me into this mess." I assumed he was referring to the girlfriend the police had been watching before CPS got involved.

I walked into the room to take pictures when I noticed a bag of pill bottles laying on top of another duffle bag. I picked them up to see if they were prescription and turned to ask Dad about them. He had already left the room and I could hear him talking to Natalie again.

"Sgt. Watson, can you come in here?" I called. He must have been right behind me because it only took him a few seconds to make his way into the room.

"What is that?" he asked.

"Pills. Dad said they are his," I replied.

"Where were they?" he asked.

"Those on the table were right there, haven't touched them. The ones on the floor are still there. And then this bag was in the duffle bag. I picked it up to ask him if they were his. He said they were."

Sgt. Watson called for the other officers and they began looking up the descriptions of the pills to identify them. Nothing was labeled and everything was within reach of the kids. As they searched, the boys arrived home on the bus. Natalie greeted them to keep them from seeing everything going on inside of the home.

"Mr. Williamson, come here," Sgt. Watson called. Dad returned to the room, clutching a cigarette pack in his hand.

"Sir, are these pills yours?" Sgt. Watson asked.

"Yes, they're mine," he said.

"Sir, these are a controlled substance and not in your name."

"I know. I know." He sounded defeated.

"We are placing you under arrest for possession of a controlled substance," Sgt. Watson told him.

Dad didn't fight or even complain. He already knew what was going to happen. He turned around, clutching the cigarette pack, and put his hands behind his back, cooperating with the officers. Natalie entered the room, the boys heading to the office with another investigator who had just arrived. We would see them again and handle the mountain of paperwork when we returned.

"Mr. Williamson, we are removing your children for neglectful supervision. They'll be placed into foster care unless you know of anyone else who can care for them. Any information you have will be helpful," Natalie said. The more the parent helped, the less dramatic it was for the children.

"I don't have anyone else right now. Their birth certificates are in the tubs at the top of the closet. You can get them if you want to. Their immunizations are in there too. Get whatever you need from it," he said.

Natalie attempted to pull down the tubs from the closet but couldn't reach them. One of the officers unlocked Dad's handcuffs so he could help. He lifted a plastic storage tub out of the closet, handed it to Natalie, and then put his hands back behind his back, ready to be cuffed again.

"I'm not going to fight anyone. This was bound to happen, and it will probably serve me for good. Maybe I can get clean," he said. He handed one of the officers the pack of cigarettes he was clutching, who turned around and handed them to me. I wasn't sure why I had them but since I did, my immediate reaction was to smell them. It wasn't cigarettes in the pack. Detective Black stood next to me and I raised the cigarette pack to her nose without saying anything. She snapped her head around and met my stare, surprised.

"Smell like cigarettes to you?" I asked.

She laughed. "Not the kind you'd buy in the store."

Everyone tried to move so Sgt. Watson could take Dad out of the bedroom. There were so many of us in the way we herded toward the bigger areas of the house. I found myself with Detective Black in the kitchen.

"Can we open them and see what's really in here?" I asked her.

"I don't care," she said.

I opened the pack of cigarettes, Detective Black watching intently, and dumped them out onto the counter in front of us. Out fell a few cigarettes and multiple rolled joints of what appeared to be marijuana cigarettes.

"Shit. Let me call Sgt. Watson over here," Detective Black said. "I don't know if this is a legit search or if we can use it.

She had to be joking. She just told me she didn't care what I did, she watched me do it, and she had smelled the pack before we opened it. What did she mean she didn't know?

She called him over and explained the situation. We possibly had a new offense for Dad, but it was a CPS investigator who had found it while the detective watched. We weren't sure how this worked. Neither did Sgt. Watson. He called the DA's office and explained the situation, hoping to get an answer.

"The DA said the search is legit. We're adding an additional charge to Mr. Williamson's already lengthy list of charges. Draft an affidavit for us if you would and good job," Sgt. Watson complimented me.

As Natalie and I left the house, she gave me her famous *really* stare. "You just had to add more work by finding that, didn't you?"

I shrugged and chuckled. Maybe she would stop assigning me drug cases. I doubted it though.

Chapter 6

May 2012

Tension wasn't just building in the office, it was also building at home. My husband didn't like the number of hours I put into the job as it left almost no time at home. We never knew if I'd get called away during a family dinner or a holiday. The long nights and early mornings of constant work caused regular arguments between the two of us. The day our house burned down wasn't any different. I'd just finished dropping off children at their foster care placement, after working a drug raid with law enforcement, when my husband called. It was just after 7:00 p.m.

"Honey, you need to come home now. The house is burning down." His voice was calm, sounding no different than if he'd told me to pick up bread on the way home.

"That's crap. Don't joke about things like that. It doesn't make me able to come home any faster." I thought he was calling to see if I'd call his bluff and dart home so we could fight about what it took to get me home.

"I'm not joking. Why would I joke about that? The house is burning down and you need to get home now."

He was serious. I'd heard sirens in the background before he hung up. I turned around and took Wesley Street at speeds I'll never admit to. If I'd learned anything in the police academy, it was how to drive like a bat out of hell and not kill anyone. I put everything I'd practiced into play as I made the road my own runway.

I could smell the fire before I saw the billowing black smoke. It was the smell of melting plastic, burning trash, and pollution. I arrived just as two firefighters standing on the roof fell through, disappearing into the smoke. There wasn't a house left.

"You made it," my husband said as I climbed out of the car. All thoughts of fighting about my work schedule vanished as we stood next to each other, watching the flames.

"Why's your car still under the carport? It's melting." I asked. I was thinking about the next steps we had to take, my mind functioning the way it always did an emergency. Calm, collected, sorting through the steps needed to contain the situation.

"I couldn't move it. The keys are inside."

"I have the spare. Let's move it before we don't have a second vehicle." I handed him the key.

He took off toward the car but was stopped by one of the firefighters. Moments later he ran back.

"They said leave it. It's too hot now. The tires will probably pop if I move it," he explained.

"Okay, we'll add that to the list for the insurance company. Why are you barefoot?" I'd just noticed he didn't have shoes on.

"I didn't have time to get my shoes."

That made sense.

"Guess I'll start making phone calls. The insurance company has an after-hours number. And I'm sure my family would rather hear this from me instead of someone else. Probably time to tell people I'm pregnant again. Everything we had for the baby's gone. Have you already called anyone?"

"I called Julia. She's on her way."

"What's she going to do about it?" I was still in emergency mode, survival mode. It hadn't occurred to me to call anyone for moral support. That's what made the two of us different.

Julia Laurence pulled up seconds later with drinks. She handed my husband a beer. "Might as well have a party. Rebekah, I brought you a Diet Mountain Dew. I know you don't drink. Sorry about the house. You know I'm just trying to keep the mood light, right?"

I nodded. It helped, seeing her laugh and joke around with my husband.

I called my mom first, sending her into tears. She'd call everyone else while I called the next person on the list, Natalie. I had to call her so she wouldn't assign any cases to me in the morning. I figured it would take me until the morning to get things figured out.

"Hey, what's up? I'm at dinner with my family." Dinner with her family was code she was with her husband. He didn't like the constant CPS calls like my husband, so when we said the code, we called another time unless it was an emergency.

"I understand. I just wanted to let you know my house is burning down. I'd really like to not have any cases assigned to me tomorrow," I said.

"Okay, crap. Is everyone okay? Do you know what you need? I'm on my way." She was gearing up for action, as if we had an emergency case.

"I don't know yet. My work computer was in my car, so that's okay." I was still in work mode.

"What? That's not what I meant. What personal items do you need? What do your boys need? Do you have underwear?" I hadn't thought about my boys or underwear, just about insurance companies and notifying family.

"Oh, right. I was thinking about bigger issues and just assumed everyone was fine. My husband didn't say anything. Let me find out."

"Okay. I'll make some phone calls. We'll get you guys set up with food, clothes, and things for the boys." Exactly like handling a case.

Justine called as soon as I hung up with Natalie.

"Hey, that isn't your house is it?" She was concerned.

"Yes, yes, it is. Can you see it from there?"

"Of course. I live behind you. I just didn't want to believe it was your house."

"It is. It's gone."

"What can we do for you? What do you need? We'll help in any way we can. How are the boys? Is everyone safe?"

"I don't know yet. Natalie's on her way."

"Okay, I'll call her. Don't worry. We'll take care of you guys," she assured me before hanging up.

"Where are the boys?" I yelled at my husband. I was worried about our two youngest boys. My older stepchildren lived with their mom, and my oldest son was out of state visiting family.

"Our neighbor has them. They're fine. They were only in diapers though. No clothes." He and Julia were drinking, watching the blaze.

Friends, family, coworkers, and people in the community came together and helped. We were set up with a place to stay, emergency clothes, food, everything we needed. I'd always been the one to help someone else in a situation like this, whether it was from a personal side or work. Now our family was in need and we were being supported by what felt like the entire community. I couldn't express my gratitude enough.

I took the next day off and then went back to work. I had too many cases, and the removal I'd just finished, to take off more than a day. Audrey had been on my butt to get my old cases closed. All they were missing was the documentation as the investigation had been worked. She agreed to give me week to finish and close them before she took the next step, which was generally some type of discipline action. That's all the time she could allow, even with a house fire.

My coworkers appeared genuinely concerned about my wellbeing. They rallied around me, finding donations and dropping them off in my office until my office was so packed I couldn't see the floor. Their support stopped when they learned I was again pregnant. I just couldn't keep it quiet with a house fire.

Natalie knew I was pregnant and had known since the day I found out, but we knew it would cause contention in the office. Some of it was personal. A couple of my coworkers had fertility problems and took personal offense that I'd had two children in such a short amount of time. The other coworkers disliked that I'd get another three months off for family leave. Short one investigator, they would have to work harder.

Tension in the office started to build but I tried to ignore it, convincing myself I was imagining it. I continued to drown in work and focused on my cases, keeping mostly to myself. I overheard gossip, comments about things they didn't like, comments directed at me. I brushed it off. But it continued to the point that Natalie reached out to Audrey and Marissa Moss, Audrey's boss, explaining the gossip in the office was too much for it to go away on its own. Audrey and Marissa continued to insist the problem would go away without intervention. They had seen the same thing in other offices and it always eventually went away. The bigger problem was closing cases and keeping up with the demand.

Chapter 7

June 2012

"Rebekah, you're being assigned the Krank case," Natalie yelled from down the hall. I had no idea what she was talking about. "Judge Fench just ordered us to take custody of her."

"What do you mean, *ordered* us? Is she already in care?" I asked, confused. We were barely into the month of June and it was the summer from Hades already.

"No. She's getting out of juvenile detention and doesn't have anywhere else to go. You're getting it. They'll drop her off here shortly," Natalie said.

I rolled my eyes. It wasn't that I didn't want to help a child without a place to go, but I already had multiple other cases needing the same attention. When Judge Fench said to take a child into custody, you didn't question him. He had always been an advocate for CPS, so long as CPS did their job.

The fifteen-year-old teen was dropped off in our office by the detention officer. "She's your problem now," was the only statement made before he left, leaving us to take over.

We already knew she was using and manufacturing methamphetamines and smoking marijuana. Ashley had stayed with multiple family members, burning every bridge she had as she accused every one of them of sexual assault when she got upset.

The latest place that took her in had tried to get her help in rehab but then found scales, baggies, and marijuana in her bedroom. That friend, the only person left who could be a caregiver, gave her a drug test. It was positive for methamphetamines, so Ashley had taken off again, landing herself in juvenile detention as a runaway.

I located a phone number for Mom, but Mom refused to accept any responsibility for her daughter, saying she didn't want anything to do with her. Mom then refused to talk about her daughter and would not come to the office. It was harsh, probably the harshest thing I had ever heard a parent say about their child. Maybe it was because Mom was also on drugs and had a felony warrant out, so coming to the office would put her back in prison.

Ashley sat in my office, scowling, complaining, and cussing me with words I didn't even know could be used together in a sentence. She was a beautiful girl, very thin, with long flowing hair. The meth use hadn't begun to affect her facial features or her skin. She was just a teenager, her whole life ahead of her. I tried to ignore the screaming and horrid things she said.

I tried to be nice. But she had been through the system before, she knew what foster care was, and she knew her freedom to do what she wanted would be over because there would be rules. It infuriated her. She screamed she would bring me down and blow up the building. Everyone in the building could hear her. Natalie removed her from my office before something dangerous happened. After all, I was pregnant and it would be difficult for me to defend myself.

Ashley's vile screams echoed in the halls bouncing off the plaster walls into Natalie's office, where her thin door did little to dampen them. Even my coworkers, who had heard everything before from other angry teens and parents and had little issue repeating it, blushed. Clients in the office, some of them visiting their children, shifted awkwardly. A few blocked their kids' ears. Ashley wasn't stopping. It wasn't until Natalie offered to find someone else, other than foster care, to try and place her with that she calmed down.

Ashley laid on Natalie's couch, calm and gloating, and gave Natalie name after name of possible individuals who could take her in. I contacted each one, asking if they would take her and running background checks. It took hours. By 6:00 p.m., we still didn't have a place for her to go. Every person I had called told me they couldn't risk it. She would accuse them of assaulting her. The two I did find who were willing had current pending charges for manufacturing drugs. We couldn't place a child addict with anyone who had pending or past manufacturing charges. Emergency placement with a foster care shelter was the only option left.

Ashley begged, pleaded, and started screaming again, desperate to convince us to keep trying. She pulled up a contact on her cell phone and handed the phone to Natalie, begging her to call one more name. As Natalie started to call on Ashley's phone, a text message popped up. The message said to delete everything in her phone before anyone found she was sleeping with him.

"Ashley," Natalie started. "Who is James?"

"He's my boyfriend, why?"

"Why does he want you to delete his text messages in your phone? How old is he?" Natalie asked, suspicious.

"Ugh, you fucking bitch. Because he's twenty-five and he thinks he'll go to jail if anyone finds out he's banging me. But he can't go to jail because he's my fucking boyfriend and I'm not pressing charges. You can't make me. And if you put me in foster care, I'm calling his fucking ass and he's going to come get me. Now give me back my fucking phone," Ashley shouted loud enough for the entire office to hear.

One of the SI's heard her screaming and came to see what the issue was. He offered to take her to his office in hopes she would calm down again. She followed him but then promptly sat her butt

48

down in the middle of the hallway and screamed like a two year old throwing a tantrum.

"I want my cell phone back. You're not putting me into foster care. I'm calling someone as soon as you give that back to me and I'm running away. If you put me in foster care, I'm killing myself," she screamed.

I was in a different hallway and stopped by Natalie's office.

"What the hell? I thought she was laying on the couch chilled out. What happened?" I asked.

"She has a twenty-five-year-old boyfriend and he happens to the one who was hiding her when law enforcement found her after she ran away," Natalie said. "I have to call Polly and see what I need to do at this point. I don't know if I should give her the phone back or keep it. She's threatening to use it to run away and go right back to this guy."

I listened while Natalie called Polly. Whatever Polly said to do, we would do.

"Hey, Polly, this is Natalie. Can you hear me?" she began. "I know, I know. We have a teenager Judge Fench told us to take custody of. She's a runaway but there's no family to take her. None. And everyone she gave me has history or refuses to take her… No, no, that's not the problem. The problem is this cell phone of hers. She handed it to me and told me to call a number on it for one more chance to find placement. Then a text popped up and it was the twenty-five-year-old boyfriend law enforcement found her with. She wants her cell phone back and said she's using it to call her boyfriend and running away as soon as we place her in foster care." Natalie paused and looked at me with a *I'm at a loss* look on her face. I couldn't hear what Polly was saying but Natalie was nodding her head. "Yes, yes, she said they were having sex. She doesn't think it's a problem… Right, yes… She's fifteen and he's twenty-five… Inappropriate relationship or sexual assault? Sure, okay. Lock it up? Okay, no problem." Natalie hung up the phone.

49

"She said to call law enforcement to come get the phone and lock it up until they get here," she told me.

"Okay. The shelter said she couldn't take a cell phone anyway. All she can take are the clothes on her back. They said anything else will be locked up and taken away from her," I told her. The placement we had found was for teenagers who had tendencies to run away or cause other problems, such as fighting.

"I have to go get my kids. It's already late and I need to get them," Natalie said.

"Can you get mine, too? I don't know what to do with them and I'm going to be here late," I asked.

Our children attended the same daycare, which was close to where Natalie lived. There were times like this when I had no other option but to have her get my kids. She didn't have a problem with it.

Natalie left the office and I had the task of telling Ashley the news. I braced myself for another fight. Everyone else in the office had left except for Ester and Kenderick, who were in a meeting in a room at the end of the hall. Ashley was still laying on the floor in the hallway.

"Ashley, we have a placement for you. It's a shelter. We'll find a better placement soon, but right now it will be this shelter. There are other teenagers there, too. It won't be for long," I told her.

"I'm not going anywhere. I'm not going. You can't make me. You're a fucking cunt whore. I want my cell phone back," she screamed, again at the top of her lungs. I was surprised she still had a voice.

I stayed calm. "We can't give you your cell phone back. The shelter won't allow it and the police are going to come get it."

I only thought she had lost it before. She stood up and let loose, even worse. "I'm killing myself. I'm killing myself. I'm going to blow this fucking place up and then jump off a building and kill myself," she screamed repeatedly.

"Okay, I'll call Glenn Oaks and you'll go to the psychiatric ward instead. It's closer than the shelter anyway," I said. I didn't have any emotion left at this point. I was tired, my feet hurt, and this had gone on all day long.

Just as I was going to call the hospital, Ester came out of the meeting. She asked, "What is going on?"

"They took my cell phone. They took it and I want it back. I just want my cell phone back," Ashley said.

"Rebekah, then give her the cell phone back," Ester told me. I stared at her. She didn't even know what was going on nor was she my supervisor. Now she was going to get into the middle of something and make things worse.

"Ester, I can't. Polly, our attorney, told us to lock it up until the police could get it. We can't give it back," I calmly explained. Ashley was standing next to us, watching us, waiting to see which side she needed to fight with more.

"Well, I don't see a reason for that. Let's just give it back to her so she can take it with her," Ester suggested.

"Yeah, give it back to me. I want it now. You can't keep it," Ashley screamed at me. She had figured out which one of us she could work. Where she wanted to kill me, she knew she had Ester wrapped around her finger. She'd use Ester to try and get her way.

"Ashley, I can't. It's locked up and I don't even know where it is," I responded. I was getting frustrated. This girl was determined to fight about this and keep us in this office for hours.

"I'll take her into the other room so she's not screaming out here and see if I can calm her down," Ester told me. I doubted that would help but whatever.

I called Natalie and gave her the update. She reminded me not to give the phone back to her as our attorney had told us what to do and we had to follow that advice. Just as I hung up, Ester came back, Ashley staying behind in the other room.

"She said she'd go to the placement if you'll give her the phone back," Ester stated.

"Ester, it's not happening. She either goes willingly or I call the police and we take her by force. But she can't stay here screaming like this, and we've been at this all day," I said.

"I'll tell her," Ester said as she walked back to the office.

I waited for her to return with an answer. If I went with Ester, I would make the situation worse.

"Okay, she said she'll go to placement if I take the phone and give it to her at placement. She said she doesn't trust you to have it," Ester stated.

"She's not getting the phone. Placement won't even allow her to have the phone. I don't have it. She's not getting it. I'm done. I'm calling the police and she can go in handcuffs," I was raising my voice by now. I was done playing these games. "She's a child, a teenager, she can't negotiate here. We have custody of her. She's going to placement."

"Well, where's the phone right now?" Ester asked.

"I don't have a clue. I just know it's locked up. I've never seen the damn phone," I yelled.

Ester walked down the hall toward Ashley again, and I slid into my office to call Natalie.

"Hey, she's refusing to go to placement," I said. "She wants this dang cell phone and she's pushing it hard. Where is it in case she asks?"

"It's locked in my desk drawer," Natalie responded. "But she can't have it."

"I know. I just wondered," I replied as I hung up.

Sure enough, Ester jogged down the hallway again, this time with another counter. "She said she'll go to placement if I take the phone and lock it in my filing cabinet. She wants to know I have it locked up and not you or Natalie."

Ester was determined to make me give Ashley her phone. It was like she didn't care if Ashley ran off with an adult man or called someone to sell her drugs. She just wanted to butt in and try to control something she knew nothing about. And she looked like she enjoyed it.

"That's the dumbest things I've ever heard. But let me call Natalie," I replied. I dialed my phone again. It was almost 7:30 p.m. I hadn't eaten, my kids were with Natalie, and I was over this nightmare.

"She wants Ester to lock the phone up in her filing cabinet. Is that okay?" I asked her.

"I don't care where it's locked up. So long as law enforcement can get it in the morning, I don't care," she said.

"Get it out of Natalie's desk drawer and put it in your filing cabinet. If she doesn't calm down with that, I'm not kidding, the police will just have to take her by force," I said, making it clear I was done. "We have emergency custody of this girl and she is not the boss. We have to keep her safe, even if she doesn't like it."

Ester took the information back to Ashley, who finally agreed only if I didn't take her to the placement. She wanted Ester and Kenderick to take her. I wasn't about to disagree. I didn't trust this girl not to stab me in the neck if we were alone in a car. I watched from down the hall as Ester took something, the cell phone I assumed, out of Natalie's drawer and lock it in the filing cabinet in her own office. She then called Kenderick, who had agreed to come back to the office and help Ester take Ashley to her placement.

It was over—at almost 8:00 p.m. I could finally leave. I had to grab my kids, take them home, and turn around and come back early tomorrow.

Chapter 8

July 2012

"Rebekah, I really need your help. I don't know what else to do," Julia Laurence begged me while sitting in my office. I was acting supervisor during a hot July day. Natalie was in Fannin County for something and was barely reachable by phone. Julia had only been out of the CPS training academy for a month when she had landed two companion cases involving parents who were twin sisters. It was her first time using an Orders in Aid of Investigation. The sisters, Mikayla and Cosette, had thrown Julia out of their home the week before, but now they were coming to the office for drug tests. Julia didn't know what to do. One of the sisters was reasonable to work with, but the other one liked to threaten to blow us up with bombs. This was the second case we had dealt with regarding bombs. A security guard was still in place in the front office since a father a week ago had threatened to blow us up. I think the security guard was more for the State's peace of mind than ours because he slept most of the time and probably would have slept through an explosion. He also couldn't work past 5:00 p.m., so after he left we were still working, alone, without any protection.

Julia kept me on my toes and struggled managing a caseload with constant cases rolling in. It was difficult for everyone.

Everything was a priority and it was hard to weed out what was a bigger priority than the others.

"Okay, let's lay this out so it makes sense," I started. I had already worked part of the case with her, so I knew the facts and had accompanied her to some of the extended family member's homes. "If Cosette's drug test is positive, her mother-in-law-ish will take her kiddo. She already has the other one. We know Dad is in prison right now, so he's not an option. Natalie and I went to see Grandma and her home is appropriate and her background is clean. She's more than willing to take him. If her test is negative then great, she can go home. Does that make sense?"

"Sure," Julia said while she thought about it. "But what if she doesn't want her son to stay with Grandma?" It was a valid question.

"Then we have to put him in foster care. This is the only relative that has a place to live and could keep Cosette out of the house. Everyone else is either intimidated by her or they have a rap sheet a mile long. But Grandma here is excellent, it appears. I doubt Cosette will want to put him in foster care."

"And Mikayla? What about her? I think she uses more than Cosette. She's the one who actually threw me out of the house the other day," Julia explained. Mikayla was the loudest of the twins. Her kids were already in the office since her mother had called and told us to come get them. It was one of the only reasons we were able to get the parents into the office. They wanted their kids back.

"Do they live together?" I asked.

If the sisters lived together, then we had a problem. I had thought they were just in the same area, not the same house.

"No, they have different homes. But they are constantly with each other."

"If one is positive and the other is not, they have to agree not to be around the other until we know if they're clean. Remember, Julia, none of this is permanent. The goal is for them to get clean and get their kids back. We only have an issue when they refuse or think that using cocaine isn't a problem around their kids."

Julia nodded. She understood. She thought she could save everyone and if she explained it enough, they would all get clean and get their kids back again.

"Where the fuck is that stupid bitch?" Mikayla screamed from the lobby area.

Why were we always *fucking stupid bitches*? I guess no one had an imagination to use a different phrase. I banged my head slightly on the desk. This was going to be another very long day and night.

"I'll get her, hang on," Julia said while she jogged down the hallway.

The children in the office could hear their mother and started getting upset.

"We're here, where the hell are you?" Cosette yelled.

"Right here, come on back. Let's talk," Julia said, trying to calm them.

I cleared out the conference area for them to sit. I thought it would fit everyone, including their children, but the sisters were too mad about having to deal with CPS. If one of them spoke, the other one joined in, screaming at each other and us. I had Julia take Mikayla to her office, leaving me with Cosette.

"Where's your son?" I asked, realizing all the kids had left with Mikayla.

"I took him to my mother-in-law's house," she said.

I nodded. She had already done what we planned to do. "Cosette, the allegations are drug use on the case. Julia is your actual worker, but I'm helping her. You can tell it's rough dealing with both of you together. Do you mind talking to me?"

"If I have to, I guess I will," she huffed.

"We need a drug test. It can be an oral swab or you can go to the lab, but we must have it. You admitted to using cocaine and this is just part of the process."

Cosette didn't like the idea and insisted she was clean. She promised she had only used once, three months ago, during Mikayla's birthday party. I seriously doubted her, but who knew? While we spoke, I could hear Mikayla screaming in the hallway. Once again, she was threatening to blow us up and have all our jobs. She sounded more likely to be high. Cosette was at least calm.

I pulled out a drug test and explained to Cosette how to use it. It was an oral swab we regularly used, and it only detected usage from the past twenty-four to forty-eight hours. She agreed to take the swab, and afterward, laid it down on the table where both of us could see it and the results. I sat in there with her, not touching anything, waiting for the results to appear. When they did, it was clear she was positive for cocaine. I didn't confirm it with her. Instead I pulled out a drug acknowledgement form.

"This is the form we use if you want to explain what you used and where you used it. You simply acknowledge the drug of choice, the date of last usage, and where the children were when you were using. If you want to use this, then you fill it out and sign here."

An acknowledgment form was more like a confession. The form was more admissible in court than the drug test because it had the parent's signature on it. The drug test was rarely authenticated by an expert and the chain of custody was a joke with them. They could get tossed out in a heartbeat. It didn't change the fact the results were positive: it was all about how to get it into court.

"Yeah, I'll fill it out," she said. I watched her fill it out, waiting to see if she would mark a more recent date than three months ago. So far she was sticking to her three months ago usage.

"Cosette, are you sure you want to stick with that story? The results of the test you just took are right in front of you. Look at them closely," I encouraged.

I wanted her to feel the need to come clean and not force me to tell her she was lying. Sometimes parents would force the issue, and I didn't know what she would do. Unlike a pregnancy test where the line means you're positive and pregnant, these tests showed no line when a person was positive for a drug. Her test tested for six different drugs, five of which had a line, meaning they were negative. Only one drug on the test had a line missing—only one positive. I waited to see what she would say while she stared at it.

"But I didn't do marijuana or PCP, or whatever these others are," she said. "I only did cocaine."

"When did you last use cocaine? Cosette, your son is already with your mother-in-law. We want to keep him there. But that means you must be honest with us so we know you won't violate the safety plan. If you lie now, they'll see it as a risk of you lying later." I waited.

"I used cocaine yesterday, after I dropped my son off at my mother-in-law's house," she confessed, now crying. "Are you going to take him away from me?"

"No. I mean, yes, but not like foster care. He's with your mother-in-law, his grandmother. He's with family, not foster care. We want him to stay there while you get clean, if you want to leave him there, too." Having to leave your child with any person was hard, and I knew that. I also knew she was in an ideal situation where we didn't have to worry about foster care, but it depended on if she could follow the rules.

"He can stay there. He can stay there. It's okay, he can stay there," she sobbed as she added the truth to her written acknowledgment. I patted her shoulder and told her I had to go see how her sister was doing. Leaving her in the room alone, I took the updated acknowledgement and drug test with me. I set them on my desk and poked my head in with Julia.

"How's it going in here?" I asked.

Mikayla was still madder than spitfire, her mouth frothing as she gritted her teeth. Her kids were playing next to her and her diaper bag was dumped all over the ground.

"She doesn't want to take a test. She doesn't want to do anything. She doesn't want to cooperate," Julia said, frustrated.

"Mikayla, we have court orders. They order you to take a drug test. You can take the oral swab or you can take a hair test. But you must take the test. If you don't, we have to call the judge and tell him you're not following the order he signed." I looked up at Julia, suddenly wondering if Mikayla had seen the order. "Julia, you did show her the order, right?"

"Yeah, she fucking showed me. I know what the judge said. I ain't doing it. All you hoes want to come in and ruin lives. You want to take our babies and accuse us of using drugs like we ain't got nothin' else to do. I be bein' a single mom and I ain't got no help and I'm just doin' the best I can," Mikayla screamed.

She could scream all she wanted, but her children were in the room and they didn't need to hear it.

"Julia, why don't you see if they want something in the rainbow room," I suggested. "Mikayla, she's just going to take them down the hall to see the toys in the rainbow room. They don't need to hear this fighting."

Mikayla waved off Julia, giving her the okay to take the kids. After they were out of ear shot, I started again.

"We already know you're using cocaine. We already know your boyfriend sells cocaine. The problem with that type of drug is your ability to parent and whether or not the children are exposed to it in the home…"

"I ain't been doin' no dope in my house," she interrupted. "I don't understand why my kids can't stay with my mom. I told y'all to put them with my mom if y'all was gonna remove them like kidnappers. My mama told me you guys done tooked them without any notice. Y'all just want the money for them."

We had tried to put them with her mother, but the placement fell apart in less than twelve hours. She had called us, panicking, saying she couldn't do it anymore and we had to pick them up immediately. The idea had been to prevent a removal and try for the lesser intrusive step of Family Based Safety Services. I had suspected her mother was on drugs, but the drug test was negative and she didn't have any CPS history or criminal history. It didn't fit with the family's history, but it tied our hands and we had to try. After we collected the kids from her mother's house, she had called Mikayla and told her we had taken them without any notice and for no reason.

"Mikayla, you know your mom called us and told us to get them? Right? She was flipped out of her mind and screaming like she had lost it. We couldn't get a hold of you and she sounded like she was losing her mind," I explained.

Mikayla looked up at me in surprise.

"She's fucking back on crack again, I knew it," she said. Well, that answered that. "I thought she was using that shit again. That shit'll fuck you up." I was a little confused.

"We were told you used cocaine, too," I said, questioningly. "Why are you mad about her using it?"

"Cause I be using the real shit. She be using crack. Crack'll mess a bitch up," she snapped. "I don't use that cheap shit. I use the real shit."

"Okay, that makes sense. Do you want to take a hair test to confirm just what shit you use? Or do you want to take an oral swab and do it that way?" I asked.

"I'll take your fucking oral swab. Where you putting my damn kids?"

"They're going to have to go to foster care. We've tried every name anyone has given us. Your family has all kinds of history and Cosette's mother-in-law can't take on two more kids."

Mikayla nodded. She had calmed down and was taking the test. It was positive for cocaine, just like her sister. She signed the acknowledgment as well. Since she was calm, I let her go back to her sister. Everything seemed to be calming down and working itself out.

Then Ester came to see what we were doing.

Julia told her we had to remove the kids from both parents. She told her about the usage three months ago by Cosette and the negative test she had two days before. Then she told her about Mikayla's alleged cocaine use and that she hadn't taken a test yet. I hadn't had a chance to tell Julia that not only had Cosette used just yesterday, but both Moms had signed an acknowledgment admitting to it. Julia and I didn't expect Ester to butt in like she did, but she got mad and flew into the conference room where Mikayla and Cosette were sitting.

"They can't remove your kids. I don't know why they told you we were taking your kids. We can't take anyone's kids if you haven't been using drugs," she yelled at the sisters. "I'm calling our attorney right now and telling her this is wrong. Your kids need to go home with you right now."

That's all it took for everyone to be mad again and the screaming to commence.

"Ester, Cosette's positive for cocaine. She took a test. Mikayla admitted to using and took a test. I have their acknowledgments right here. What the hell are you doing?" I yelled.

"You're lying. You've falsified those tests. You're just trying to take these kids," she yelled back.

I was completely dumbfounded. Not only had she butted in, she had just accused me of falsifying the tests the sisters had taken. This woman had to be completely crazy, and she continued with this story as she called our attorney and told her the same thing.

However, I had already told Natalie about the confessions and acknowledgments, and Natalie had already called our attorney. We already had permission for the removal and our attorney already knew the full story. I shot Natalie a text telling her what Ester was doing because I knew things were about to get even worse.

Sure enough, Polly called Natalie asking her why we were removing children if the tests were negative. Natalie told her they weren't and that we had acknowledgments signed. She also explained we had family for one of the sisters' kids and had to use foster care for the other. Polly backed down, but it sounded like she didn't believe Natalie. Natalie gave me the go ahead to continue and Julia calmed the sisters again.

I stepped into Julia's office to find a diaper for the youngest kid. The diaper bag was still dumped everywhere with papers and toys scattered. After I found the diaper, I stood up to head back to the families and noticed Alison watching from down the hallway. I didn't know she was still here. She spun around and went back toward her office.

"Thanks for the help, Alison. Glad you could chill while all of this was going on," I smarted off, loudly. I headed for the conference room as Ester was storming out.

"You're wrong for removing these kids. You're fucking wrong for it," she yelled at me.

This wasn't even her case. I didn't even know if she knew the parents' names or if she knew which one was which as they were identical except for their hair.

"You don't have a clue about this case. You have no idea what's going on. You have no idea what the test results were. You need to butt the hell out of this case and let us do our jobs. Don't you dare ever accuse me of falsifying anything ever again," I yelled back. Thankfully Julia had closed the door so the parents couldn't hear us very well.

"You're done. You are so done. You just wait," Ester said as she walked away. That woman was scary. She had only been working for CPS for thirteen months, three of which were in the

CPS academy. But something made her feel like she knew more than everyone else. She often bragged about being best friends with one of the assistant district attorneys and many of the other attorneys in town, going as far as saying she had dinner with them on a regular basis. She bragged she was best friends with Polly, too. Something wasn't right if all it took was a phone call from her for Polly to suddenly not believe the facts in a case I worked. Polly had never addressed anything with me before and had never rejected a case I had worked.

I had a sick feeling in my gut but had to push it aside to keep moving along. I didn't want to work this case all night.

Chapter 9

August 2012

Tensions were mounting in the office as summer passed. Rumors flew, tempers flared, and I tried to avoid it all by staying to myself as much as possible. By the end of August, I had three months before the baby was due and I just wanted to survive. Our new house wasn't finished, so we still lived in the tiny duplex. I regularly pulled twelve to fifteen-hour days and no one wanted to help. Usually when someone had a big case or lots of children to interview, others would jump in and assist. It didn't matter who I asked, there was always a reason they couldn't help. We had never behaved this poorly to each other before.

I caught Alison in my office, digging through my drawers. I asked what she was doing. She said she was looking for an extra battery and thought I had one. As our offices were never locked and we were mobile workers, I couldn't complain. But I knew she wasn't looking for a battery.

Things had gotten so severe, Natalie was reporting to Audrey on a regular basis, trying to gain control of the office, but Audrey and Marissa still didn't think it needed to be addressed formally. Natalie tried to persuade them to let us switch offices when Alison was caught eavesdropping on a conversation between Natalie and Audrey about me. Alison darted to Ester afterward and repeated, word for word, what had been said during the confidential conversation. We were stunned. The gossip and backbiting had stooped to a new low.

Natalie addressed the problem with Rachel Amaru, Ester's supervisor, but Rachel didn't want to be involved. Natalie then begged Marissa for help. Marissa and Audrey both advised her to keep me out of the office as much as possible and hold any conferences, something that was required monthly, or conversations, out of earshot from the other investigators. If they couldn't hear anything, there would be nothing to gossip about.

I was forced to stop talking in the office. Natalie often accompanied me on my cases, not because she was helping me more than the next person, but because if she needed to discuss a case with me, hold a conference, or do anything a supervisor had to do, she had to take me out of the office so no one could eavesdrop. Anything we said inside was passed around and construed into something else.

The only people who didn't have a problem with me or Natalie was law enforcement. Because I was constantly around Natalie, partly for my protection, I was standing next to her when they called for assistance. I wanted to escape and let her assign it to someone else, but it was too late. I would be the official investigator on it.

"This is Detective Fumer," I heard through her phone, "We have a case involving a sexual assault. We're about to go to the Child Advocacy Center and watch the interview. Right now, it appears to be a police matter only, but could you come just in case? Mom is acting hostile and we aren't sure if everything is okay."

"No problem," Natalie replied instantly. "We'll be right there."

Children were interviewed at the Advocacy Center, what we called the CAC, so they didn't have to go through more than one interview, if possible, when there were allegations of sexual abuse or severe physical abuse.

Mom and Angel, her daughter, were already at the CAC when we arrived. We hustled to Kris' office where we suspected to find them.

"Amy, this is Natalie and Rebekah. They're with CPS and are here to help on the case. Rebekah, Natalie, this is Amy, and this is her daughter Angel," Kris said.

"Why're they here?" Mom asked.

"We asked them to come and help," Kris explained.

"Why? I made a police report. I brought Angel here. Why does CPS need to be involved?" Mom pushed. It was clear she didn't want us anywhere around her or her daughter.

"They're just here to make sure everything's okay," Kris said.

Kris had a soothing voice and usually helped interviewees feel comfortable. It wasn't working this time. Detective Fumer stood next to Natalie, giving her the *I told you something isn't right* look. Why was Mom on the defense? I didn't know anything about her, her history, or much anything else this case, but already something seemed off.

"There's no reason for them to be involved. I done everything I'm supposed to. They ain't got no reason to be here. We don't need to be here anymore." Mom gathered her things and took her daughter's hand, ready to leave.

"We're going to have a problem if you leave. CPS is here because I asked them to come. If you want this guy prosecuted then we have to have this interview. You made the report, you want to help your daughter, now let's get to the bottom of it. We can't prosecute this guy any other way," Detective Fumer explained. I peered around the two of them to see how Angel was responding. Generally, we kept the victims in a different room while Kris gathered basic information from a parent or caregiver. But this case had already started off differently, having been initiated by law enforcement and not exactly falling under CPS' jurisdiction. Angel didn't seem too bothered by the commotion.

"I do want this man prosecuted. That's for sure." Mom relaxed enough to let us continue.

"Okay, good," Kris continued. "How about Detective Fumer takes you to the lobby area and I'll go with Angel to the interview room? Is that okay?"

Mom nodded, finally willing to comply.

We waited in the hall next to Kris' office, Angel sitting on the chair inside the office, all of us in an awkward silence.

Detective Fumer came back shaking her head in frustration. "That's why I wanted you guys here. That woman isn't making any sense."

Natalie grimaced, glancing at Angel and back at Detective Fumer, trying to remind her not to say anything about Angel's mom in front of her.

"So," Kris said, trying to get everyone back on track without the awkwardness. "Angel, how about we go into the interview room and talk some more, shall we?"

Angel nodded and followed Kris down the hall to the interview room. It was a simple room with a small table with two chairs, a calendar, a tissue box, crayons, and paper. Each item served a purpose. The small table allowed the two to sit closer together, helping the victim, in this case, Angel, feel comfortable and more like this was a conversation rather than an interview. The calendar allowed Kris to establish the recorded date and time and often assisted the victim in remembering when something had happened. The paper and crayons were used by both. Some were blank pages for doodling or taking notes. The other pages contained a drawing of a boy and girl so the victim could explain what happened using pictures. The tissue box was for wiping tears, but it was also used as a demonstration tool. In the upper corner of the room was a small camera that recorded everything with a live stream into the observation room where Detective Fumer and CPS investigators could watch.

"I don't know what's wrong with that mother," Detective Fumer continued to mumble while we waited for Kris to get situated. "Something's not right. Mom made the report, but when we tried to set up the interview she got hostile, like she didn't want her daughter to speak to anyone. I don't know if she's not protective or if she's just... weird."

"Well, we haven't called in a report yet," Natalie explained. "We can go ahead and get it started. Anything else we need to include in it? Do you have any other information?"

"I have their address and the name of the suspect and all. I can give you that."

"Rebekah, do you have your computer?" I nodded. "Go ahead and start the report. We'll see if it goes anywhere."

I logged online to initiate the report to Statewide Intake. Statewide Intake, the centralized call center in Austin, handled all calls of abuse and neglect for children and adults. Reporters could call them or report abuse online. Calling resulted in a faster response time. It was the ideal way to report abuse if there was an immediate danger to a child that wasn't a life-threatening emergency for 911. The report was usually sent to a screener the same day it was called in and then forwarded to the investigation's division so contact could be made with the victim.

If the case involved abuse or neglect but the victim was not in immediate danger, or in our case, CPS was already with the victim before a case was generated, reporting online was appropriate. Online reports usually took forty-eight hours to process, which wasn't a problem since we were already with the victim. All we needed was to generate an official case number.

I began inputting the limited information I knew at the time, focusing on Detective Fumer's comments about the lack of cooperation from Mom and lack of protectiveness.

Law Enforcement asked CPS to accompany them to a CAC interview they had already set up. Law enforcement is unsure if the case will fall in the jurisdiction of CPS as the suspect does not live in the home. Law enforcement is concerned the mother is not protective as she was hostile with them when trying to set up the interview. However, the mother did bring her daughter to the CAC for the interview.

While typing, I listened to the interview. Angel was soft spoken but detailed every encounter she could remember, claiming all of them were consensual. She sounded like most hormonal teenage girls, except for the part where she was dating a nearly fifty-year-old man. Her assailant's name was Gary Booksire and she confirmed he didn't live in her home. She had known him for a while, and it sounded like he had acted like other sexual predators. He had convinced her they would get married, have children, and so on.

Kris asked her why she was willing to tell anyone about the relationship and she said it was because her mother had told her she had to. She said she wasn't supposed to be with an older man because she was only sixteen and a half years old and it wasn't legal until she was eighteen. She was right. In another eighteen months it wouldn't legally matter how old her assailant was. She promised not to see him again because that's what her mother wanted.

Angel continued talking openly, not only about herself, but about other girls, too. She named other girls Mr. Booksire had been with, names Natalie and I recognized from other CPS cases. Mr. Booksire was the same man who neither CPS nor law enforcement could prove had assaulted the girls in the other cases. The girls wouldn't come forward or they had recanted their statements, leaving us without evidence. Finally, these girls would see justice after years of waiting because Angel wasn't afraid to tell someone.

"Well, she sounds off, like maybe she has a learning disability, but I don't think that outcry could've been any clearer. I'll have a warrant within a week for Mr. Booksire," Detective Fumer announced after the interview. "But I still want you to call in a report on the mom."

"Really?" I asked. "For what? Mom's the one who made the report."

"Just do it. If nothing comes of it then nothing comes of it," Natalie said before Detective Fumer could answer. "But go talk to Mom first and see if she can add anything else."

I pulled Mom into the meeting room next to the lobby to give us some privacy.

"Your daughter was very clear in her interview," I said. "There are some victim forms you can sign, and the CAC can provide counseling at no cost."

"I ain't signing nothing," Mom growled. "I did what I was supposed to. I done it all. I took Angel to the police and asked for help. I done that. I brought her here. Why I got to sign anything?" She vented her frustration on me and I started to understand how hostile she could be. "Where's my daughter?"

"She's in the room with Kris. She's just fine," I explained, pointing to the wall. Kris' office was on the other side. "Let's talk for a min. Part of my job is to speak to the parents and get information so we know how to help."

Mom refused to respond. Her face had no feeling, no emotion, nothing. I wondered if she was ever diagnosed with flat affect, a complete lack of emotional expression, but I tried again.

"Can you tell me where you work?"

No response

"Is Angel's father involved?"

Nothing.

"Did you know Angel was sneaking out of the house?"

Again, nothing.

"Look, Amy. I have to ask these questions. We're investigating everything. It looks like you're hiding something and if we don't find out what it is, then we'll have to do something more drastic. We have to get a social history from you. That's our job."

"I'm not speaking to you."

"I just need the basics. Where are you working?"

"I can't answer that. It's confidential."

"Confidential? Why?"

"I have a security clearance. I can't answer that." Was she on drugs? "Look, it's a basic question. Where do you work?" She stared straight ahead, no emotion, no expression.

"Do you use have a history of drug use?"

"I don't use no drugs. Why you think I use drugs?"

"I'm asking because you're acting like you're on something. Will you take a drug test?"

"I'm not taking no drug test. I ain't doing nothing for you people. I asked for help from the police. Not you people."

I wasn't getting anywhere and the situation was escalating. I thought Natalie might get through to her, so I didn't waste any time in grabbing her from the hallway.

"Amy, maybe we can try this again," Natalie said sweetly as she entered the room. Mom responded to Natalie and ignored me. "We need a drug test and a few questions answered. Okay?"

"I already said I ain't takin' no drug test. I ain't done drugs in my life."

"Look. You're acting like you're on something. We have a job to do. If you don't do it willingly, then we'll just have to ask a judge for court orders to make you cooperate. And we really don't want to do that."

We waited, giving Mom a chance to make up her mind.

"Fine. I'll take your stupid test, but I ain't on no drugs."

I was willing to bet money she was. Her behavior, gestures, and speech were unusual. I pulled an oral drug swab kit from my bag and made note of the number. Kit 153-22 #22. I kept track so we knew what test was used and on which individuals. Mom grudgingly took the test and swabbed her mouth. The test was clear: she was clean.

"I told you people I don't do drugs. Every time something happens and I ask for help, you people come in and tell me what to do. You never believe me. You always say it be my fault."

"What are you talking about?" I asked.

"It don't matter no how. I want my daughter. We leaving."

"You're not leaving yet. We have more to discuss. We need to make sure Angel is safe before we can allow her to leave with you," Natalie said.

"I took your drug test. I ain't talking 'bout nothing else. I ain't doing nothing you people want."

"I've had enough. Come here, Rebekah," Natalie said, gesturing to me to follow her. We stepped outside of the room. "I don't know if there's enough to remove or not, but something's wrong. She's hiding something or she knows something. She won't even tell us where she works. And if there's not, I want someone else telling me there's not enough."

I agreed. We'd call our Polly, ask her, and then do whatever it was she advised.

"Polly, I need to staff a removal with you," Natalie said on the phone. She gave Polly the rundown of why we were here and what led up to this point. "We had her take a drug test and it's negative… No, the suspect doesn't live in the house… Yes, the police think they'll have an arrest warrant within the week… Yes, Mom took her to the police station and made the report… Yes, she brought her here, too… No, she didn't make any other outcry… No, she said Mom didn't know anything about it. She snuck out of the house. Really? Okay. Thanks."

I knew Polly had said there wasn't enough to remove Angel.

"I'm calling Audrey. Maybe we can at least safety plan Angel out for the night and figure out what to do tomorrow."

"Audrey, I need to staff a case with you," Natalie began as she went through the entire case again. I saw frustration written all over her face as she hung up. "We don't even have enough for a safety plan. But she and Polly both said to see if Mom would come back tomorrow with Angel for another interview with law enforcement. If she doesn't agree then we may do something. But maybe today has just been too much happening at once. And, she keeps referring to us like we've done this before. Let's see what's in her history. We'll need time to look at that."

"Amy, you can take Angel home now," Natalie said when walking back into the room. "But we need you to come to the office tomorrow and speak to Rebekah about this some more. Can you agree to that?"

"No. I can't take off work," Mom replied instantly.

Natalie was about to say something else but Angel and Kris walked in.

"Oh, sorry. I thought y'all were done," Kris said.

"We are now. Angel, you can go with your mother. Thank you for talking to us," Natalie said, patting Angel on the shoulder. Mom didn't waste any time. She grabbed Angel by the wrist and rushed out the door.

"Ask Detective Fumer if she's available tomorrow. Then call Mom back and talk her into coming to the office," Natalie said.

Detective Fumer had already left so I called her on my back to the office.

"Sure, I can meet tomorrow. How about 3:00 p.m. or something?" Detective Fumer agreed. I called Mom next, leaving a voicemail when she didn't answer. Surprisingly though, she called me back within minutes.

"I'm calling Rebekah back," she said.

"Amy, this is Rebekah. We really need you to come to the office tomorrow and speak to me and to Detective Fumer again. Can you please come in at 3:00 p.m.?"

"No, I told you. I have to work."

"Look, we have to investigate. For all we know you're going to let Angel go right back to Mr. Booksire's house tonight. You wouldn't even answer the question of where you work. We have to make sure everything is okay."

"Angel ain't goin' to his house. And I don't have no money for gas. I have to work. I can't take off work."

"You live two miles down the road. We can meet later tomorrow afternoon. We can do it after 5:00 p.m. if you need. I'll stay late. I'm sure Detective Fumer will also." If she had a problem, I had a solution.

"I ain't got the money for gas."

"We'll go to your house instead. That way you don't have to drive all the way here."

"You people ain't coming to my house. It too small. No."

"Then I'll pick you up. Or I'll fill up your gas tank. Whichever way you need."

Mom only lived two miles down the road but if it took filling up her gas tank to get this figured out, then that's what I'd do.

"Do Angel got to be there?"

"Yes, please."

"I don't know. I have to check." She hung up. I had no idea if she would show up or not. Either way, I'd be ready.

I shot Natalie and Detective Fumer a text, updating them with the conversation before sitting down in my office to finish filling out the intake report. I hadn't learned much more from when I started the report, so I checked Mom's CPS history. There were two cases, but one was too old to access. I opened the more recent case and summarized the information into the report.

Victim made a valid, detailed outcry describing what happened and where. Victim said she is in special education classes and may not be functioning at the average level of a sixteen year old. Mother made the initial report to law enforcement after victim arrived home late and mother learned what victim was doing. Interview was attempted at the CAC, but mother was not cooperative. She did submit to a drug test, which was clean. Mother is supposed to come to the office in the morning with her daughter for a full, detailed interview with both CPS and law enforcement. A search in Impact showed mother has prior history. Mother works full time. Based on the past CPS history, the last case being five years ago, victim may have special needs. Victim may need medication. Mother might not be protective.

I submitted the initial report, wondering if I would learn something different tomorrow. It wasn't unusual as the investigation progressed to learn facts that contradicted everything in the initial report. If Mom cooperated tomorrow, we might be able to fill in the missing pieces.

Mom and Angel showed up the next day before Detective Fumer. Mom was pleasant with a completely different attitude than the previous day.

"Amy, hi, I'm glad you could make it," I said as she shook my hand. She smiled back. "Do you mind if I speak to Angel first?"

"Go ahead. I'll wait here," Mom said.

I took Angel back to my office so I could ask questions the CAC interview didn't cover.

"Do you remember me from yesterday? We barely were able to say hi to each other," I asked as we sat down.

Angel wore a purple t-shirt and cutoff blue jean shorts. The shorts made her long legs look even longer.

"Yes, I remember you."

"Everything go okay when you got home?"

"Yeah. It was fine. We ate supper and watched TV."

"Did you go to anyone's house?" I tried to make the mood light and see if she knew where I was going with the question.

She laughed. "No. I stayed home."

"Not even when everyone went to bed? I remember being a teenager."

"No." She laughed again. "They watching too much."

I laughed with her. "Tell me about school. Do you like it? Don't like it? Something else?"

"I like it okay. I don't miss any days."

"Who are your teachers?"

"I have Ms. Mapps for math and Ms. Shay for reading. I'm going into 11th grade next year.

"That's great. One more year and you'll graduate. You said something about being in special education classes. I don't really know how to ask this, so just forgive me. You don't seem like you need to be in special ed. I don't understand."

She was speaking to me coherently, like a regular teenager. It was different than yesterday, but we also weren't talking about her assailant.

"I'm not in special ed like with the others. I just don't read too good. I had to do sixth grade again one time because I couldn't pass the test. And I have ADHD."

"So, you have special classes to help with reading, but you're in regular classes with the other kids?"

"Yeah. It's so I can pass the tests."

I finally understood out what she meant. She wasn't special needs in the sense of mentally handicapped; she had a learning disability. Being in special education classes allowed a work around for students to manage the state mandated tests.

"Okay, I get it. Do you take medication for the ADHD?"

"Yeah, I take it when I'm at school."

"Your mom or someone make sure it's filled?"

Angel nodded.

"Tell me about your family. I'm confused on who lives where. See, I tried to draw a family tree and it's all messed up."

Angel laughed again and took my notebook from me.

"It's confusing, I know," she said as she drew her family members. She labeled each one, naming who was married to who, who worked where, and who stayed in what house.

"Thank you for that. It really helps. Are you scared of anyone at home? Or anyone anywhere else?" I asked. She shook her head. "Would you tell me if you were?"

"Yeah. I'm not scared of nobody. I haven't been whooped in a long time," she replied.

"Whooped? What did you get whooped for?"

"I don't know. It was a long time ago." She shrugged, unconcerned.

"Okay. I just have a few more questions. Anyone in your house do any type of drugs?"

"Well, my uncle drinks beer. And I tried a joint one time."

"Girl, who gave you weed?" I was surprised she admitted to it.

"A friend. I only did it one time last year. Don't tell my mama. She'll whoop me for sure. I never doing it again. I don't hang out with that person anymore. She wanted me to smoke K2, but that'll kill you."

"How do you know that?"

"I heard stories. I don't want that stuff."

"Did anyone whoop you for sneaking out of the house?"

"Nah. But they sure watch me now."

We continued to talk about everyday life for her. She didn't have many friends and didn't seem to mind. She knew which medication she took for her ADHD and said she took it at school. She knew the last time she went to the doctor and she knew where to go if she ran into problems. I questioned her again on whether or not she was scared of anyone, whether it was family members or friends or if anyone gave her a hard time. She insisted she was fine. She just couldn't sneak out of the house anymore.

I walked Angel back to the front of the office where Detective Fumer had joined Angel. They were chatting with each other, unlike yesterday.

"She's back," I announced as Angel sat down next to Mom. "You good to stay here while we talk to your mom?"

Angel nodded.

"Then let's go." I waved toward the interview room, and Detective Fumer and Mom followed behind me.

"The room's small, sorry about that," I said while we crammed into an interview room with an oversized desk. "You look better today."

I sat next to Detective Fumer with Mom sitting across from us.

"I am. I'm sorry 'bout yesterday. Y'all showed up and I thought it was over. It's how it's always been," she explained.

"I know. I read your history today. I couldn't see all of it, but I can imagine this was scary."

She nodded, understanding.

"Amy," Detective Fumer began. "We're working on a warrant for Mr. Booksire. If everything goes as planned, it will be issued tomorrow. Has Angel gone to see him again?"

"Nope. She ain't goin' to that man's house again. We make sure of that. She has an earlier curfew and we all watch to make sure she stay home."

"Good, that sounds good."

"I'm glad you gettin' that warrant. He needs to go away for a long time."

"And you didn't know anything about Angel's excursions?"

"No. I work in Garland. I'm gone all day. She's supposed to be home when I get home. She wasn't this time. She kept trying to tell me a story about where she was. I wouldn't stop asking 'til she told me. I didn't know she would tell me that though. That's why I took her right to y'all."

"That's good. That's good." Detective Fumer was making notes. "Rebekah, you got anything?"

Now it was my turn. "Well, Amy, remember that social history I mentioned needing yesterday? Can we go over that now?"

Mom was agreeable this time. She openly talked about her background, her daughter, and their home life. She apologized for not understanding why we were there yesterday and explained she had a hard time in social settings. She never could understand how to act around other people. I had read about that in her case history. She confirmed the same things Angel had already told me about the ADHD and content mastery classes I had referred to as special education, and she was proud of her daughter for being on track to graduate.

"How about Angel's phone? Where's the phone?" Detective Fumer interrupted.

"We took that away. Her father gave it to her and we took it away. She can't call no one anymore."

"Can I have it? I want to see if there's anything on it that will help us with Mr. Booksire's arrest."

"Sure. It's at the house. You can have it."

Detective Fumer returned to taking more notes, her cell phone continually ringing as we interviewed Mom. Finally, she pulled me out of the room.

"Rebekah, I don't think Mom had anything to do with this. I was concerned yesterday. I mean, her behavior was horrible. You said she was negative on drugs?"

I nodded.

"I've spoken to everyone in the family. They've all got the same story. And they've been cooperating. Angel helped with a lineup yesterday. I really don't think Mom knew about this and I don't think she condones it. I don't think you guys need to be involved."

"I'm getting the same impression," I said as her phone went off again. "Who's calling?"

"It's another case I have. My phone is blowing up. There's a guy trying to take his kid and threatening to stab the kid. A couple of other detectives are on it already."

"That wouldn't be the Langston case, would it?"

"Yeah, how do you know?"

"Because I was assigned that one this morning. Natalie's been on the phone all day with someone out there. I have to go there as soon as I'm done with Mom."

"Well, then I guess I'll see you in a bit. But honestly, CPS doesn't need to be involved with Angel's case. We'll have an arrest warrant tomorrow and be done with this."

Detective Fumer left and I returned to Mom.

"Sorry about that. It looks like we have everything. Can you do something for me though? Can you get Angel into counseling? I know you don't want to use us, but can you get someone?"

"Yes. I'll get her into the one she's used before. She got to know she can't be seeing a fifty-year-old man."

"You're right. That's not appropriate at all. But Detective Fumer assures me she'll have the warrant tomorrow."

I walked Mom to the front where Angel was still waiting and watched as they left together. Their family was unusual but being unusual didn't give CPS a right to interfere.

"Hey, Detective Fumer said it's a police matter and they don't think we need to be involved. Mom did a complete 180 and is fully cooperating with police," I said as I poked my head into Natalie's office. "We're out of it."

She nodded in agreement and called Polly and Audrey to give them the update. They both agreed it was a police matter and we needed to close the case. CPS didn't investigate cases where the suspect didn't live in the home, Mom was being protective and fully cooperating with police, the suspect would be arrested tomorrow, and no one condoned Angel's behavior.

Since we had an official case already filed, I still had to document the last two days' worth of interviews before I could close it and that would take some time. I needed to rush off to the case involving the violent father and his kid. Documenting Angel's case would just have to wait.

Chapter 10

September 2012

Ester, Alison, and Justine continued to report to Natalie and Audrey concerns that I was violating the Fourth Amendment.

The Fourth Amendment specifically addresses searches and seizures in cases pertaining to public servants and what we could or could not do inside of a home. We had some basic training from the CPS academy regarding it and knew of the clarifications from the Gates case in 2008. We had to have court orders, exigent circumstances, or permission to enter and remain in a residence.

My coworkers kept insisting I would barge into someone's house and search their home for drugs. Or I would force myself into their home without asking for permission first. They accused me of tampering with drug test results to make a parent positive for drugs when they were not. Every time they came up with an accusation, I had documentation to back up the truth.

They pulled apart my Facebook account, claiming my posts were about cases, something they felt was a violation of the Fourth Amendment. Those posts were never work related. Still, they blatantly said they were and passed them up the chain of command. If I mentioned anything about seeing a parent on their public profile, I was once again accused of violating their rights. The fact it was a public account didn't seem to matter.

Management called Natalie constantly about the complaints, wanting her to address them with me. My coworkers felt Natalie allowed me to get away with everything and never addressed problems with me. They didn't understand the complaints because none of the parents complained, and they decided the complaints weren't serious because it was only gossip and bullying.

Someone, a few someones, told Audrey. They formally wanted to complain I was controlling Natalie's mind and had a supernatural power over her. Audrey thought they were joking. They weren't. The complaint irritated management enough that they no longer took anything else about our office seriously. Had that last, out of this world, insane complaint never gotten called in, management might have allowed us to move offices, formally address the bullying and gossiping, or even transfer workers to put a stop to everything. It's hard to take anyone seriously when you have people complaining of mind control.

Natalie and I decided to have a special conference on September 12, 2012, a day after a mandatory Fourth Amendment training, to show we had discussed the concerns. While management might not have taken the complaints seriously, the Assistant District Attorney and our CPS attorney did. Coordinated by Polly Patterson, Assistant District Attorney Karen Bacon held a special Fourth Amendment training on September 11, 2012.

Everyone was supposed to attend. I hated it. I didn't hate what the training was about but the fact they wanted every single worker in Hunt County to cram themselves into a government building on 9/11. It had always creeped me out and I tried my best not to be anywhere near a building on that day. But the training was mandatory, and I wasn't going to admit my fear over something that had occurred eleven years before.

For two hours, every single worker, including Audrey Lauren, sat in the court house for a refresher on how to enter a home, when we could search a house, how we could search, and what protections we had, such as immunity. We had been trained since the academy that if we did everything we thought we were supposed to and someone sued, we would be protected by immunity and CPS or the Attorney General's office would represent us in a lawsuit. I didn't expect to learn anything new, but I paid attention anyway. I didn't want to make any mistakes.

Usually someone from the Regional Training Center handled these types of trainings. This time a criminal assistant district attorney, someone who had never worked in family law other than as an advocate, was discussing how the Fourth Amendment applied to us.

Karen Bacon reviewed the same things we had heard from day one. In order to enter a residence, we had to have permission, exigent circumstance, or a court order. We were never to barge into a house without one of those three. Even if law enforcement was with us, we still had to have permission to enter if we didn't have any of those three options. She passed out the landmark case from the Fifth Circuit, Gates v. Texas Department of Regulatory Services as an example. The Texas Department had been sued because the investigators didn't have permission or a court order to enter. Though the Texas Department had won the case, they pushed for us to use an Order in Aid of Investigation more often if we could not gain entrance. That was a large reason I had the orders to find Daisy. Karen also used Miranda v. Arizona and Terry v. Ohio, two other landmark cases for law enforcement, as examples. I wasn't sure how they really applied to CPS, but I was familiar with them because of my past law enforcement experience.

The biggest thing I took from the training was her assurance that if we were ever in doubt, ever, even a tiny bit, we could ask our CPS attorney, or law enforcement if they were with us, if it was okay to do what we thought we could do. She assured us, if we had their approval, we would be protected. She assured us if we documented we had permission to enter or search, we would be protected. It was a bit odd she suggested we record the home visits and interviews with the parents for proof we had permission. I understood law enforcement had the ability to record, but it was against CPS policy at the time and we didn't have the equipment to do so. Everything else she recommended was normal. She continued to assure us court orders, exigent circumstances, permission, and discussing it with our attorney and law enforcement beforehand, was adequate to ensure our protection against any type of lawsuit. It was nothing we hadn't all been trained on before, but it was odd she was pushing it so hard this time.

She used examples of cases from other investigators and workers, explaining what was wrong with them, though it was more of an *it could have been done like this instead* correction rather than *that was the wrong thing to do*. I waited to see if she would use one of mine, but she never did. I thought it meant she didn't have any complaints on my cases or no one had made her aware of anything for her to review. In my mind, I had done everything she had said to do, and I knew Natalie was on the phone with Polly more often than she was on the phone with Audrey. Polly knew every move we wanted to make, and we listened to everything she told us to do or not to do.

I left the training feeling assured things were fine and that the law and policy were being followed. If anyone ever tried to sue me, I would be protected by immunity and represented by an attorney, because I had done, and always had done, everything she had explained. It never occurred to me to think about a criminal prosecution.

The next day Natalie and I held our conference out of the office so no one could eavesdrop. We made sure to address the Fourth Amendment issues and add the conference notes to our reported discussion.

It was brought to my attention that people alleged Rebekah and another worker were violating clients' Fourth Amendment rights and there was an issue with work information posted on Facebook. Rebekah stated she understood Fourth Amendment rights as she worked in law enforcement prior to coming to CPS. She stated she has not violated anyone's Fourth Amendment rights and is careful to document permission in her narrative. She stated if there is a drug issue or drugs in specific places she has law enforcement with her. Rebekah stated if there is something specifically mentioned in the report she does ask the family and they typically will show her. She stated she documents this. Rebekah stated if the family denies entering the home or anything else she does not push the issue. She staffs the case and gets court orders when necessary.

I also addressed with her the issue of Facebook and asked that nothing pertaining to work be posted to Facebook. I specifically asked her about the Facebook post regarding an affidavit. She stated both the comments and post say she had to call the police because two men were found fighting at her residence. Rebekah stated the affidavit was written for the police officers that responded to her home in regard to the incident. She stated she understands the Facebook policy and will not post anything about work.

To both of us, it appeared everything had been sufficiently handled if not even redundantly reviewed, rehashed, and documented in multiple places. We could return to work and handling the cases staring us down before I went on maternity leave.

Chapter 11

September 2012

"You have got to get this backlog off before you pop and someone else has to take them," Natalie nagged me. She was getting nagged by Audrey, who was getting nagged by Marissa, who was hearing it from her supervisor, and so on. The reports and numbers showed our backlog to the full chain of command, and those numbers were more important than anything else.

I sighed. Part of me wanted to throw in the towel and tell them all where they could shove it. Only four days before, I had completed an emergency removal for four children. I had spent five hours at the house trying to find family to take the children, and when no one could I stayed to find foster placement who could keep the children together. It was next to impossible to find foster placement for that many kids in one family. Mom had stayed with me, taking care of her children, so I could focus on placement.

It had been one of those cases where you really didn't want to remove because you knew Mom had the potential to be a great mother—if she would put down the meth. Worse, she had used while pregnant and her youngest one was positive for it. By the end of the day, I had found one place that could keep all four children together. It had been a victory for both Mom and for me. Mom could focus on overcoming her meth addiction and praying her new infant would not have severe withdrawals because she knew her children were together. I had ordered pizza at the office, fed the kids, and hung out with them until it was time to take them to placement. Thankfully, one coworker of mine had felt bad enough watching me waddle around with four children and a ton of paperwork to do that she helped me with the kids and then helped take them to placement.

I still hadn't finished the case's paperwork, but backlog was more important. I sat down on September 24, 2012 to finish documenting Angel's case. I finished the safety assessment first and then called Angel's mom to check on the counseling. Mom assured me she was taking care of it and was not about to discuss it with CPS. We didn't have grounds to force it, so I let the counseling drop. That phone call triggered a phone call from an uncle, Mr. M. who didn't live in the home. He spoke to Natalie, wanting to make sure nothing new had been called in. Mom was concerned, and he wanted to put her mind at ease. After calling Mom back to obtain permission to speak to Mr. M. about the case, we told him everything was fine and we were just following up.

I contacted the school and verified Angel was attending classes. They said she was and expressed no concerns. Because the allegations hadn't concerned the home and she was sixteen-years-old, a home visit wasn't needed. I sent a request for the police report regarding Angel's assailant. Policy allowed us to use that interview when law enforcement had conducted it, and I didn't want to leave it out of the documentation.

As I started the risk assessment, my phone rang. It was Greenville PD calling me directly.

"Rebekah, I need your help. Please. Like right now if possible." It was Officer Hilton, someone we worked with regularly on raids. I knew him from before when I was at Greenville PD, and I recognized concern in his voice.

"Okay, what's wrong? Where are you?" I asked.

"I'm just down the road. I've arrested a mother and we have an infant here she left alone in her apartment for about three and a half hours before someone realized he was home alone, in his crib," he said.

"Like a baby baby?" I asked. I was putting my boots on and gathering my things to rush out of the office. We didn't have an intake on this case, but I wouldn't leave the officer hanging. There was a baby to take care of.

"Yes, a baby baby. She went to work and just left him here. I think maybe Grandma was supposed to come get him or something. I don't know. I just need help."

I ran out of the office and shot a text to Natalie letting her know where I was. Once again, nothing was getting closed on my workload. She wanted me sitting on my butt documenting cases, but instead I was adding more. This one might turn into an emergency removal depending on what Dad and Grandma had to say.

I met Officer Hilton at the apartment complex. The infant appeared unharmed, though hungry, and there were multiple individuals outside of the apartment, waiting to speak to me or an officer.

I began to interview each of them, learning Mom had left for work, assuming someone would get there to take the baby. She had told one of her coworkers about it, who had told her to get home immediately and get her child. While interviewing Dad, he admitted to not showing up on purpose and telling Grandma he had shown up, so Grandma didn't pick up the child. He wanted to teach Mom a lesson. Dad insisted I look at his phone for text messages for proof. I took his cell phone and searched through, as requested, and found he had deleted most of his messages.

Officer Hilton and I went upstairs to the apartment where Mom sat on the couch in handcuffs. I told Officer Hilton I needed Mom's phone to verify Dad's story. He nodded in agreement.

"Ms. Childs, can I have your cell phone and search the text messages and call logs to verify Dad's story? He's telling me you told him he could get the baby," I asked.

"Yes, it's right there. I'd get it for you, but I'm handcuffed," she said.

"Ms. Childs can you say that again so I can make sure my mic picked it up. Does the investigator here, Rebekah, and I both have permission to search your cell phone?" Officer Hilton asked again.

"Yes, you can both search my fucking phone. I'll even give you the password. Yes, yes, yes. I said fucking yes. I don't know why this is such a big deal. He was only alone for three hours," Mom scoffed at us. In the back of my mind, I wondered if anyone would complain about me searching a cell phone with a police officer.

"He's only five months old. Why would you ever think this was okay?" I asked.

Mom just shrugged.

Officer Hilton and I found the proof we needed. Mom had intentionally told Dad not to come get the baby. Grandma had no idea she was supposed to get the baby. The parents were doing this out of spite to each other. I had another emergency removal on my hands since Grandma said she couldn't physically care for the infant long term. She thought foster care would teach the parents more and that keeping the child in the family would enable the parents to continue this behavior.

After taking the infant to the office, I commenced on yet another emergency removal with yet another stack of horrendous paperwork. The backlog would have to wait again.

Chapter 12

November 2012

I was due in three weeks. I had roughly twenty-eight cases left on my workload that I wanted closed before I went into labor. The investigations on all of them were done, but the documentation needed to be finished. Audrey and Natalie were getting nervous. If it wasn't done, other workers would have to finish it and they already complained about every move I made.

I returned to Angel's case, trying to finish documenting it and then close it. Upon opening it, I noticed none of my previous documentation was there. I knew our computer systems had problems, but I had never seen this before. I went to tell Natalie about it at the same time she was coming to tell me she had just read in the paper Angel had run away. We weren't sure what to do. CPS doesn't investigate runaways, but I also had an open case.

Natalie staffed it with Audrey, who wanted me to call the police department. Even though they hadn't notified us she had run away, we needed to know if they thought the family had anything to do with why she had run away. I followed Audrey's direction and spoke to Officer Banter, who told me, in no uncertain terms, he did not suspect the family had anything to do with the missing teenager. In fact, Mom had reported it to the police as soon as she knew her daughter was missing. The police were treating it as a runaway and not a CPS matter. They would call us if anything to the contrary came up.

I had copied some of the case's original documentation into a Word document when I first wrote it, something I did when trying to spell check it or was concerned the internet would crash. Thankfully I still had most of it, and I could paste it back into case. I was still baffled about how it mysteriously disappeared. No one had access to my cases unless they went through my password or through Natalie's password. I brushed it aside and continued. My safety assessment and risk assessment, at least, showed I had completed them back in September. They were time stamped so they couldn't be messed with.

Statewide Intake had generated Mom as the perpetrator in the case, probably because we were initially concerned about her protectiveness. Because she was listed as a perpetrator, I had to make a ruling next to her name. The only logical ruling was to rule her out for any type of abuse or neglect. I knew she had done everything she could and had the same challenges as any other parent raising teenagers.

The other perpetrator was Mr. Booksire. I should have administratively closed out the allegations under his name because he did not live in the home with Angel. It was what policy required—but I wasn't thinking about policy. He was linked to the sexual assault of multiple other girls, and in every single CPS case he was involved in, he had been administratively closed because he did not live in the house. It meant none of the cases would follow him, and if he got out of jail and he could potentially continue to assault young girls. Any background checks would show he was never a part of the CPS system. This upset me. Without thinking about policy, I ruled him *reason to believe*, something that would tag his name and keep him in the system, hopefully to protect future children. It was truthful—he had assaulted Angel, but I should have closed it out differently per CPS policy. Either way, Angel's mother was not guilty of any type of abuse or neglect. I closed out her case, finally, and didn't think anything else about it.

The next day, after reading the paper, we learned Angel's body had been found on the side of the road in a different county. No one knew what happened. No one had called me or Natalie to tell us. We simply read it in the paper.

My coworkers whispered about the case and me. They wanted to know why I had closed it. I told them it was my case and none of their business. The man listed in my case had been arrested and was still in jail. Nothing about her death was related to my case. My coworkers claimed we knew her body had been found and still closed the case. No one had known she was dead and the police had ruled it wasn't a CPS case, but they didn't believe me.

Natalie wanted to host a baby shower for me to replace the things I had lost in the house fire on November 14th at the office. On the day of the shower, my coworkers made their thoughts about me blatantly clear. They staged a walkout. Twelve out of my sixteen coworkers, every one of them, stood up and walked out of the office twenty minutes before my shower started. Only Natalie and Lori Wright were left. Julia came in later, having forgotten what day it was, and Scarlet Hart had left an apology note and gift, as a doctor's appointment had already been scheduled. The other twelve coworkers, the same coworkers I had considered my comrades and would have taken a bullet for without a second thought, got up from their offices, announced they wouldn't be attending, and walked out.

I called my husband and begged him to join us. I tried to hold back tears and pretended like it was just a great big coincidence. I knew it wasn't. I smiled and laughed with Lori and Natalie while we ate cake and opened gifts, but the pit in my stomach told me something ugly was brewing.

Chapter 13

November 2012

My water broke while I was working at home. I was two weeks away from my due date, but I was experiencing mild contractions. Natalie and I had decided I would accomplish more working from home and away from the office tension. I thought if my body relaxed from the stress, the contractions would probably ease, and they did. They stopped completely.

When my water broke, I was rather surprised.

My family and I had moved out of the duplex and into our new home a month earlier. My husband was home from his hitch, trying to finish the back deck before company arrived the next day for Thanksgiving. We had the full meal planned and family coming over for dinner. The boys happily stayed outside, watching him work and leaving me alone to document cases.

I was documenting the final cases left on my workload with the help of Julia and Natalie. Our goal was to ensure no one in the office had any of my cases dumped on them. It was a burden being assigned someone else's cases when you struggled with your own heavy workload, and it usually happened when someone quit without notice or suddenly went on medical leave. I didn't want to do that to anyone, even if my coworkers didn't like me anymore. Julia was making home visits on the cases with younger children.

Natalie was reviewing my cases as I sent them to her. Since most of my workload consisted of removals, the children were already out of the home and I just had to finish documenting, which was the biggest task.

I sent Natalie a text after my water broke. I figured I would tell her first and then tell my husband whenever he came inside. Natalie sent a text back ordering me to go to the hospital. I said I would—I just didn't tell her when and continued finishing cases. She called after I sent her two or three more.

"Rebekah, why am I still getting cases?" she yelled.

"Because I'm still working?"

"Your water broke. Why aren't you going to the hospital? You have to go to the hospital."

"The contractions completely stopped. I have time," I replied.

"It's your fourth kid. Labors go faster each time. Go to the hospital."

Maybe for her they went faster, and for most mothers. I had never been in labor for less than thirty-six hours. My first lasted for fifty-four hours and three hours of pushing. It was only because of my pure stubbornness and the good health of my son that it didn't end in a c-section. My second child, Korben, was a natural, completely unmedicated birth with a midwife, and it hit the forty-eight-hour mark before it was over. My last one was induced three days early because of pre-eclampsia and still lasted over thirty hours. Each labor might have gone faster but not by much. With no contractions since the night before and only my water breaking, I still had time. But I assured her I would go ahead and pack for the hospital, something I hadn't done yet.

Instead, I closed out five more cases, sending them to her for approval, causing her to call me again and threaten an ambulance if I didn't go. Those last five cases closed out my workload. No one was stuck with anything. Well, except Julia. She had agreed to take four of the newest cases I had received a couple of weeks before and weren't ready for closure, but those didn't count. My workload and backlog were empty, and no one would have anything dumped on them.

After calling the nurse at my OBGYN's office and causing her to have a complete panic attack, I finally went to the hospital. My doctor was extremely laid back and remained calm when I told him I had waited twelve hours before going in. I still wasn't having any contractions, so he sent me and my husband for a walk and a drive, asking that I check in every hour to make sure everything was still okay. I think the nurses wanted to punch him, but he wasn't worried. When nothing started the contractions again, he gave me Pitocin, the devil's drug, to start the contractions and gave me Ambien to sleep. Kragen was delivered the next morning with me drugged out of my mind screaming I would never take Ambien again, ever. Twenty-four hours later we were home with a new baby. My husband returned to finishing the deck and I prepared the day after Thanksgiving dinner for everyone coming over. You would have never known I had just given birth.

I had left personal belongings at the office, not expecting to go into labor early and not return back to work after Thanksgiving. I asked Natalie if she would grab them for me and bring them to my house. I was concerned about one item, which was supposed to be in the bottom right-hand side of my desk drawer. It was a bag of drug paraphernalia leftover from a case two years ago. I wanted it out of my office before my coworkers ransacked the place.

"I have something in the bottom drawer on the right side of my desk. I need that, too," I told her while on the phone.

"Okay, I'm looking," she replied.

I was giving her a play by play about what to grab. My office was a complete mess with things I didn't know what to do with or wasn't aware of. Some items needed to go to foster placements, other things were donations from the fire, and yet other items that

Natalie described to me I had no idea what they were for or why they were in my office.

"There are some files in the drawer," she said. I knew about the files. I didn't want those.

"Under the files then. It's an evidence bag of that paraphernalia from way back when."

"You still have that? I forgot all about it. There's nothing here. I pulled everything out. It's just a few files," she said again.

"Natalie, that drawer was packed solid. What do you mean there's just a few files?" I was confused. Last I used it, I could barely wrestle the drawer open it was so jammed with stuff.

"I took everything out. There are only a few file folders and a onesie for the baby. Otherwise, the drawer is empty," she replied. "I looked in the other drawers, too. Nothing is here."

Someone had already taken my stuff out of my office. Even if they knew the story behind the paraphernalia, I doubted they would tell truth about it. I left it alone for now, not wanting to alarm Natalie and cause her to stress. Instead, I just asked her to bring me the rest of the stuff still in the office.

She came over that afternoon, bags of clothes and my personal things in hand. It had been a week since I had given birth and nine days since I had gone to the office.

"What's wrong?" I asked as I opened the door.

"It's nothing. I'm just stressed is all," she lied. "Here are your things. And can I see that beautiful baby?"

She sat on the couch holding Kragen, making baby faces and baby talk. She tried to act happy, but I wasn't an idiot. Too much had happened over the past few months and I knew her better than I ever had before. At the start of the year we were coworkers: she was my supervisor and I was her employee. By the end of the year, with the constant influx of ridiculous complaints against me, we had become friends, something not often possible between a supervisor and employee. I couldn't control her mind, but I could read it.

"And now, you're going to tell me what's going on," I demanded.

"I don't know. I really don't know. I just know I was called by OIG and told there's an open investigation. I'm not supposed to talk about it," she replied.

"What's OIG?" I asked.

"Do you remember that other CPS worker in the other county, a long time ago, who was investigated and accused of falsifying visits?" she asked. I vaguely remembered something about it.

"Kind of?"

"Well, it was OIG that investigated her after someone said she was falsifying visits. She wasn't. She might not have documented very well, but it was proven she had actually made the visits. OIG insisted she was falsifying and tried to press criminal charges against her. They weren't able to because they can't file criminal charges against anyone, but it made life pretty miserable for her and everyone else," she explained.

I didn't understand. What did it have to do with Natalie?

"Now there's an open investigation again and I guess it's on me."

"What the hell? What did we do to involve OIG? I thought they only investigated Medicaid fraud."

"They do, and I guess they still investigate us. I'm supposed to interview with this guy and I don't know why. I was told it was all confidential but everyone in the office is whispering about it. They all know about it already. I wasn't going to tell you anything. I didn't want to stress you out right after having a baby," she apologized.

"Is it about me, too?" I asked

"I think so. He called and wanted to speak to both of us. I told him you were on maternity leave. He sounded like he was going to call you anyway, but I wouldn't give him your phone number."

"I still don't get why we'd be investigated." And I didn't. I couldn't think of a single reason there would be an actual investigation.

"I think it's because of Angel's case. Everyone keeps talking about it like we did something wrong. I filled out the 2701, the Notification of Child Fatality, and sent the case to the Child Safety Specialist. It went all the way to the top and we were told everything was okay and not to reopen the case. We called Marissa after we closed it and she reviewed it and said it was fine. You shouldn't have RTB'd Mr. Booksire but that was a minor issue. I asked her if she wanted us to fix it and she and the child death unit said no, not to touch it, and leave it exactly as it was because it was fine. And then I got a call from one of the assistant district attorneys asking for a copy of your case. I gave it to them. I figured it was for Mr. Booksire's criminal case. But everyone in the office is whispering about it."

I sat there in shock. What could they possibly be accusing us of? No one would investigate because the case was old and backlogged. If that happened, then over eighty percent of CPS would have to be investigated. If the Child Safety Specialist and Marissa didn't want us to change the RTB to an admin closure, then that shouldn't be investigated either. I was at a complete loss.

"Have you ever dealt with OIG before?" I asked.

"No, I've just heard stories. Audrey has. She said OIG thinks they are above everyone else and they have no training in any of our policies or procedures. They tried to exceed the scope of their position in that last case, but that was years ago. It was a war between OIG and CPS back then with OIG thinking they controlled CPS. And I know they investigate child deaths now if a child dies on an open case. That's why I wanted to make sure everyone knew what happened with Angel's case and filled out the forms. They said it was fine, so this didn't come from them. What makes me so mad though is that everyone else knows about it and no one bothered to tell me. Instead, I answer the phone like a dumbass when he called and Alison is sitting right next to me, smirking."

"When's your interview?"

"I'm not sure yet. I'll tell you about it. Though I'm sure I'm not supposed to. Everyone else can talk about it, but I can't."

"Do you have to speak to him?"

"I think so. It's administrative. Not speaking to him would be like refusing to speak to your supervisor if they questioned you about a case," she explained.

"If it's administrative, then how could they file criminal charges in that other case you mentioned?" I was more than a little confused.

"They couldn't. They tried to, but they couldn't," she said. That didn't tell me anything. "I should go. I know everyone was watching me, wondering what I was doing. That guy told me I couldn't speak to you but that doesn't make any sense either."

"Why don't you tell him to call me. I don't care if I'm on leave or not. If he wants to talk then he can come over here and meet me here and we can talk." I was ready to get this over with, whatever *this* was.

Natalie left stressed and upset. I was more confused, and a little mad, at not knowing what was going on. She was right to not want to tell me while I was on leave, but it stressed me out even more.

I didn't have to wait long for an update. Natalie called the next day, whispering on the phone.

"Rebekah," she said. "He searched your office. There were drugs in your office. I was just in there and there wasn't anything in there."

"Were they in an evidence bag?" I asked, unfazed.

"I think so. I couldn't see much. When he saw me looking, he shut the door. Then he brought the bag to my office and told me he found them in your office. I was so shocked I didn't know what to say. And then he called Greenville PD and made them take it. They weren't there when I was getting your stuff together to take to your house." She was in tears.

"Natalie, calm down. That's the paraphernalia I asked about. From when I found the dope in that mom's house and I couldn't get Greenville PD to take it. You remembered the other day. Just calm down and think."

"Yeah, I remember that case. Is that what this is?"

"Yes. I had asked the officers with me to take it and they were the ones who told me to keep it. They said they couldn't take it because Mom denied it was hers. Then I called Wood and Richards and asked them to come get it. They wouldn't take it either and told me to keep it. They said they didn't have an open investigation and had nowhere to put it. Richards gave me the evidence bag telling me I was lucky he had them because they generally just used a paper bag. Do you remember them coming into the office and laughing they finally got to put me into handcuffs? And then just laughing about the entire thing?"

I was trying to jog her memory. Every single person in the office knew about that incident and they had known about it for two years, including two detectives and two officers.

"We decided to bag it all and have it just in case we needed it for court. I couldn't throw it away because it was evidence and that was illegal. But the detectives wouldn't take it either and Mom was denying it was hers. I didn't want to leave it in the house because it was in the baby's bed. There's even a field-testing kit in the bag that the officers gave me to test the substance in the baggies. Everyone in the office knew about that case. They've known for two years."

"I remember, I remember. Then where was the bag when I was digging through your office?" She was finally realizing something wasn't right.

"Your guess is as good as mine, but I'm thinking it was hiding in someone else's office. I caught someone digging around in there one day a couple of months back. I could name potentially six or seven coworkers that would do this. I'm sure they put it back just before OIG went in there so he would *find it*. You and I both know it wouldn't have been sitting on top of the drawer like that. Did the police make a report?"

"I think so. The one who went in there didn't want to take it, but the OIG guy made him. I think he made a report."

"Don't worry about it. I'll make some phone calls and see if I can get my hands on the report," I assured her.

She suddenly hung up.

I turned around and called a friend of mine, asking for a favor. All I wanted to know was what type of report it was. It should be paraphernalia, class C, if it was anything at all. And it wasn't anything. The officer hadn't even made an offense report. He wrote an Information Report. That type of report was like an FYI report. It stated he was contacted by someone with OIG, told there were drugs in the office, he went out to speak with them, OIG said there couldn't be drugs in my office and requested he remove them. The items listed as *drugs* on the Information Report consisted of a weed grinder with residue in it, an empty sandwich bag, two empty baggies, and a field-testing kit.

If this was what the OIG investigation was about, I wasn't worried at all. I had everything documented in detail in the case the drugs were related to. According to the Fourth Amendment training we had in September, we were supposed to be able to rely on the police officers and their advice if we found ourselves in a situation we weren't sure how to handle. I had done just that and had every word of it documented. Mom had even written a statement and testified in court what had happened. If anyone had a problem with any of it, it should have been addressed two and a half years before.

Not to mention, if they tried to nail me with possession, they would have to prove who was in possession of it when I hadn't been there in almost two weeks, the office was never locked, and the office was accessible to everyone.

In the end, I still didn't understand who or what OIG was and what they could actually do. I only knew there was an investigation and rumor about it dealing with Angel's case. There was an evidence bag of *drugs* found in my office, but the drug case was extensively documented and Angel's case had been cleared by upper management. There shouldn't have been anything to investigate.

Chapter 14

November 2012

"She was interviewed for seven hours," Julia told me as she entered my home. She had stopped by to see the baby and update me on OIG.

"Seven hours? You can't be serious," I scoffed, fully believing she was exaggerating. Julia could be overly dramatic at times. It was her nature and something I love about her.

"Well, if it wasn't seven hours, it was almost that long. She went in at like 9:00 in the morning and then didn't finish until 4:00 or maybe even 5:00. I think she had to go to the police station for the interview. She came back to the office once, made some copies, looked like she was crying, and then went back. I'm telling you, it was seven hours." Julia sat on the couch next to Kragen, watching him sleep. She didn't like to hold babies, so she just watched.

"I've been researching OIG and there's not much on them. All I can find is how they work federally. I can't find their policies or procedures online or even what exactly they investigate when it comes to CPS. They aren't transparent at all."

"I don't know. I just know everyone is talking about it. I know Alison, Justine, Rachel, Ester, Teri, and Lori interviewed with him already. They did it a couple of days ago or something, I don't remember. I haven't been called in for an interview." Kragen started fussing, wanting to eat again. I pick him up, snuggling him against my chest.

"Really? You've heard rumors? I thought this was supposed to be *oh so confidential* and no one could talk about it," I said sarcastically.

"Right. I guess it's only confidential for you." She laughed. "Everyone's talking though. They try to not talk around me because they know we're friends, but I still manage to hear things. They gossip about everything."

"So, what's the rumored gossip? What am I being investigated about?"

"I keep hearing it's about that case where the girl died and the drugs in your office." She acted like it was common knowledge.

"Oh hell," I snapped. "Seriously? I worked Angel's case. Why do they keep bringing it up? None of them had anything to do with that case. They never even met her. I met her. I spoke to her. She was with me in my office, not theirs."

"I don't know. I don't know. I just know they keep saying you didn't do anything on the case and you closed it knowing she had died. And then you didn't care because you didn't wear purple, her favorite color, the day everyone else did."

"First, I did wear purple. They're just too stupid to remember. Secondly, I did work the damn case. Natalie and I both worked it. From her forensic interview. To interviewing her mother twice, once with a detective, to staffing the case with Polly who said we didn't have grounds for anything. It was a police matter. Why is this everyone else's business?" I was infuriated other people, who knew nothing about the case, were poking their nose into my business.

"Chill out. It's okay. I didn't mean to set you off. I had no idea. I didn't know anything about the case." She was leaning away from me like I was going to explode. "I have some Xanax if you want."

She always joked about wanting to shove a chill pill down me, but I wasn't joking today.

"Funny. You're hilarious. This is serious. This isn't anyone's business. We did our job. We had Audrey Lauren and the Child Safety Specialist review it. Natalie even filled out a 2701 just in case we were told to open the case again. It went all the way to the top and they, upper management, said leave it alone, it was fine. Why is this anyone else's concern?"

"You know how it is. They see drama and jump on it. You should've seen them when that OIG dude searched your office. I got there in the middle of it. We weren't allowed to go down the hallway on that side while he was there. I know a couple of police officers were called and they took stuff out of your office. Everyone said you had drugs in there. If I had drugs in my office, I would've smoked them so no one found anything. Kidding. You know I don't use drugs. Might be nice though." She was trying to make me laugh, but I could feel my blood pressure ringing in my ears.

"I didn't have *drugs* in my office. I had stuff left over from a search, a search I had permission to conduct, a search that Mom and a case worker helped with, where *two* officers and *two* detectives refused to take what was found. They gave me the evidence bags. I mean, damn. I guess I should have flushed it down the toilet like that FBSS worker did. That didn't seem to go over so well, but she's not in trouble for having drugs in her office."

Julia's eyes got big. "What? When did that happen?"

"It was a few months back. An FBSS worker went into a house for a home visit to check on a kid. There was marijuana and some cocaine sitting on a dresser. Instead of calling the police, like I did when I found shit, she flushed it down the toilet." My voice grew louder and faster as I got more upset. "She didn't even take pictures of it. She flushed it. Then the people who were supposed to be taking care of the kid denied knowing anything about the drugs. They blamed it on someone staying there, someone who wasn't even supposed to be there. Then those people claimed they didn't know anything either. It was a whole mess because she flushed evidence and now there's nothing to prove why the kid could be in danger even though coke was within its reach." I was practically yelling, standing up and holding Kragen, who was fussed louder as I grew more stressed.

"Guess where the kid is? Still in that home. Probably snorting coke because the crack heads still live there. That FBSS worker just keeps going on with her work, but I have an OIG investigation for taking dope out of the house when police officers wouldn't? Which way do they want it? It's like we aren't supposed to ever find ourselves in a situation like that. It's like CPS thinks we're just supposed to mosey into a house and be welcomed with open arms by parents who are begging for us to save them. Like anyone wants to be told they suck at parenting. And then when something *out of the ordinary* happens, management scrambles around figuring out which worker to blame and telling us what we should have done after they've had a week to discuss it. They aren't out there with us. They aren't in the situation with us. And if I hear *take law enforcement with you* one more time… We have no damn idea what we're walking into. There are not enough officers out there to do that with us. What does the damn Department expect from us?" I screamed over the top of Kragen's screaming.

Julia looked on the verge of a panic attack. "Let me take him. Calm down."

It must have been bad. She never held babies and now she was volunteering to take Kragen. I gathered my composure, trying to relax.

"It's damned if you do and damned if you don't. Damned if you do what your CPS attorney tells you to do. Damned if you do what upper management tells you to do. Damned if you have to make a split-second decision because the policy makers are in their cozy offices playing solitaire and never created a policy for something out of the norm."

Julia quieted Kragen and when I was calm, I took him back and started feeding him.

"Well, alrighty then. On that note, I'm gonna head out. I'll let you know if I hear anything." She gathered her things and left. This was going to be a nightmare maternity leave. I could only imagine how Natalie felt.

I sent Natalie a text asking if she was okay. She responded she was but said she couldn't process anything. She needed time to think. The most she could tell me was it was a horrible experience and the investigator hammered on her for almost seven hours. Julia wasn't exaggerating. I couldn't believe he had any authority to interrogate her like that.

I spent the next two and a half months of maternity leave researching everything I could find about OIG. There wasn't anything available. It was like they were ghosts, left to their own devices, without any official rules or guidelines. Worse, there weren't any policies or procedures for how those being investigated were supposed to handle it. I couldn't find anything that explained whether we had to speak to them, if they could interview us for seven hours, if they could search our offices, or even if we could have an attorney with us. I would return to work with no idea of what rights or protections I had, if any.

Chapter 15

February 25, 2013

"Hey, Rebekah, you're back," Julia announced when she saw me in the hallway. I had just passed through a line of death stares. Alison, Ester, and Justine had been wasting time chitchatting when they saw me walk in. They had immediately quieted and stared at me like I had a third eye. The tension in the air was so thick it was hard to breathe.

"Hi. Yeah, I'm back." I smiled. I glanced behind me to see if the three had scampered off to their holes. Thankfully they were leaving, Alison taking one last glance behind her toward Natalie's office.

"Shut the door," Natalie said.

I shut it and sat down on the couch next to Julia.

"So, that was fun," Julia said, stating the obvious.

"Woman, you knew I'd be back today. Why'd you have to announce it like that? You know they can't stand me."

She laughed. She could make any situation awkward.

I turned back to Natalie. "So, what's up? It already feels great around here."

"They're all listening, that's why I wanted the door shut," Natalie went on. "About two weeks ago it started back up. They were asking me non-stop whether or not you were coming back.

Audrey had to tell Rachel to mind her business. They were blowing up her phone, too. They don't want you here, but Audrey and I both told them there's nothing they can do about it."

"No kidding? I couldn't tell."

"I know, I know." Natalie shook her head, frustrated. "My guess is you'll have your interview soon. Who knows what will come of it? I mean, I'm still here."

After her interrogation, she had continued to work like nothing happened. It was like everything was on hold. "I don't want to assign you cases yet, because we don't know what will happen. And it's too hard to work cases and focus on this investigation. I don't want to do that to you. Not to mention, I sure don't want you to get into the middle of something and give those guys something else to complain about."

"Yeah, that's why you get to help me instead," Julia squealed.

I glanced at her suspiciously. "Help you?"

"Yeah, she's backlogged, bad. You two are going to close her cases. She's to sit in your office and dictate to you what she's done and you type. She has to get her workload cleaned up. I'm having a hard time holding off Audrey. She'll probably end up writing me up if this doesn't get cleared off."

"Really? You mean to tell me you came over to my house, while I was on maternity leave, had me type for you then, and you're still backlogged?"

Julia glanced around the room, pretending she was oblivious to my question.

"Wait, what?" Natalie asked. "You helped her while you were on maternity leave?"

"Who, me?" I played dumb. "I was practicing my typing skills."

"You were supposed to be resting."

"This is supposed to be all about me, not your typing skills," Julia chided.

It was fun to banter back and forth with each other again. I was usually excited to come back after maternity leave, see everyone, and get back to investigating. This time, it had been torture. Julia's attitude helped lighten the mood.

"It is all about you. Someone who can't sit down long enough to document." Julia could work a case just fine but sitting her down long enough to type was next to impossible. Typing was boring. Being out in the field was exciting.

"Go get to work. I'll let you know if anything happens, but I'm sure you'll get an email or something about the interview." Natalie had her own work, too, so Julia and I headed for my office.

Julia cheerfully rambled on about her cases, excited she would get undivided attention to help clean up her workload. My mind was elsewhere though, thinking about the investigation that had plagued my mind for the past three months. Part of me was disappointed I had ever thought things would blow over. Things had gotten worse and I had no idea why.

"Let's get this done," I said, opening my office door. It was the first time I had been inside my office since I went on leave. It didn't feel the same. "Close the door. They don't need to hear us talking, though they've probably bugged the office anyway."

"Really? You think they'd do that?"

"No. Well…" Maybe they really would do that.

Julia pulled up a chair next to me and opened her laptop, resting it on her lap. I opened my email for the first time in three months. The first email I saw was from Marissa telling me there was a pending investigation. It said I would be contacted soon by the investigator for an interview. Above all, the investigation was confidential. I laughed out loud.

"What? What's so funny? You scared me."

"It's confidential. The email says the investigation is confidential." Julia busted out laughing, too. Tears rolled down her cheeks.

"Confidential to you maybe." She laughed some more. "Only to you. Everyone else already knows everything about it. You're the only one that doesn't know. I think they're violating your First Amendment right to free speech." We laughed even harder.

"Don't think I didn't think about that. Wait."

Someone was talking on the phone in the hall. I held my finger to my mouth, signaling Julia to be quiet. Tiptoeing to the door, I listened intently, trying to force my ear between the tiny opening at the doorframe.

"She must've left, I don't see her car," I heard Alison say. "Yeah, I know, I can't believe it either. Yeah… Okay… I'll call him tomorrow with the new case. Hopefully this time it'll work." I couldn't hear anything else.

"What was it?" Julia asked, her face wrinkled in worry.

"I'm not sure. Maybe nothing. But I have a really bad feeling."

Chapter 16

February 2013

"OIG can't interview me until next Tuesday, March 5th. I just want this over with."

Natalie and I sat in her office, avoiding coworkers. It was only Wednesday, but it felt like weeks had passed.

"Is it the same investigator? That Juan Carlos guy?" Natalie asked.

I nodded.

"Did he give you any indication what it's about?"

"No. I tried. I figured I'd play nice guy and be all chipper and sweet and see if that got me anywhere. I asked how long it would take, knowing how long he kept you in there, and all he said was, 'It shouldn't take too long.' So, I know nothing."

Natalie nodded in acknowledgment, typing at her computer. I felt out of place in her office as much as I did in the entire building. It didn't make things any easier waiting on Julia to get back from seeing the kids in her cases. I was used to working my own cases, going constantly, and working in the field. Now I was locked in an office with gossiping coworkers. "I think I'll go hide in my office for a while. I don't have anything else to do."

I made my way down the hall, trying to avoid everyone. To reach my office I had to pass either the SI offices or the other supervisors, and all the investigators. One way or the other, I'd run into someone. It was Alison.

She was on her phone, oblivious of my approach, her high-pitched voice echoing off the walls. I thought about avoiding her but decided against it. It was time to see if she'd tell me what the problem was.

"Hi, Alison. How are you?" I asked, stopping her from passing me. Her head snapped up, surprised and disgusted at the same time. She didn't even try to hide it.

"Hi." She rolled her eyes and kept walking.

This was ridiculous. Alison had attended my wedding. We had worked multiple cases together. Now she was telling new investigators to stay away from me so I didn't get them fired.

I'd never gotten anyone fired.

I changed course and decided to check on Lori. On the way to her desk, I ran into Ester. She was talking with Sierra, another investigator who stayed to herself. They were discussing a case Sierra was working on with parents using K2, a synthetic marijuana. Ester was insisting CPS couldn't remove the children, even with the concerns that the children weren't being fed, weren't getting medical care, and had random bruising on their bodies. Alison was agreeing with her, but Sierra thought the children were in danger. Having had a similar situation in the past, I spoke up, wanting to help Sierra. I hadn't predicted the reaction I'd get from Ester and Alison.

"You can remove for it if it's posing a danger to the children. K2 can cause parents to go completely off their rockers," I offered.

Sierra looked uncomfortable and Ester continued as if I hadn't said anything. "It's not even illegal. It's fake marijuana and we can't test for it. We don't know for sure if the lack of food or medical care or the bruises are related to the K2, or if it's even abuse. They're on probation anyway, so the probation officer can test for it if they want to. You just need to close it."

I couldn't stay quiet. She was suggesting leaving a three-year-old in a house with, what sounded to me, abuse.

"Ester, it is illegal, and you can test for it. If they're on probation, ask the probation officer to test for it. That's how we found it in my case. The parents were so out of it that they were falling on the floor in the grocery store, screaming about dragons trying to burn them down. After they were taken to the hospital, I found out Mom was on probation. The probation officer was able to get the test and send it for confirmation through their department. You could try that route." I was immediately sorry I had said anything.

"No one asked for your opinion. Why're you even here? You're a worthless piece of shit and no one gives a fuck what you say." She looked me straight in the eye without hesitation.

Sierra turned on her heels and hustled back to her office. Alison didn't stay either, mumbling, "She's not wrong."

Ester puffed out her chest and pushed past me, knocking me in the shoulder and into the wall.

Lori sat in her chair, at the front desk, her jaw hanging open.

"I'm sorry for her bad luck?" I shrugged.

"File a report against her. That was assault."

"And say what? That she's a bully? Somehow, I don't think anyone around here cares."

"That's because everyone's scared to death of her. You don't know what she's capable of."

"What's she capable of? What aren't you telling me?" Lori shook her head. Whatever she was talking about had scared her too much to say anything else. "Do you know where Natalie is?"

"Break room, I think. I think I heard Justine with her."

Lori was worried about something. I needed to know if it was related to the investigation. Hopefully Natalie would tell me. As I reached the break room, I heard Justine having a panic attack.

"I need to take off. I need medical leave. Rachel keeps assigning cases and won't approve the ones I'm closing. She's having me do stupid stuff on them and refuses to read them. She's making me harass families. Literally everything's done on the cases. Interviews, contacts, records, everything. She just won't approve them. If Ester wants to close a case Rachel lets her, without a question. She's scared shitless of her so she's taking it all out on me. She's going to write me up. Just me. I can't work like this."

Natalie spoke calmly. "I'll take over your workload. Go to the doctor, get a note, and take leave. She can't question you if you have a doctor's note. Get your head together and when you come back, you'll have a clean workload."

"Thank you, thank you, thank you." Justine sobbed.

"That sure was nice of you," I said.

"I know what you're thinking. I would do this for anyone. This investigation is giving her problems, too. She wants to talk about her interview, but OIG told her she could go to jail if she says anything. It's stressing us all out."

"You don't think she has anything to do with this? You're crazy to think that."

Natalie was still too trusting. She wanted to think the walkout before my baby shower was a coincidence.

"I have to go to Corpus tomorrow and help my dad while he's getting radiation treatment. I'll take her cases with me. If everything's done on them, then I can close them. If things aren't done, then I'll bring them back and Rachel will reassign them."

"I'm sorry about your dad."

Natalie's father had stage four cancer and wasn't doing very well. Between her father's illness and her recent divorce, she was hanging on well and still willing to help someone in another unit close her cases. She had a big heart and always tried to help everyone. I was nervous about her leaving. I felt more confident when she was around, and I could handle negative comments better knowing I had backup. I'd get over it. She had more important things to do and my interview wasn't until next week.

With Natalie out of the office, Julia and I stayed in my office, behind closed doors, and worked on her cases. We submitted them to Natalie in Corpus so she could approve and close them. When we finally made a dent in her workload, I saw Marissa's number ring on my caller ID Friday afternoon.

"Rebekah, it's Marissa, are you where we can talk?" Her voice was professional but rushed.

I hurried out of my office to sit in my car for privacy, leaving Julia alone. "I'm outside in my car again. It's the only place I can talk. What's wrong?"

"Rebekah, I'm sorry, I don't know what's going on, but we are putting you on administrative leave, effective immediately. It's for your protection. Take your computer and your cell phone and leave the office, immediately."

I was stunned. I didn't know what administrative leave was.

"What do you mean? Leave? Am I fired?"

"No. You still have a job. It's for your protection. I've never dealt with this before. I don't know what's going on except it has something to do with the OIG investigation. Don't speak to anyone, don't say anything, just get your things and leave. I'm sure there will be emails and phone calls, so keep your email up and answer your phone. I'll call you when I know more." She hung up. I didn't care if she told me not to talk to anyone, I was calling Natalie.

"Marissa just told me I'm on administrative leave and I have to go home," I blurted when Natalie answered. "What's administrative leave?"

"What? I have no idea? What do you mean you're on leave? No one told me," she said, clearly confused. "Wait, Audrey's calling me. Hold on, I'll call you back." She hung up. I impatiently waited for her to call back, failing and calling her again moments later.

"Sorry," she answered. "I was still on the phone with Audrey. They just called and told me I'm on leave, too, and so is Audrey. I'm freaking out. It doesn't make any sense. I've been working since I had my interview. Why now?"

"I don't know. I'm getting my stuff and getting out of here. Marissa said I could take the computer and phone. Call me if you find out anything else. I can't talk while I'm in the office getting my stuff."

I ran back into the office and took a deep breath before opening the back door. I didn't want to appear as if anything unusual had happened. I didn't want to spark more gossip or give them reason to gloat.

"Oh hell. Something's wrong. What happened? Tell me!" Julia said when she saw me. Her voice sounded like it could carry to the other end of the building, even with my door closed.

"Shh, shut up," I snapped. "There's too many ears around. Just help me get my stuff. I have to go home."

Julia helped pack my things and carried them to my car. Once we were outside, she asked, "What's going on?"

"I'm on administrative leave. I don't even know what that is, but I'm supposed to take this stuff, leave, and not talk to anyone." I threw my things into my car. "Natalie and Audrey are on leave, too. Don't say anything to anyone. I just want out of here."

"You know I wouldn't say anything."

My tone must have sounded harsh. "I know, I didn't mean it that way. I'm just stressed. I don't know what this leave is, what it means, how long it will be, or anything."

"But you're not fired, right? And you haven't even had your interview yet."

"I'm not fired and you're right. I haven't had an interview. Natalie wasn't put on leave before her interview. Something isn't right."

"What does that mean for me? I just realized I don't know who to talk to or who to answer to."

"Honestly, I'd go home. There's no telling who's acting supervisor and why bother right now? I'm sure you'll hear what's going on long before I do. That seems to be the pattern. Everyone probably knew I was going on leave before I did."

"You're right. I'm out of here. I'll call you tomorrow." She ran back inside.

I pulled out of the parking lot, a million thoughts racing through my head. Maybe everything would be fine. Maybe this was just a precaution. None of it made any sense, but then again, it hadn't made sense from the start.

Once home, I unloaded everything and dragged it into my house. I wanted to see if I had any emails or phone calls that would explain what was happening. I plugged in my computer and waited for it to connect. An error message popped up. I tried again. Another error message. It wasn't connecting to anything. Suspicious, I sent myself an email from a personal account. It bounced back as undeliverable. I turned to my state cell. I couldn't make any calls. I tried to call my work number from my personal cell. The familiar beeping of a disconnected line rang in my ears.

I called Natalie's state cell and heard the same disconnected number beeping, so I called her on her personal number. "I'm locked out of the system. Are you? Your other phone isn't working."

"I don't know. I've been busy with my dad. Let me see... Yes, I can't believe this. Just like that and we don't have access to anything. This is wrong."

In less than forty-five minutes after being told we were all on administrative leave, for our protection, we had all been completely locked out of the system, as if we had never existed.

Chapter 17
March 5, 2013

"You must be Rebekah. I'm Investigator Juan Carlos with the Office of the Inspector General. How are you today?" Investigator Carlos stepped off the elevator in the records' lobby of the Greenville Police Department, the location he insisted using. He was a Hispanic man in his late forties, slightly overweight, and wore a suit. His handshake was limp and weak, a style I didn't like.

I had waited almost half an hour for him.

"I'm fine," I lied. I was nervous, if not scared to death. He had interrogated Natalie for hours, to the point where she cried and begged for it to stop. She had believed full heartedly she'd lose her job if she hadn't cooperated with him. I didn't know what he planned to do to me. I knew something was wrong with how the investigation was being handled, but I had no idea what was off. Being placed on administrative leave a few days earlier made me even more suspicious. I was so uncomfortable with the situation I had tried to hire an attorney before the interview. I had called every attorney in town, but no one knew anything about OIG except for an attorney in Dallas. Problem was, he was out of the state this week.

"You ready to go upstairs?" he asked as he pushed the elevator button.

"Of course I am," I lied again. I wasn't ready for anything.

We stayed silent during the short ride up to the Criminal Investigation Division or CID. Investigator Carlos wanted to use one of CID's interview rooms. Leading the way, Investigator Carlos opened the door to the lobby and I followed him down the hall toward the interview room. I had been here before, but on the opposite side as an investigator working a case with a detective. I hadn't ever been the interviewee. I stared straight ahead, wondering if I would run into the detectives I had worked with. Did they know what was going on? I assumed everyone in town knew with as much as my coworkers were running their mouths.

Turning the corner, I saw four familiar faces lined up against the wall, chatting amongst themselves. Two of them made eye contact and gave me *the nod*. It meant a lot of things, but this time it meant they knew what was happening and were silently supporting me. I nodded back. Maybe I was imagining the support or just praying for it, but I knew I wasn't imaging the body language on the other two. They refused to look at me, purposely turning their bodies the other direction. I had a good idea who was involved from the office. Now I was certain I knew which detectives weren't on my side.

The interview room was a few feet past the detectives. Investigator Carlos opened the door, entering first, taking a seat, and leaving me in the doorway. I stood there, refusing to enter. The small room had a tiny table, two chairs, and a lamp. On the table sat a single file folder. Natalie had told me when she interviewed there was a massive pile of folders and papers Investigator Carlos had used to dig through, read, and show her. She didn't know if he was just unorganized or if he had meant it to intimidate her. Now there was only a single, thin folder.

"Come in," Investigator Carlos ushered. I stepped in, but I wasn't going to sit down until he told me to. He caught on. "Have a seat. Please. Have a seat. Can I get you something? A drink? Do you need to use the restroom? Anything I can do to make you comfortable?"

He shut the door to the room, leaving the two of us alone. I didn't believe his sincerity. He was using the same tactic we were all taught in law enforcement. Pretend to be their friend, build a repour, and they'll tell you whatever you want to know.

"I'm fine." I sat down in the chair, hands in my lap, feet in front of me.

"Okay, just let me know if you need something. Like I said, my name is Investigator Juan Carlos. I'm with the Office of the Inspector General Internal Affairs Division."

"Can I see your badge, please?" I interrupted.

"Yes, of course. Absolutely." He couldn't hide his surprise. He reached inside of his suit jacket and pulled out a small wallet, flipping it open like an actor on TV when they open their FBI badge, flashing it at the suspect and quickly putting it away.

"No, let me see it. Hand it to me, please."

He gave me a suspicious look but pulled it out again, this time handing it to me. As I opened it, his cell phone rang.

"I have to step out of the room and take this. I'll be right back."

"Sure thing."

He closed the door behind him. He told someone he had another interview at 2:00 p.m., but everything else was muffled.

I expected his badge to look like ours, which was nothing more than a keycard with our picture, name, and the state seal. His badge was completely different and was similar to a federal agent's badge. It was rectangular, fitting snugly in the wallet. Embossed on it was a silver colored Texas Seal with *Office of Inspector General* in large, bold letters around the top and *Health and Human Services* in smaller letters around the bottom. The title *Investigator* boldly stood above his name. Natalie had told me the investigation was only administrative. Audrey had told her the same thing. But this badge didn't look like anything I had seen on a civilian investigator.

He had also said he was with the Internal Affairs Division. The only time I had ever heard those words was when it was police related. Was Investigator Carlos an officer of some type? Maybe OIG had a law enforcement division. I thought about looking at the file folder sitting on the table. Maybe he wanted me to look. Maybe this was a setup, a camera watching me, to see what I'd do. Maybe he left on purpose. I decided not to look.

He stepped back in, apologizing for having to take the call. He was slightly shaken but gathered his thoughts and started again. I returned his badge and watched as he slipped it back into the inside pocket of his jacket.

"Do you have a business card on you, too? You know, so I have it just in case?"

"Of course." He pulled a card out of a wallet in his back pocket and gave it to me. I held it in my hand, feeling the thick cardstock and sharp corners. Nerves shook my hand slightly, and I pressed a corner into my palm, trying to keep my nerves in check.

"Like I said, my name is Investigator Juan Carlos with the Office of the Inspector General Internal Affairs Division. I'm investigating a criminal case, case name Natalie Reynolds number 11134-13."

An alarm exploded in my head like a hydrogen bomb. Everything when blank, wiped out, leaving only a loud ringing in my ears. He didn't say administrative anything. He said criminal. What did he mean criminal?

"Can you pronounce your last name again?"

"Thonginh. It's Thonginh." My voice sounded foreign to me. I wasn't sure if I had spoken out loud.

"Thonginh. That's a hard name to pronounce." He chuckled softly, looking at the folder. Why was he laughing? There wasn't anything funny about this. "I need to ask you some questions. Are you willing to answer some questions for me?"

I gathered my thoughts, trying to clear the explosion out of my head so I could sort through what I knew and figure out my next move. I remembered Natalie telling me this guy had threatened Justine, telling her she'd lose her job or face criminal charges if she said anything about her interview or the case. Natalie and I were placed on administrative leave for *our protection*. Investigator Carlos carried a badge that looked like an officer's or detective's badge. He told me he was investigating a criminal case. Civilian investigators didn't investigate criminal cases, only law enforcement could do that. Therefore, logic dictated, Investigator Carlos had to be law enforcement.

"Criminal case? I was told this was an administrative investigation." My voice held steady.

"No, it's a criminal case. I have the case right here." He pointed to the file next to him. "I'm sending it to Robert Locker, the district attorney this afternoon. In fact, I emailed him this morning to let him know. Do you know the DA, Robert?"

My heart pounded out of my chest, my head wouldn't stop spinning, and the siren going off in my ears almost drowned out his voice. He was trying to intimidate me by dropping the DA's name. That much was clear. But calling the DA by his actual name and not his nickname caught my attention. No one referred to Robbie as Robert. If Investigator Carlos had, even once, met Robbie in person, he would know to call him Robbie, just like everyone else.

"I know the DA. I work with him on a regular basis." I carefully thought about every word I said.

"So, I'm sending Robert the case, but I need to go over a few things before I file it with him." The way he kept his back straight, smirking and nonchalantly waving the file, told me he had every intention of doing whatever it took to pry information from me for his case. "You do have to cooperate, I'm sure you've been told that."

I nodded. "You're filing the case with the DA? Not anyone else? Just you?"

He nodded.

"Okay, am I a witness or a suspect?"

"You're a suspect."

I should have known that's what he'd say. It sent my head spinning again. *Suspect, suspect, suspect.* The words echoed in my ears. I was a suspect in a criminal investigation. I didn't care if I was told to cooperate. I didn't care what he said next. There was only one way to respond, one answer to give, one way to handle this.

"I want an attorney." The words surprisingly sounded confident. Especially since I didn't know if I had any rights. This wasn't any type of criminal investigation I had conducted or been involved with.

"What? You want an attorney?" He acted like he couldn't believe I had the audacity to say such a thing, as if no one had ever lawyered up. Maybe no one had. I knew Audrey and Natalie hadn't.

"I want an attorney. You said you were investigating a criminal case. I want an attorney." I was winging every word, trying to sound like I knew exactly what I was talking about and as if he didn't have a choice in the matter. I watched him, waiting for a reply. Any indication of what he was thinking. Something.

"You want an attorney?" This time he was the one fumbling around, trying to cover up something and figure out his next move.

"Yes, I want an attorney. If you're investigating a criminal case, then I have the right to an attorney. You should know that, right?" I said, stating it as a fact and not a question. I hoped he would go with it, agree with me, and let me out of this room. I didn't even know if I could leave.

"Um, yes. Of course. Yes, yes, you do." He shifted in his chair. "But even so, you should cooperate and continue with the interview."

I wasn't cooperating with him without an attorney. "I want an attorney. And I want to leave."

He stared at me, silent, like I would change my mind.

"Okay, so you're not willing to cooperate?" He seemed irritated, like I had ruined his day.

"I never said that. I said I want an attorney. You said this is a criminal investigation. I said I want an attorney. I have the right to an attorney." I felt like a broken record. "And I want to leave. Am I free to go?" It was starting to feel like I was under arrest. I stood up, attempting to walk out, but he stopped me.

"I did say this was a criminal case." He was frustrated, almost mad at me for not speaking to him. "You can't leave. We aren't done." He was crazy. He had to be crazy. He was forcing me to stay in this room.

"Am I under arrest?" I was afraid to ask, fearing if I wasn't yet, then I was about to be.

"No, you're not under arrest. But, well, I have to read you this statement. And I have to record this conversation. I should've been recording this entire conversation."

I couldn't believe what I was hearing. I wasn't under arrest, but I couldn't leave. And why wasn't he recording? Why start talking to someone before you hit record? Did this guy know how to conduct a criminal investigation and interview a suspect? I thought that was why he picked this room, in the police department. I assumed he had been recording the entire time. But maybe not. Maybe he didn't want anyone to hear him threatening me with criminal prosecution. Or maybe whatever statement he was about to read should have been read at the beginning. Had he tried to coerce information out of me without following procedures? I had a hundred questions, but I mostly wanted to know what the statement was and why he was backtracking.

"Sure, go ahead. Record."

He pulled a small, hand-held recorder from his pocket, pushed a button, and laid it on the table in front of us. He started again.

"My name is Juan Carlos with the Office of the Inspector General. Today is March 5, 2013. I am here on criminal case Natalie Reynolds, case number 11134-13. We are at the Greenville Police Department located in Greenville, Texas. I am with… State your name," he paused, waiting for me to speak.

"Rebekah Thonginh."

"I need to read you this statement. *You are being contacted to solicit your cooperation in a matter under investigation which could constitute a violation of law, which could result in criminal prosecution of responsible individuals. You are advised that the authority to conduct this interview is contained in Texas Government Code §531.102. Before we ask you any questions or you make a statement, you must understand the following warnings and assurances. You have the right to remain silent and refuse to answer any questions at any time. Anything you say may be used as evidence in any future criminal proceedings involving you. You have the right to terminate the interview at any time.*" He stopped, looked up. "I just need your signature on this line showing you're willing to cooperate and continue with this interview." He had to be joking. I grabbed the paper and looked for the signature line. A statement was typed above it.

WAIVER I understand the warnings and assurances stated above. I am willing to make a statement and answer questions. No promises or threats have been made to me and no pressure or coercion of any kind has been used against me.

"No way. I want an attorney. I'm not signing this."

Investigator Carlos was trying to sneak this by, trying to get me to sign so I would *waive* my right to remain silent. He just tried getting me to talk first, before letting me know I had a right to stop this whole mess. That's why he hadn't been recording. That's why he got upset when I asked for an attorney. What kind of investigation was he doing? Had he done this to the others, too? Is that why they felt pressured into speaking to him? Had he told

Natalie she didn't have to speak to him? She told me she hadn't signed anything until she was forced to write an affidavit. She made no mention of the statement I had just been read. This was shady investigating.

Did he not have any ethics or morals?

"Did you hear me? I want an attorney and I want to leave. Now."

Chapter 18

March 5, 2013

"This interview is concluded at 11:23 a.m." Investigator Carlos turned off the recorder and tapped his fingers on the table, like he was waiting for something.

"So, am I free to leave?" I asked. I wanted out of the room, away from him. I tried to stay calm, but nauseating panic was building. I didn't know what he would do next, and I was in uncharted territory.

"You know, the reason for this interview was to get your side of the story before I send this to the DA's office. Your side could help me understand. I really hoped you'd explain."

Instead of terminating the interview and letting me leave, he was trying to convince me that telling my side would help my situation. A common tactic, one more attempt to convince someone to talk. Generally, people want to talk, even after requesting an attorney. It's human nature to keep talking. They may believe their actions are justified and after explaining, the investigator will understand and let them go. Or they may believe their story will play on the investigator's sympathy. Sometimes, people just want to confess because they feel guilty or they think being honest and confessing will get them a better deal. Whatever the reason is, people keep talking, and it rarely helps anyone except the investigator. A good ol' fashion statement or confession solidifies the case, leaving a defense attorney with his hands tied. I had nothing to confess, nothing to feel guilty about, nothing to explain, nothing for him to understand. I had no reason to still be there.

"If you want my side, then how about I leave right now, get my attorney, and then come back and talk?" I only offered so no one could accuse me of refusing to cooperate.

"I can't do that. If you leave this room, it's over. I'm filing the case if you leave. Even with an attorney, you won't have a chance to ever tell your side. This is your only shot."

I stared at the beady-eyed, coercing, threatening man who called himself an investigator. He was flat out threatening me. First, he told me he's ready to file the case, and now he told me he's filing it if I exercised my right to an attorney. If this was how OIG handled their investigations, I didn't want any part of it, no matter the consequences.

"I want to leave, right now." Anger and adrenaline overpowered the panic and nausea.

"If you're sure then, okay. I mean, the DA's about to have the case, whether or not you talk to me, but once they have it, it will be too late."

"I'm getting an attorney and I'm leaving right now. I want this interview terminated." I felt like I was being held against my will. I was done waiting for permission to leave. I was walking out that door and he could either let me or tackle me to the ground.

"Okay then. That's your choice. I'll walk you down." I caught his surprised reaction at my insistence. Leaving the file on the desk, he opened the door, allowing me to exit first. I didn't waste any time and bolted down the hallway, trying not to appear like I was running from him. He kept up with my pace, staying right next to me. We passed the same detectives, still standing in the hallway. The two, maybe friendly detectives looked at me, glancing quickly at their watches, and then back at me. Maybe they realized I wouldn't talk. I caught the irritated glance of the other two but didn't care.

"So, you used to work for Greenville PD?" He asked when we reached the elevator door.

Why was he still speaking to me? I begged the elevator to hurry up. "Yes, yes, I did. And this building has eyes and ears everywhere. There're like sixty cameras in this place listening to every word you keep asking me. I don't want to talk. I want an attorney." It was an exaggeration about the cameras, but I didn't care and I doubted he knew the difference. I just wanted him to know someone could be listening.

The elevator doors finally opened, and I could get away from this guy. But he followed me in and we rode in silence all the way to the lobby floor. My mind was reeling, planning my next move, adrenaline surging. I kept my focus on the doors in front of me, ready for them to open, trying to appear calm and collected on the outside. The elevator stopped, the doors opened, and we were in the lobby, the exit doors straight ahead.

"It was nice meeting you. This actually works out. I can file the case before heading back to Austin."

I wanted to slap the smirk off his face.

"You have fun with that. I want an attorney."

His smile disappeared and I marched myself to the exit doors. *Stay calm, stay calm, stay calm.* I could hear my heartbeat in my ears and had to make a conscious effort to march and not trip over my own feet. Throwing open the exit doors, I practically ran to my car.

Crawling into the driver's seat, I tried to pull myself together. I was going to lose it. Tears of anger and fear were brimming in my eyes. My stomach churned, ready to spew. I wanted to call Natalie and Marissa and tell them what happened. I wanted to scream at Marissa for not telling me it was a criminal case and warn Natalie to get prepared for shit to hit the fan. But I remembered there were at least two sets of cameras that watched the parking lot. Investigator Carlos could be watching. Maybe he wanted to see what I did next or if I made a phone call. I needed to be out of sight before I did anything.

Leaving the parking lot, I thought fast. When I called attorneys before the interview, all I could say was that I had an administrative OIG investigation against me. Now I could tell them it was a criminal investigation. Criminal was criminal, whether it was OIG or the local police department investigating. I should be able to get an attorney now.

I found an empty parking lot and pulled over. I called Marissa, who answered right away.

"This is Rebekah. I'm done with the interview."

"Already? I thought it just started."

"I left. He said it's a criminal investigation. It's not administrative. You never told me it was criminal. The interview."

"I didn't know anything about it being criminal. You didn't stay and talk to him?"

"He said it was criminal. He read me my rights, like I was under arrest. No, I didn't stay and talk to him. I told him I wanted an attorney."

"He said it was criminal?" She sounded like she just figured out what the word meant.

"Yes, criminal. I told him I'd come back and interview with an attorney, but he wouldn't let me. I don't even know what I'm accused of doing. Do you? Can you tell me what the allegations are?" I hoped she would tell me or at least have words of encouragement.

"If you had stayed and interviewed, you'd know by now. You didn't have to leave. This will just delay everything. I don't know what'll happen next."

"Why would I talk to him if he's telling me I'm under criminal investigation?" Was it common practice for CPS employees to just sit and talk to someone, waive their right to shut up, and lay it all out for them? Even if they didn't do anything wrong, anything they said could be twisted and turned around. Just like with what happened to Natalie. "So what happens now?"

"I don't know. This is the first I've heard of it being criminal. I don't know." She hung up, almost sounding mad I didn't stay and talk.

I would find an attorney today, and there was only one that came to mind. I didn't know Jack Wilford personally, but I knew he was a former prosecutor, had been around for many years, and had the personality of a cop. His staff told me he didn't handle administrative investigations, but this was criminal now. I didn't have an appointment, I didn't call ahead, I just drove. His office was only a couple of blocks away. I thought about what I would say. For the first time in my life, I was a suspect in a criminal investigation, facing charges I knew nothing about. The thought made me sick.

I pulled into the parking spot directly in front of Mr. Wilford's office door. Reaching for the gear shift to put the car into park, I realized I had been white knuckling it the entire way. My hands hurt from holding on so hard. I shook it off and took a deep breath. It felt like I hadn't breathed since leaving the station. Calming myself, I closed my eyes and focused on the task in front of me. I could do this. I put my hand on the door handle, opening the door slowly, when my phone rang. It startled me, and I answered it without looking at the caller ID, something I never do.

"Hello?"

"Hello, is this Rebekah?" A male voice was on the other end. I knew the voice but couldn't think straight.

"Yes, this is Rebekah." My voice came out in a rough growling croak. Hearing myself speak reminded me I wasn't calm at all. I was rattled worse than I thought.

"Rebekah, this is Scott Libby. I wasn't sure if I had the right number. I tried calling your state cell, but it was disconnected. Anyway, I was calling to see when you could come in and speak to me about your case."

Everything went black. I felt myself spewing, vomit flying across the dash, splashing down the passenger's side window and on my seat, destroying the inside of my car.

"Rebekah, are you there? Are you okay?" He was still speaking. I hadn't moved my phone away from my ear before blowing chunks.

"I'm fine," I managed to muster while cleaning off my face.

"Okay, if you're sure. I need to talk to you for a few minutes if you'd be willing. I'm the prosecutor on your case and it goes to trial next week. I need to know your side of the story and what exactly you did. Can we get a time scheduled by the end of the day?"

Investigator Carlos wasn't joking. Maybe he had already sent the report to the DA's office back in November after he interrogated Natalie. Maybe he was lying the whole time about giving me a chance to tell my side and the whole time the DA already had it. Maybe OIG cases were fast-tracked somehow. I wasn't thinking clearly or rationally. I didn't know what to do, so I did the only thing that came to mind. I hung up on him.

Chapter 19

March 5, 2013

Every step toward Mr. Jack Wilford's office felt like walking through quick sand. My legs were unsteady, my head dizzy, tears rolling down my cheeks. I wasn't the stone-cold investigator from before. I was the vulnerable, scared suspect accused of the unknown.

I pushed Mr. Wilford's office door open and walked straight to the secretary, keeping my eyes focused on her and nothing else. She sat on the other side of the glass separating the lobby from the rest of the office. I knocked on the glass and opened my mouth to speak. Nothing came out. I tried again. Tears were falling and my nose was dripping.

Surprised and concerned, she handed me a tissue, and then another, and another. "It's okay. Try to tell me what you need. We'll try to help."

"I just left an interview with OIG. He's filing criminal charges on me. I don't know what for." I was outright sobbing and a complete mess but kept trying to get the words out. "I wouldn't speak to him. He tried to make me, but I refused. I wouldn't talk. I told him I wanted an attorney. He tried to force me to talk, but I kept telling him I wanted an attorney. He wouldn't let me leave, but then I did. I kept telling him I wanted an attorney. I don't know what I did. I just need to speak to Jack." I didn't know if I was making any sense. The more tissues she handed me, the more I sobbed. I felt completely out of control.

"Hold on. Hold on. Okay. Just hold on. Don't say anything else." She hurried to the door separating the lobby from their offices. "Come here, come on through. That's right. Don't say anything else, just come on."

I followed her, having no idea where we were going. She took me into a room, pulled up a chair, and gently guided me into the seat. I was shaking so badly the chair was rattling.

"Try to calm down. Try to calm down a little. We are trying to get in touch with Jack. He's handling a Federal case right now, but we're getting in touch with him. Can I get you some water? Anything?" She was genuinely concerned, maybe even frightened by my behavior.

"A trash can. I think I'm going to throw up again. Or the bathroom." I really hoped I wouldn't throw up, but my stomach had other plans.

She grabbed the nearest trash can and set it down next to me. "Here, the bathroom is down the hall, but if this is easier then you can use this. Whatever you need that helps. I'm going to get you some water, too. You wait here." She left and immediately returned, water in one hand, a box of tissues in the other.

"I need to know a little bit about what's going on so I can tell Jack. You don't have to go into detail but tell me a little bit. It was kind of hard to understand you a minute ago."

"I work for CPS. There's some type of investigation against me. I think against Natalie, too, and maybe her supervisor Audrey. We were told it was an administrative investigation, but then when I went to my interview today, he said it was criminal." My voice was calmer, the tears starting to slow.

"Who? Who said it's criminal? Who's conducting the investigation?"

136

"OIG. OIG. It's the Office of the Inspector General. It's like internal affairs but for CPS. But it's not administrative. He said it was criminal." My voice started to rise again.

She patted me on the shoulder. "Do you know what the charges are?"

I violently shook my head. "No. He didn't tell me. No one's told me. I don't know anything." More tears exploded with more sobbing.

"I'll be right back. Just sit here. I'll be right back." She left the room, this time longer than the first. I knew I had to gain control of myself if I was going to be able to explain anything. I tried to take some deep breaths. I tried to control the shaking. Every pent-up emotion I had experienced while being stuck in the room with Investigator Carlos was exploding inside me, finally released. It was all coming to a head, all at one time.

The secretary returned—I didn't even know her name. "Jack said he won't be back for about one and a half hours, but he'll talk to you. We can schedule for another time or you can wait. He doesn't mind if you want to wait."

I couldn't imagine waiting until tomorrow. "If he's willing to see me today, I'll wait. I can wait in my car if I'm in the way."

I suddenly felt very in the way and afraid all the sobbing had disturbed their work.

"No, Honey, you're not in the way. You can wait here. He just wanted you to know how long it would be. He also wants to know if you said anything to the OIG investigator. Anything all. And don't worry, anything you say is confidential, so don't be scared."

"I told him I wanted an attorney and I left. All I said was I want an attorney. I wouldn't speak to him." I suddenly started second guessing myself. "Should I have said something?"

"I'm just asking. I need to tell Jack. Just hold on." She left me alone again.

As I waited, I wondered if I had done something wrong by not speaking to the investigator. The door swung open, interrupting my thoughts, and one of the other attorneys entered. It was Cason Cuff, the family law attorney. I had forgotten he worked in the same office.

"Rebekah," he carefully started. "Don't answer anything else, other than the three questions I'm about to ask you. Do you understand? Don't elaborate, don't add to it. Just answer these three questions and only these three questions. Understand?" I nodded. I really didn't understand, but I could follow directions. "Just these questions. Do not tell me anything else. Question one, is this investigation against you?

"Yes."

"Is it a criminal investigation?"

"Yes."

"Is your supervisor also involved?"

"Yes."

"Okay, I actually have two more questions. Don't tell me what they are, but did he tell you what the allegations were?"

"No."

"Did you refuse to speak to him?"

"Yes."

"Okay, that's all I wanted to know." He left.

I wasn't sure what had happened, but I didn't have time to think about it as the secretary came back.

"Jack and Jim are on their way back. They are going to speak to you together. They will be here soon. Can I get you more water?"

I shook my head. I was doing better. I had managed to stop the tears and I didn't need to throw up anymore. I leaned my head back against the chair and closed my eyes. Two hours had passed since I arrived, but it felt like only minutes. I was exhausted.

"Rebekah." Jack's voice boomed as he walked through the conference door. "We're so sorry you had to wait so long. This is Jim, he offices with me. He's going to sit here with us if that's okay."

I nodded as they shook my hand. I didn't know Jim London. I had only heard stories about him, and they weren't very nice stories. He sat quietly at the end of the table, intently watching me.

"I hear you've had a rough day," Jack began.

I chuckled and nodded. "You could say that."

"Well, I want you to know anything you say in here is confidential, whether we can take your case or not. I have to warn you, though, we think we might have a conflict of interest already. That's why Cason asked you those questions. He does so much family law, we aren't sure if we can separate this case from his. But we're going to talk to you anyway and see if we can figure it out. Does that sound okay?" Jack explained things clearly, giving me a much better understanding of the events over the last few hours.

"Your interview was today? Do you know when this started?" he asked.

"I think it started right before I went on maternity leave. Natalie interviewed back in November. She said her interview lasted seven hours."

"Seven hours? That's not an interview. That's an interrogation." Jack sat back in his chair, appalled.

"That's what I told her. He wouldn't let her go, but he never told her anything about it being criminal. She can't even tell me what the allegations are. He never told her either. She can only speculate. After her interview, she went back to work and has worked this entire time. Until Friday. We were all put on administrative leave on Friday."

"She can't tell you because she's not allowed to tell you or she doesn't know?"

139

"She doesn't know. He never told her directly. She's only guessed based on the questions he kept asking her."

Jack and Jim exchanged looks, telling each other something without speaking. I didn't think they believed me.

"So, what happened today?"

"Last week I came back to work after maternity leave. The OIG investigator scheduled an interview with me. Natalie and her supervisors said I had to speak to him because it was administrative. But when I got there, at the police department, he said it was a criminal investigation and I was a suspect. He wanted to know my side. The case name was Natalie's name. He said he was sending it to Robbie's office today." I was speaking as quickly as I could, trying to get it all out and not forget anything.

"Okay, that's odd. I didn't think they could do that. He said he was sending it to Robbie's office?"

"Yes, the file was sitting on the table. I saw it; it was in Natalie's name. He said he'd already told Robbie about it and he'd file it today with the DA's office."

"Okay, and then what?"

"Well, when he said it was criminal, I told him I wanted an attorney and I wanted to leave."

"And then?" Jim interrupted Jack. "That's it? You just asked for an attorney and that's it?" Jim really didn't believe me.

"Well, he kept telling me I only had this one time to talk to him. He said if I got an attorney then I couldn't speak to him at all, even with an attorney. He said he would send the case to Robbie's office."

"And you stuck to it. You didn't say anything else at all to him?"

"Well, I told him my name." I didn't know what else Jim wanted me to say.

"That's not what we meant. Are you sure you didn't say anything else? Not even a little bit?" Jack took over again, still questioning me like they didn't believe me.

"No. I didn't say anything else. I kept saying over and over again I wanted an attorney. He even tried to get me to sign a waiver. He said it was a statement that said I had the right to remain silent and the right to leave. He wanted me to sign it and keep talking. But I read it. It said if I signed it then I was waiving that right. So I told him no. I kept telling him I wanted an attorney. He finally let me leave. I didn't even ask him what the allegations were. I just wanted an attorney and I wanted to leave." Maybe if I kept repeating myself, they would finally believe me.

"Wow." Jack and Jim laughed, again, talking to each other without speaking. I didn't think anything was amusing. "That's amazing. Do you know how many people can't stick to that? Everyone talks. Well, nearly everyone. People come in here all the time telling us they didn't say anything and then we find out they really made a statement or even outright confessed," Jack explained. "If you had continued with the interview, you'd know the allegations, maybe. But you didn't, and that's good, but now we are here. Here being we don't know what charges you're facing." They both sat quietly, thinking.

I remembered I hadn't told them about Libby calling.

"Well, Scott Libby called me right as I got to your office. He said he wanted to talk to me about my case. He called before I came into the office today. He said he's taking it to trial next week and wants an answer today on when we can meet. What do I do about that?"

"What? He called?" Jack shook his head. "There's no way Scott was calling about this case. Whether or not OIG sent the case over, there's no way Robbie's even looked at it. It will sit in Robbie's office for months before anyone even takes a glance. Scott had to be calling about something else. Maybe one of your CPS investigations?"

"He didn't say. Just said he wanted to talk to me about my case."

"Any of your CPS investigations going to trial soon?"

I shrugged. "I've only been back from maternity leave for a week. And then I was put on administrative leave on Friday. I have no idea where any of my investigations stand."

"That's got to be it. Robbie's office doesn't move fast on anything. It will take months before anything happens on this case, even if OIG filed it today."

Had I been in the right frame of mind, I would have remembered a criminal case doesn't go to trial overnight. I still had to be arrested, indicted, and allowed to hire an attorney and defend myself. Jack and Jim helped get my head straight.

"But we still have the issue of not knowing what the charges are," Jack continued.

"Criminal is criminal, isn't it?" I hadn't hired an attorney for a criminal case. To me there were only two kinds of law, family and criminal. I thought attorneys handled everything in one of those two categories.

"It is, but we're under an ethical obligation to make sure we know enough about the case to know if we can represent someone on a particular charge before we can agree," Jim explained.

"Maybe I shouldn't have walked out after all. If I had stayed and talked, then we'd know what I was charged with."

"No!" they both said, leaning forward in their chairs.

"It was the right thing to do. No one does that, just walk out like that. We usually have a confession and then have to deal with that on top of the case itself. Trust us. You're already ahead of the game. Just be sure to continue to keep your mouth shut. You never know who's listening or who's watching." Jack said.

Jim nodded in agreement then asked, "Can you give us any idea of what you think this might be about?"

"I know my coworkers blame me for that girl dying. They said I should've removed her. I didn't because her mother was protective. My case was about the sexual assault and the guy that assaulted her went to prison. But they keep saying I should've removed her."

"That's bullshit. CPS doesn't have anything to do with that case. It's a criminal case and CPS needs to stay out of it." Jim's reaction surprised me.

"Okay." I thought harder. "I know my coworkers accused me of illegal searches. They said I searched houses without permission. OIG searched my office while I was on maternity leave and found an evidence bag with drugs in my office. He made the police department take it. They made an information report."

"How'd you end up with dope?" Jim asked suspiciously.

I explained the case to him, telling him about the search and the police officers who wouldn't take the evidence. I explained how the detectives gave me the evidence bags and how long everything was in my office.

"How much dope was there?"

"Just some residue left on the baggies. The information report said the bags were empty. There wasn't enough to use or smoke. I had wiped them clean trying to test them with the field test to see what kind of dope it was."

"Robbie would never prosecute for something like that. Not only do we not know whose it really was, you weren't in possession of it. Anyone had access to that office. And Robbie won't prosecute for such a tiny amount. When I was the DA, I would have. But I'm an asshole and I like being an asshole. Robbie isn't. What else. Any other rumors you've heard? Any accusations you've ever had? Even if they seem like it doesn't matter, it might matter now." Jim was pushing. He seemed genuinely concerned, genuinely trying to figure out what was going on. Jack let him keep pushing.

"Natalie mentioned a couple of things she was questioned about in her interview. She was asked about taking a cell phone away from a teenager we had in foster care. The kid wanted to run away from foster care and wanted her phone to call her boyfriend. He asked if she knew about the stuff in my office. I don't know what else. He asked if I did illegal searches a lot. Something about bragging about searching. A whole bunch of Fourth Amendment violations."

"This sounds crazy. If this was about a Fourth Amendment violation, it would be a civil matter, not criminal. Like, a parent could sue you for violating their rights. No one's prosecuted for violating the Fourth Amendment. I don't even know what that'd fall under. And taking a cell phone away...isn't that your job? Aren't you the kid's parent while you're taking care of the kid?" Jack looked a bit bewildered.

"I hate CPS. I always have. They have done some stupid things in my time and I have no issue saying so, but this beats it all," Jim growled.

"You know if we take this case, you're looking to spend at least $50,000.00, right?" Jack asked. I nodded. I hadn't considered the cost to defend myself, but I knew I'd do whatever it took to fight.

"Who were the parents on the case you mentioned before, with the dope you found? That seems to be the only case that could possibly be worth charging you with," Jack asked.

"The parents were Carson and Kasey Jackson." Jack and Jim both let out hearty laughs. "No kidding? You're kidding us, right?"

I shook my head. What now?

"There's our conflict," Jack explained. "We were worried about Carson because of the family ties, but now we have an actual conflict. If this actually becomes a case, we have an issue because we've represented Carson in criminal cases, a lot of them. If those cases and your case collide, well, ethically we can't do that," Jack explained.

I felt despair coming back. I didn't know who I would turn to next.

"But don't worry," Jack continued. "We are going to send you to another attorney. He's never done family law in his life, so I don't think he'll have a conflict. Go down there and talk to him. I bet anything he'll tell you how to handle Scott Libby, too. He's been around for a very long time."

"Okay, I'll do that," I said as I stood up. "Thank you for meeting with me. I feel better. You've made some things make sense. What do I owe you?"

"Nothing. Nothing at all," Jack said. "This is a professional courtesy. Don't even think about it. And hey, good job on keeping your mouth shut. That took some guts."

"Yeah, he's right. Not many can do that. I'll be interested seeing how this plays out. It doesn't make any sense," Jim said as he shook my hand.

I thanked them again and left their office feeling more confident, even if the worry hadn't completely left. It wasn't quite 5:00 p.m., so I rushed to see Daniel Golden, the next attorney. I didn't expect to see him that day, it being so late, but luck was on my side and he was there.

We had a quick and simple meeting. I filled him in on what happened. He agreed with Jack and Jim, CPS had nothing to do with Angel's case and I couldn't be prosecuted for an illegal search, only sued. He suspected the drugs found in my office were the issue. He didn't think they would prosecute it though, because he'd remind them of what was in their own desk drawers and maybe even in a drug test if they took one. Jack and Jim were right, not only did he not have a conflict, he knew exactly what to do with Libby and he knew secrets about the prosecutor's office I didn't even want to know.

Golden couldn't represent me yet. Like Jack and Jim, he didn't know for sure what the charges were. But he would be my attorney if I was charged with the drugs in my office. He said he'd check weekly with Locker to see if OIG filed the case and try to catch it before it went to grand jury. I didn't have anything to worry about. If they tried anything, the most he thought it would be was for possession of controlled substance, but he doubted it would ever to come that. For now, I needed to meet with Libby and find out what he wanted.

Chapter 20

March 2013

"Libby, this is Rebekah." Daniel Golden had told me to call him, be straight with him, and assured me Libby would tell me the truth. "I can talk now. What was it you wanted?"

"Hi, thanks for calling me back. You worked a case back in 2011 that's finally going to trial. I wanted to speak to you about it before the trial started. See what you'd say and all if I called you as a witness."

I breathed a sigh of relief. It really wasn't about my pending case, except now I had to tell him everything. Daniel had told me exactly what to say.

"Libby, I have to tell you something."

"Okay... What is it?"

"I found yesterday, right before you called, that I have a criminal case pending against me. I'm being investigated by the OIG."

"Oh, well that explains it. I thought something sounded wrong when I called. You didn't sound like yourself. What's OIG?" I suspected OIG was a ghost if even the prosecutor's office didn't know about it.

"OIG is like internal affairs for a police department, but for CPS. Your timing was horrible." I laughed, remembering the two hours it took me to clean the vomit out of my car. "I don't know what the allegations are, but I wanted to tell you so it didn't mess up your case. Oh, and we're on administrative leave while the investigation is pending."

"I appreciate that. Who's the investigator? Who's he with? We haven't heard anything about that around here." He sounded confused, and I wondered if OIG had filed anything.

"His name is Juan Carlos. He's with the Office of the Inspector General, OIG."

"Is Natalie under investigation also? I need to meet with her, too."

"I think so. The case was in her name."

"Can you call her and have her come in with you? I'll ask Robbie if he's heard anything and if you don't hear from me before, just come in Thursday, and Natalie, too, and we'll discuss it."

Everything happened exactly like Daniel had said it would, almost word for word. Daniel really had been around a long time.

Thursday rolled around and I went to the courthouse to meet with Libby. I arrived early, before Natalie, and waited patiently in the DA's lobby. Walking into the DA's office used to be normal, but now it was uncomfortable. I had some mysterious criminal charge hanging over my head. Hopefully Libby had some new information.

"Rebekah." Libby greeted me in the lobby. "Come on back. Thank you for meeting with me."

"Of course." I followed him to his office. It was dark and dreary, like most of the offices in the courthouse. Files were piled around his desk and a yellow legal pad waited in front of him. I noticed our names, and Audrey's, written on it.

"So, it's been a pretty rough week for you, I bet." He laughed like something was funny. I hadn't worked with Libby as much as I had the others, so I wasn't sure if he was trying to be funny or if he didn't know how to start a conversation. I shook my head. "Well, let's wait until Natalie gets here so I don't have to talk about this twice. Is she coming for sure?"

"I think so. Let me ask her." I sent Natalie a text, confirming. "She's coming. She's parking right now."

"She's on administrative leave too, right? And what's the other one's name?"

"Natalie's on administrative leave with me, and Audrey is the other. She's on leave, too. We're all on leave. We're getting paid to not do anything."

"And you had an interview with this OIG guy?"

I was suspicious of the question, but Daniel told me to tell him the basics. "I was supposed to. I mean, I went to it. But he said it was a criminal investigation, so I said I wanted an attorney and left."

Libby looked a bit taken back, his eyes wide.

"You refused to speak to him? Really?" He acted like this was the first time anyone told him they had refused to speak to an investigator.

"Yes. Even after he threatened to file charges and not let me go back with an attorney, I still refused to speak him. Anything I said would be used against me." I didn't believe the shock on his face.

"Well," he shook his head, smirking. "I probably would have done the same thing in your situation. So, you don't know what this is about?"

I shook my head.

"Sorry I'm late." Natalie interrupted, rushing in and frazzled.

"It's okay. Thought maybe you wouldn't want to come." Libby was trying to be funny again. "I'm sure you're stressed about this, too."

"Just a little." Natalie wore sweat pants, a t-shirt, and looked like she had been awake for days.

"From what I can put together, this OIG guy, this Juan guy, whoever this guy thinks he is, has a target on your back, Rebekah. He wants you and it looks like Natalie and Audrey are collaterals, whatever a collateral is. He has a problem with your investigations or something. But I've never seen anything hinky about your investigations. I don't see anything hinky in this one here. I know that Greenville Police aren't investigating you, the Hunt County Sheriff's office isn't investigating you, the Texas Rangers aren't investigating, it's just this OIG guy, whoever he thinks he is. I really think this will go away." He seemed confident. He really thought this was no big deal.

"Wow, okay. So, you've been checking into it, I see. Does everyone know about it?"

"I've asked Robbie about it. He said he's heard something about it but isn't sure what's going on. He also said if anything comes of it, he'll bring in a special prosecutor. Evidently it's already dividing the office."

I didn't know what "dividing the office" meant, but it made sense to have a special prosecutor come in. It would be weird to be prosecuted by the same people you worked with on a regular basis.

We continued to talk about the upcoming case, the one he needed our testimony for. We planned out how to work around the criminal charges and not mess up the case. When everything was covered, Libby walked us to the lobby.

"I really think this will all go away. I'm curious though, Rebekah, what did you do to piss off this guy so much?" He laughed at his own question, not waiting for an answer. "Just hang in there."

"Sure, I'm hanging all right," I said as we left.

"You were really quiet in there," I said as we stood next to our cars, talking before going home. Natalie was never quiet.

"I don't know what to say. I don't even know what to think about this mess." She looked awful. Her hair was barely combed, she'd lost even more weight, and her eyes were sunken in. "Do you think he told us everything?"

"No. But I think he came close. He said too much to not know something was going on. It was clear I made Investigator Carlos mad. I just hope I haven't made him too mad. I'd hate to see him react because I hurt his ego."

"The DA's office wouldn't allow it." Natalie really trusted these people.

"Not if they knew about it. I have a feeling Investigator Carlos plays dirty."

"I think so, too. I guess all we can do now is wait."

Chapter 21

July 2013

"OIG has cast a net so wide, we can't contain it. Your reputation is ruined. There isn't a judge, attorney, or professional with the State that doesn't know about this." Marissa let the words sink in. "I'm sorry. I really am. I have never seen such toxic hatred for someone as I've seen against you. Your coworkers hate you, the CPS attorney hates you, the OIG investigator hates you. I'm sorry."

The words hit the very core of my being. What had I done to these people to deserve this? I was speechless. I couldn't cry, I wasn't angry. I was in shock. Marissa wanted to meet today to discuss the case. My husband drove me to Dallas so I didn't have to go alone. Even though Marissa didn't tell me what the meeting would be about, part of me thought I'd leave without a job. I never thought I would be told I was hated. I knew people didn't like me. But to say there was a toxic hatred was harsh.

"Why?" I managed to ask.

"I don't know. Sometimes people just attack someone like animals do. For whatever reason, they picked you. Maybe they were intimidated by you. Maybe they just didn't like you. I don't know. I do know there's no recovering from this."

"Then what's next? Are you firing me?" I asked. I didn't know where to go from here.

"I don't want to. I tried to find a place for you. If you were willing to commute, I would have put you anywhere else. But the state is small. As soon as someone finds out where you are, they'll tell everyone and your reputation will be torn down so badly you'll never be able to testify in court and a judge won't ever trust you."

I couldn't believe what I was hearing. "What did I do wrong? I don't even know what I did."

It had been five months since Investigator Carlos told me I was under criminal investigation. For five months, Natalie and I spoke every single day, checking on each other, re-hashing everything, trying to make sense of it all. We still didn't know anything.

"Nothing. You didn't do anything wrong. There's just nothing I can do. It's gone too far. Never in my wildest dreams did I think it could reach this point."

"Well, clearly it has." The tears started to flow as questions swarmed my mind.

"I can tell you this, OIG doesn't have a clue how we work cases. They haven't ever been trained on our system. They don't even know basic terminology. Nor do they want to learn. We spent hours and hours trying to explain it to them. And then the legal briefs. One after another after another. It was awful." I had no idea what she was talking about. What legal briefs? Explaining what?

"What does OIG think I did wrong?" I needed answers. I needed something. I had waited too long to still not know anything.

"I guess, misconduct. That's the overall allegation. We were told there was a legal case pending, but we've tried to contact the DA's office and they won't tell us anything. We hope the legal briefs took care of any criminal case. Surely it would."

I didn't say anything. There was nothing to say. "

OIG thinks you falsified a risk assessment in Angel's case."

"What? That's crazy. I didn't falsify anything."

"I know. We looked at the risk assessment and for every answer you put, you explained, in detail, why you chose that answer. I don't know how he could think it was falsified. Besides, it was clear the mom was protective, and the man was arrested for the assault. There wasn't anything else to do."

"What else did he say I did?"

"He tried to say you conducted illegal searches. Let me ask you about these while we're talking about it. First, there was some purse you searched that belonged to some mother. I think it was Mikayla's or Cosette's case."

"I remember that case. It wasn't mine, but I assisted on it for like two hours. I don't have any idea what he's talking about though."

"Okay, and something about you searching a cigarette pack belonging to the dad? I think it was the Williamson case?"

"Yeah, that was the case where I found the marijuana. But there were six officers there with us. And, immediately after I found the marijuana, the lieutenant called the DA's office and asked them if we could use it and told them exactly how I found it. The DA's office said it was a legal search and told the lieutenant to charge Dad with the additional possession charge. I wrote an affidavit and everything for their criminal case."

"Well, OIG didn't include that in their report." She looked annoyed.

"You can call the DA's office and ask them. Or, just pull the file and read my case. It's all in there." She nodded, like she had heard enough.

"How about this cell phone on Ashley Krank's case?"

"We took a cell phone away from a teenager who threatened to kill herself? She said she'd use the phone to call her boyfriend, he was twenty-five, I think, and have him pick her up from foster care. She also said she'd go right back to dealing and using drugs because we couldn't stop her. Polly told us to call law enforcement and lock up the phone until law enforcement could get it. She said it was an inappropriate relationship on the man's part. So we did just that. Called law enforcement, just like Polly told us to."

"Mm, Ms. Patterson…"

"What about Polly Patterson?"

"Nothing. Let's continue." I suspected Polly had called in the report and Marissa didn't want to tell me. I made a mental note to dig deeper, later.

"And this last one. Evidently you searched a house for a missing baby?"

"Yeah, like back in 2011. I wrote an affidavit, had Orders in Aid, deputies with me, one of my lovely coworkers. I put it all in the second affidavit I wrote, too. Spelled it out in black and white. Why? Is he saying that was wrong?"

"Yeah, he's saying the orders didn't authorize you to do anything like that on the case because the parents weren't home."

"Did you read my affidavit? Or the case?"

"No, I haven't read it. But surely whatever happened, you had law enforcement with you and they would've said something if you had done something wrong. They wouldn't have let you do something you couldn't do." She was posing it as a question and a statement.

"I had law enforcement, and Natalie was telling Polly everything as we went along. Polly said to do whatever it takes to find the baby. We had court orders. I didn't go barging into a house alone."

"But the parents weren't home?"

"No, they ended up not being home. But we had court orders authorizing us, me and the deputies, to enter the house by any means necessary. Why? What should I have done? Walk away?"

"Well, generally we don't enter a residence if no one is home." She wasn't making any sense to me.

"I had court orders. I didn't just barge into the house. And I spelled it out in all my affidavits. I mean, if I did something wrong, it's in black and white with my signature and has been for almost two years. So, seriously, what should I have done? Because there isn't any policy to tell us what we should have done in that situation. Policy says we have to have permission, or exigent circumstances, or a court order. I had a court order. Polly had drafted the petition and orders. She didn't have an issue with it." I was frustrated. Of all the things to complain about, she was focused on a case where I had court orders signed by a judge.

"Let's move on."

"You're not going to tell me what I should have done? What happens if someone runs into the situation again? Missing baby? Drugs? Past CPS history on the parents? Doesn't know if the baby is alive or dead? Do they just walk away?"

"We have to ensure we follow policy when we investigate. I'm sure if you did anything wrong, the deputies would have said something." That sounded like political sidestepping. She hadn't answered anything.

"But let's move on. The other problem he had was thinking you shouldn't have been able to close out all the cases that were on your workload. He insisted you left children at risk. So we took every single case you had on your workload before you left for maternity leave and had them reinvestigated. I believe there were twenty-eight cases. We sent them to different investigators throughout the State. Get this, OIG even thought some of the cases were called in again after you closed them. He didn't understand that the investigation is closed even though the case continues if you removed a child. He had no concept of how the system worked. We tried drawing him a picture and he flat denied we knew what we were talking about. He believed whatever it was

156

he had made up in his own mind. We even went around in circles over the risk assessment, for hours. He's a nightmare."

"He sounds like someone who sees conspiracies in everything, even when they don't exist. I'm glad I walked out of that interview. He would've twisted every word I said." Things made a little more sense, hearing how he wouldn't back down even when policy was laid out in front of him.

"I think walking out was the best thing you could possibly have done. I didn't think so at first. In fact, I was upset you left. I wanted this over and thought if you just spoke to him and explained whatever he wanted to know, you could go back to work. But it would've just been worse. Walking out was the best thing."

"How did the reinvestigations turn out? Was anything wrong with them?" Surely something had to be wrong. OIG couldn't make things up because he had his own idea of how something should be done. Could he?

"Rebekah, every single case came back great. I've never seen that in all my career. Usually there's something that someone could have done differently. Maybe you could have done something differently or better. But not in yours. There were absolutely no recommendations for anything you could have done better. They re-contacted the parents and caretakers and asked them about the case. Everyone confirmed that whatever you said you did in the cases was actually done. Nothing was falsified, nothing was missing. Children were safe whether they were left in the home or removed. You did excellent work." She looked proud, happy to say those words. But they upset me. I was still about to lose my job.

"What's the point of doing excellent work if OIG can make up things and cause me to still lose my job?" It was like getting a back-handed compliment.

"I know. This got out of hand. I should have listened when Natalie and Audrey told me there was some major gossip in the office. I should have allowed you guys to change offices. I should have taken this seriously. I thought it was just small-town gossip. I thought it would work itself out. Never in my wildest dreams did I think something like this would happen." She looked apologetic, not that it mattered now. "It doesn't make anything better. And to make it worse, I need to know if you want to resign or be fired. There are pros and cons to both."

I pushed the pros and cons around in my head. It was clear I was leaving without a job. I'd never been fired before and I didn't want to start now. If I resigned, I could leave on my terms and never have to explain anything to future employers. Besides, who would want to continue working with cruel, dishonest, manipulating coworkers? I had better things to do with my life.

"Just to clarify, would I be resigning in leu of being fired?" I had to double check.

"No, not at all. We just have to do something. You've been on paid administrative leave for the past five months. The press is starting poke around and ask questions about employees on paid leave because of some other unrelated things going on. And I've exhausted any other options of where to put you."

"What's happening to Natalie?" Natalie knew where I was, and I assumed Marissa would call her next. I was worried about her. My husband and I had already planned for the *what ifs*, but Natalie needed medical benefits for her kids.

"You know I can't tell you that. That's confidential."

"She knows I'm here. She'll know something's wrong if I don't call her when I leave and it's going to stress her out. If I tell her I quit, she's going to assume she's next."

"She has a job. I'll call her as soon as you leave. Please give me time to do that." I assured her I would.

"Okay, then I'll resign." My husband was in the lobby, waiting for me. Even though we had planned for the *what ifs*, he saw no reason I would have to leave here without a job. I had tried to explain how bad it was in the office, but he thought I was exaggerating. In his mind, if it was as bad as I said it was, then management would have stopped it.

"Okay, I'll get the paperwork going. Draft a letter of resignation and email it to me. Let some time pass. You'll get another job. I'll give you a glowing letter of recommendation, too. I promise." She patted me on the shoulder before embracing me in a hug. "You've been through a lot. I can't imagine how hard this has been."

It was over. My career with CPS began five years ago. The investigation against me started eight months ago. Both were over.

"You don't look so good," my husband commented as I left Marissa's office.

"I know. I quit. Five years of my life down the drain. But we can move on and put this all behind us."

"It's all over? She said it's over. We don't have to think about it anymore?"

"No, it's over. I don't want to talk right now. I just want to go home." I didn't want to think about it again. I wanted to put it behind me, pretend it was a distant nightmare. In the back of my mind, I wondered if the criminal case really had gone away. Marissa didn't seem to know for sure. It was clear OIG, or at least Investigator Carlos, believed they were superior and could make up their own rules. But with months having passed and Natalie remaining employed, surely it was over. How could OIG pursue a criminal case if CPS said we didn't do anything wrong? That would be going rogue.

Chapter 22

September 25, 2013

A Deputy Sherriff's car pulled into my driveway as I situated my kids in the living room for an early dinner and prepared their plates. I warned my husband, but he only gave me a *so what* expression, a forkful of spaghetti in his hand.

"What do they want?" he asked.

"I don't know. Why would I know what they want?" I tried to sound like I didn't care, like it was no big deal, but deep inside, I knew something was wrong. Officers always called first when I worked for CPS. It didn't matter if it was morning or midnight, they called. They never showed up in our driveway unannounced.

My kids jumped up from the coffee table and ran to the window, peering outside.

"I'm not opening the door," I whispered.

"Why not? What's wrong with you?" He took another bite, staying at the couch. Maybe I was paranoid, but after everything that had occurred over the last year, I didn't know what to think.

Our front door quivered with the officer's pounding knock. I stood behind the door, gesturing to my husband to open it.

His eyes questioned me as he approached the door.

"Don't let him inside," I said as he turned the knob.

My boys piled around their father's legs, excited to see the police officer. They had been taught police officers were good guys. If they came to your house, you opened the door and invited them inside.

This time, I didn't want him inside.

"Hi. Is Rebekah here?" It was Officer Ballard, the warrant officer. My stomach dropped to the floor. No one had told me I had a warrant, and with my history with the police department and my CPS managers, I would have expected a warning out of professional courtesy. I casually planted my foot at the bottom of the door, preventing both my husband and Officer Ballard from opening the door any further.

"Yeah, she's right here." My husband gave me a quick glance. I could read his mind. *What the hell are you doing?* I was probably over reacting.

"I'm here," I said as I slid from behind the door, trying to look normal.

"Hi, Rebekah. I have some bad news. Can you step outside?" No one had ever confirmed OIG had dropped the criminal case, but Natalie had returned to work as a supervisor. I hadn't done anything wrong, but I wasn't going outside.

"Nope." My heart raced, but I stayed still and confident.

"Rebekah," he whispered uncomfortably. "You don't want your kids to hear this."

My constant anxiety since my resignation exploded. I was going to be arrested. My husband herded our boys onto the couch, out of earshot. I remained at the door, my foot still stopping it. My husband returned, and I strangled his arm, desperate to remain in control of myself.

"Rebekah, there are five felony indictments for you. I need you to come with me." He stayed professional and polite, giving me a chance to respond.

Felony? Indictment? FIVE? Surprise, confusion, and furry battled within me. Indictment meant the case had already been presented to the grand jury. When had that happened? Why hadn't anyone told me?

I glanced behind me at the back door and the massive field beyond our property. I could make a run for it. I could slam the door in his face and be gone before he knew what happened. He wanted to arrest me on five felony warrants and hadn't brought backup. That was his problem, not mine.

"Honey?" my husband asked, snapping me back to reality. Was I really thinking about running? Now I knew why officers were taught to always be prepared, why I was taught to be prepared. When that fight or flight reflex kicks in, there's no telling which one will take over.

I chose not to run.

When I still didn't respond, my husband took over. "Is she going to have to spend the night in jail? How long will she be gone?"

"What are they for?" I interrupted before Officer Ballard could answer. "Do you have the hard copies in hand?"

Hard copies meant the officer already had confirmation the warrant was legitimate. I wanted to see them.

"No, I don't have the hard copies. I don't even know what the warrants are for—"

"How about I just go in the morning and turn myself in?" I wanted a plan in place, bond money set aside, a bonding company ready to bond me out. Otherwise who knew how long I'd sit in jail.

"There's a judge already there, waiting specifically to arraign you. You can make bond and be back home in a few hours, but we have to hurry."

It was almost 4:30 p.m. Judges never arraigned anyone this late, not here.

"Natalie and Audrey are already there. We really need to hurry. I don't want the judge to leave before you get there." He sounded concerned.

Natalie and Audrey. It wasn't just me they were rounding up. I wouldn't make them go through this, whatever this was, alone. Besides, I was worried Natalie would fall apart, if she hadn't already.

"Okay, I need to change clothes."

I wanted something to wear that I could burn afterward. They were going to take a mugshot, and I never wanted to see the shirt I would wear again. I replaced my shoes with cheap flipflops. My wired bra for a sports bra. I removed everything from my pockets and took the clip out of my hair. I pulled off my belt and twisted my pants so they wouldn't fall off. I didn't want to waste time checking in and out property.

"Rebekah, you really need to hurry. I don't know how much longer the judge will wait," Officer Ballard called.

I opened the bedroom door to yell I was almost ready and saw Officer Ballard inside my house. My husband had let him in—I guess it didn't matter now. I was going willingly anyway.

As I approached the living room, I realized my cell phone was in my bra and stopped at the kitchen.

"Honey, can you come here, please?" I asked

"What? What's taking so long?" he asked.

"Here's my cell phone. I want you to keep it. If for some reason I can't get out, go drop it in the septic system. I mean it. Get rid of it."

He looked puzzled. I'd have to explain later.

"How much is her bond?" he asked Officer Ballard back at the door.

"I don't know. I haven't seen anything yet. But she can get out tonight, well, I guess depending on the amount of the bond."

"Honey, google a bondsman. Call them. Tell them to get me out. The retirement check is on the counter. Use it." I realized there was a reason I'd thought to take out my retirement and a reason my unemployment was approved in record time. It wasn't chance. It was divine intervention. My unemployment had been approved the day before and the check from cashing out my retirement sat on the kitchen counter. We could afford bond and hire an attorney. "Honey, did you hear me?"

"Yeah. Okay." It didn't look like he was processing anything.

My boys were smiling at us, oblivious.

"What did you tell them?" I asked.

Officer Ballard answered, "That I'm picking you up and we're going to the office so you can help me on a case."

"Are you going to handcuff her in front of them?" my husband asked.

"No, no, not at all. She's going to ride in the front seat so it will be just another normal day for the kids," Officer Ballard said.

I was appreciative of the gesture. I never wanted my children to see police in a bad light. Arresting their mother in front of them would scar them worse than the house fire.

I followed Officer Ballard out the front door, willingly crawling into the front seat of his car. My children were piled at the window, watching every move I made. I smiled and waved. My husband watched from the doorway.

"Don't forget to call the bondsman," I yelled. "The check is on the counter for them." His blank stare worried me and I hoped he understood what to do. I was under arrest. Under felony arrest. I needed his help.

Officer Ballard tried chatting as he drove, telling me he didn't know what was going on except that he had heard something about that girl who had died. He said we'd done our job and weren't responsible for whatever had happened. I smiled and shrugged, not saying anything. He had been professional, patient, and kind. I trusted him, but he was a cop. Anything I said could be used against me. The right to remain silent was my motto. He seemed to understand, and turned up the radio, rather loudly, so we could listen to music for the rest of the drive.

Once we arrived in Sally Port, Officer Ballard handcuffed me. Sally Port was the underground garage that led into the actual jail. No one exited the squad car until the garage doors were closed. If anyone tried something stupid, like run off, they couldn't get outside. The jailers would have yelled at Officer Ballard if he hadn't cuffed me and I understood why. Even the calmest suspects were known to flip from calm to crazy in milliseconds when they heard the first set of doors slam shut. If their hands were loose, it was a free-for-all, often ending with injuries for one or more parties. Even I had thought about running when he had shown up at my house.

But I wasn't going to lose it. I wasn't going to act like I was crazy. All that would accomplish would be me strapped down in the rolling chair they used for those refusing to cooperate or so drunk they couldn't walk. I had my reputation to maintain, even as shattered as it already was, so I was determined to stay calm. At least on the outside. On the inside, I saw red. The handcuffs had sealed the deal, and I went from taking one step at a time to seeing fireballs shoot out of my eyes.

Officer Ballard apologized again for the handcuffs as he led me to the double doors and buzzed the jailers to let us in, but I only stared at the doors. In the past, the doors meant another bad guy was off the streets. It meant the end to a father or mother beating their child. An end to someone feeding their baby cocaine because they were too high to realize they had mixed it with formula. An end to a man sexually abusing a teenage girl. In the past, it meant a child would finally be safe. I didn't know what it meant now. I was the bad guy this time. Escorted in by the good guy. I was about to experience jail from the other side, and it infuriated me.

Chapter 23

September 25, 2013

"Open up. We're still waiting," Officer Ballard yelled into the intercom. He glanced at me, an uncomfortable chuckle in his throat. "They seem to be taking their time today. Sorry about this."

I bit my lip to keep from saying anything. I didn't need to take my anger out on him. It wasn't his fault. I would be doing the same thing in his position.

The familiar buzz alerted me a jailer was unlocking the door from the control panel. The door opened and I had to move forward. Through gritted teeth I picked up one foot and placed it in front of the other, ready to face my new future.

We walked forward two steps and stopped again. Each door we walked through closed behind us before the next one opened. It was a safety protocol so no one could turn and run. I wasn't thinking of running anymore, but I was still treated as if I could. When the last door slammed behind me, I was officially inside.

The inside of the jail was exactly how it always was, cold and loud, voices echoing everywhere. Inmates were yelling from their holding cells, shouting, cussing, screaming. It was always the same, no matter who was in jail. The inmates yelled at the jailers, and the jailers yelled their standard "quiet" back to them. The inmates then ignored the commands. This continued back and forth until

166

someone banged on the cell doors, telling them to shut up. I think the jailers felt like parents tuning out their child's whining until they were pushed too far.

"Is she with the other two?" Officer Johnson asked Officer Ballard. I hadn't ever met this one and didn't particularly want to get to know her. Her tone annoyed me.

"Yeah, she's with them," he said as he tried to unlock the handcuffs. He fought with one of the cuffs, slightly bent over in front of me and jerking on it. I almost slipped my wrist through them because they were so loose, but he had done me a favor and I didn't want to make him look stupid. I looked over his back for Natalie and Audrey, expecting them to be in jumpsuits, handcuffed and seated in one of the cold, bare holding cells. I breathed a sigh of relief when I found them uncuffed, sitting on metal chairs in the hallway just a few feet in front of me. They wore their regular clothes, and Natalie still sported her favorite three-inch heels. They both looked out of place in a comedic way, but it was hard to laugh when we were the ones living it.

"Got it. I think I need a new key or something," Officer Ballard said after removing the cuff. "I'm going to get your paperwork finished so you can get out of here."

He gave me a quick smile and walked down the hallway to the interview room. It was the same room every officer used when they arrested someone. I had done the same paperwork before. He would turn on the junky, dinosaur of a computer and type my information into the system. He'd write a summary about arresting me and print everything for the intake jailers, who would finish booking me into this lovely, shithole county jail.

"Let's go," Officer Johnson barked. She was stern but level-headed and not on some power trip like some of the other underpaid, overworked jailers. Sometimes those power trips got ugly.

As I followed her down the hall, more irrational thoughts crossed my mind. I wondered why I was following her. Normally she'd walk behind inmates to keep an eye on them. Behind her, I could grab around her neck and pull her to the ground before she knew what had happened. No one had frisked me—I could have a knife on me. Maybe she assumed I was frisked. Maybe she assumed I wasn't a danger to anyone. Maybe I was paranoid about assuming she was assuming. I needed to focus on something else. She hadn't done anything to me.

We passed Natalie and Audrey on the way. Natalie had been crying, but I couldn't read Audrey. They both made eye contact with me.

I mouthed, "This is bullshit."

I was thoroughly confused why Audrey was arrested, though I assumed Natalie was here because she was my direct supervisor. Then again, Libby had called both of them *collateral damage*.

"Do you have anything on you?" Officer Johnson asked as we stepped inside the empty room where they searched most of the inmates. I wasn't here on a drug-related charge, so I wasn't sure how far this search would go. I had visions of being strip searched and bending over to spread 'em. I had strip searched women before, and I swear I hated it more than they did. I was thankful I had showered, shaved, and wore clean underwear. That was hard to do with three toddlers running around in the house, but this morning I had managed to find ten minutes for myself.

"No, I took it all off before I got here."

"Nothing in your pockets? Nothing in your hair?" she asked

"No, I don't have anything on me." I said, irritated.

She was just standing there. She could have patted me down and moved this along, but she did nothing. Was this the procedure these days? I didn't want her to touch me, so I pulled out my pockets, showing her nothing was inside, lifted my shirt above my waistband, pulled the waistband of my shorts forward a little, and turned all the way around. She didn't try to look any closer, which didn't bother me. No one wants to see the stomach of a woman who's had three kids back to back.

"See? Nothing."

"Okay, let's go," she said with a shrug.

Too easy.

"Sit there," she said pointing to a plastic chair in the hall near the cage where the intake officers worked. I plopped down, leaning my head back against the hard brick wall. To my right, Natalie and Audrey were still sitting in the same chairs down the other hall. I chuckled, realizing Natalie's three-inch heels were weapons. No one was worried about us stabbing anyone in the neck with her heels. She leaned forward and cried as we waited. I felt bad for her, for both of them, but I wished she'd stop. Crying was viewed as being guilty, and we weren't guilty of anything.

Another sign of guilt was falling asleep after being arrested. Once caught, you're supposed finally relax. Sleep would come naturally. I didn't want to sleep, but the adrenaline rush was fading. My anger was fading with it, and the noise around me was calming. I knew these sounds. The clanging doors, yelling inmates, shouting jailers. They were part of my past life. I had been here as a cop and as a CPS investigator. Now I was here as an inmate, a criminal waiting to find out what they were charged with. I knew I was innocent, but sleep overcame me anyway.

Chapter 24

September 25, 2013

"Ross."

Someone was yelling from the intake cage, startling me. I had allowed myself to drift away into my own thoughts and now someone was yelling. The echo in the jail was horrific.

"Ross."

Why wasn't anyone answering? He'd stop yelling if someone would answer.

"Ross, get up, come here."

I looked around, wondering who this Ross person was and found myself making eye contact with an intake officer.

"Ross, I'm talking to you. If I have to tell you one more time…" he barked again, this time pointing directly at me.

Well shit. Why was he pointing at me? I marched myself over to the cage.

"What?"

"Why the hell didn't you answer me?" he asked. "Next time I call you, you answer me immediately. Do you understand?"

Oh, hell no, he did not just speak to me like that. "Why are you calling me Ross?"

"You're Rebekah Ross, aren't you." He phrased it like a statement rather than a question

170

I didn't like his tone. I didn't like him. My mind flashed to pulling him through the small opening of the cage and stomping his ass into the ground. I needed to get ahold of my thoughts and calm down.

"No. No I'm not." I was thoroughly irritated. I still didn't know why I was there. He was using my maiden name, a name I hadn't used in years. The officer glanced at the paperwork, as if he had made as mistake.

"You haven't ever gone by Ross?"

"It's my maiden name. I haven't used it in years. My legal name is Thonginh."

"Well, it's Ross in the paperwork. You're Rebekah Ross from now on. Sign this stuff."

Anyone who thinks their case will get thrown out over a technicality because their name isn't exactly right needs to think again. If that name still means you, then it's you.

His tone and attitude gave me an epiphany. This was why otherwise non-aggressive people, those who had never been in trouble or were only in trouble for something minor, ended up landing an assault charge. Some arrogant jailer, cop, or probation officer wouldn't let something go and antagonized the person until they snapped and punched them in the face. I wanted to punch this guy square in the jaw. Between thinking about running and imagining drop kicking some jailers, I had a brand-new understanding and appreciation for why we were trained to be alert and aware of everything. Even the most levelheaded, calmest person you'd never expect to lose their mind, could flip and knock the sense out of you.

"Do you have any medical conditions?" he asked, staring me in the eye.

"No," I responded coldly without breaking eye contact. I wasn't going to look away if he wasn't. It was juvenile, but it gave me some satisfaction. He checked a box without looking at the form.

"Do you have any thoughts of suicide?"

No, but I'm having thoughts of homicide.

"No." My eyes watered from the staring contest.

"Are you on any medication?"

Nothing you need to be aware of.

"No."

He started to ask another question, but someone tapped him on the shoulder and he turned away. Thank goodness. I could blink again. It was a tiny victory over something dumb, but it was a victory. When he was done with whatever it was that distracted him, he pushed the rest of the paperwork toward me.

"Fill it out."

I took the rubber pen and half filled out the paperwork. I didn't want to tell any of them about my life or my medical needs. Maybe I would have if I was going to be there all night. It was legitimate paperwork they needed to properly care for the inmates. But I knew I was getting out in a couple of hours, so I didn't care.

Officer Ballard approached me as I finished and handed me his paperwork. "Good luck with this. I have to go. You'll be fine." He gave a nod to the intake officer but didn't say anything else. He was in a rush, maybe something was wrong, but he wouldn't look directly at me. Instead, he turned and rushed back to the doors that imprisoned me.

As I examined the paperwork in my hands, I realized this would be the first time I'd know what I was charged with. No one had ever told me, other than *misconduct* OIG thought was criminal. But before I could read it, I saw Natalie and Audrey coming toward me, paperwork now in their hands. I couldn't read Audrey's face, but Natalie looked mad. I finished examining the paperwork.

Tampering with Physical Evidence $10,000.00 bond—Felony

Official Oppression $10,000.00 bond—Felony

Official Oppression $10,000.00 bond—Felony

Official Oppression $10,000.00 bond—Felony

Official Oppression $10,000.00 bond—Felony

Five felonies and a total of $50,000.00 hanging over my head. *What the hell.*

"Get their prints," one of the jailers told Officer Johnson. I'd forgotten about printing.

"Just place your fingers here. It's inkless now," Officer Johnson explained.

It had been a couple of years, if not longer, since the last time I took someone's prints. Back then, they still used their messy ink. This time I placed my hands on a screen and the computer scanned them. One by one we scanned our prints, irritation and frustration building.

"Stand over there." Officer Johnson pointed to the wall behind us.

A pit of despair filled my stomach as I saw the infamous wall of shame. The wall where suspects stood to have their beautiful portraits taken. Mugshots that would be plastered all over the internet. Now mine would join the others to follow me the rest of my life, popping up every time my name was googled. The internet was unforgiving.

Some people smiled for their mugshot. Some looked like they had just woken up. Others looked drunk, shocked, high, or sad. After fingerprinting, I was pissed again. My mugshot was about to show just how infuriated I was.

"You two get over there, too," Another officer barked at Natalie and Audrey. We walked to the wall of shame together, and Natalie was finally close enough to talk to me without anyone overhearing.

"What's your charge?" she asked.

"Tampering and Official Oppression. Times four for the Official Oppression. It's a $50,000.00 bond. They did $10,000.00 for each one.

"I have that, too, except I only have three Official Oppression charges," she said. "Audrey just has the tampering charge. Her bond is $10,000.00. Rebekah, we didn't tamper with anything. What're they talking about?"

"I don't know. I haven't looked at the rest yet. Officer Ballard tossed it at me and took off. He was in hurry or something."

I watched the intake officers fumble around with the camera, wondering if they planned take our mugshots any time soon.

"Well, look at them. They said we tampered with something on Angel's case. And then look, the teenager's case, the case with the Writ, and Daisy's case. Official Oppression? For some search? Are you kidding me?" She was upset again.

"Look at this. I have the one with the moms that were twin sisters. That's the extra one you don't have. Nice. That wasn't even my case. I helped on it for like two hours or something. This is jacked up." The charges transformed pissed off into fury. "And how is Official Oppression a felony? I swear it's just a misdemeanor. Maybe I have it mixed up with something else."

"It says felony here."

"I see that. Something's got to be wrong with the paperwork. Or with the charge. Something is wrong with all of this," I scoffed. I knew the basics about Official Oppression from my training in the police academy. It wasn't ever mentioned in any of our trainings with CPS. We were told we could be sued by a parent if we conducted an illegal search, not dragged into jail.

"What's going on with them?" Natalie pointed to the intake officers. They were talking amongst themselves, glancing in our direction. The cage was so full of jailers, they were tripping over each other. It looked like chaos, and a feeling of dread passed over me as I imagined them losing our paperwork. It already felt like we had been here for hours.

"They sure are chatty with each other and staring at us," I said. Natalie and I quieted, trying hard to hear them from twenty feet away.

"Did you see it?" one of them asked.

"Shit ya, I saw. It's all over the damn news. There's cameras and news vans all over out there."

I groaned. "Natalie. You hear that? Sounds like shit's hit the fan."

Chapter 25

September 25, 2013

"Get against the wall," the officer yelled, pointing directly at me.

I leaned against the wall, my arms folded across my chest, steam billowing out my ears. The longer I stood there, the madder I grew. The media was going to take our mugshots and run with them, plastering them everywhere. We'd no longer have names, no one would care what the truth was, they would see the mugshots and assume.

"Turn to the right."

He had taken the front view picture while my arms were folded, I was slouched, and I was glaring daggers.

"Reynolds, stand at the wall." Natalie was trying her best to suppress tears.

"Turn to the right." Tears were flowing again. I didn't blame her. This was humiliating.

"Lauren, you're next." Audrey moved to the wall, turning to ask Natalie a question as soon as the jailer took the shot. She looked like she was smiling when hers was taken.

"Turn to the right. Okay, you're done. Lauren, you're first. Go see the judge." She followed an officer into another room.

"By the way, how is the judge here? Did you know this was happening?" I asked Natalie.

"No, they arrested me at work, in the middle of lunch, in front of my staff."

"No, they didn't. Who arrested you?"

CPS would never have allowed that. They would have pulled her out of work to avoid the bad publicity. They didn't want their employee arrested while on the job. Still, here hadn't been any professional courtesy.

"Stupid Jett Hayes and Sheriff Minks showed up while I was at lunch," she spat. "I knew as soon as I saw Jett walk in something was wrong. He told me I needed to go with him, and I realized he went there all the way from Hunt County just to arrest me. I know his wife is behind this. Alison's been waiting for this moment. He just had to insert himself into the drama and that means Alison knew about this. They probably all do."

"You're telling me the Sheriff himself and Jett Hayes drove all the way to Dallas just to arrest you? That never happens. Those were some tax dollars at work."

The story just kept getting better.

"I won't complain too much. If they hadn't, then I'd be at Lew Sterrett and I'd never get out of there." Lew Sterrett was Dallas County's jail. We were standing in paradise compared to that place. "Anyway, I told Minks I didn't know what was going on. I didn't want to go with them, I guess because I thought it was a mistake. Jett threatened to handcuff me right in front of my staff if I didn't go with them so, of course, I went. He had this stupid smirk on his face the whole time and then had the nerve to tell me he thought it would be easier on me if he was there. He's such a lying ass."

"I guarantee Alison and Jett are enjoying this. Alison always did want your job. Anyway, how did the judge get here? How is he here this late?" It didn't make any sense if none of us knew about it.

"I told Minks to call Judge Dollar. I kept telling him we didn't know this was happening and I have kids in daycare. Minks didn't believe me. He said the case went to grand jury and I kept telling him we didn't have any idea. I kept telling him, 'I was at work. I'm still working. Do you really think if we knew about this I'd still be working?' And I was crying, of course. I mean, that's what I do when I'm upset. I was begging him to call Judge Dollar, begging. I don't know if it was the fact I was still working or how badly I was crying, but he finally said it was clear no one gave us any professional courtesy. He called Judge Dollar and asked him to come and arraign us. I think Jett was irritated. Their plan had been to arrest us late enough we'd be here all night. Minks and Judge Dollar said it was crappy how it was handled and we didn't deserve to be in here all night."

Finally, something positive from one of the professionals we had worked with for years.

"Well, I'm glad you talked him into it. Thank goodness someone is still looking out for us. I'm sure no one would have done the same for me on my own."

"Reynolds, you're next. Go see the judge."

"Good luck," I said as Natalie followed the jailer. Audrey came out, standing near me. I didn't know her on any sort of a personal level. Our only communications in the past had been her hounding me about backlog or questioning me about whether or not I had permission to enter a house. I didn't know what to say, so I didn't say anything.

"Ross, you're next."

I followed the jailer into a small room. It felt like a dream, most of it a blur.

"Are you Rebekah Ross?" he asked.

I almost told him no but decided not to argue with him about my last name. We all knew who I was. "Yes, Your Honor."

"I'm going to read you the charges and then read you your rights. You're charged with one count of Tampering with Evidence and four counts of Official Oppression. You have the right to remain silent. Anything you say can and will be used against you in a court of law. You have the right to an attorney. If you cannot afford one, one will be provided to you. Do you understand these rights?"

"Yes, sir." I had the remaining silent part covered.

"Your bond is already set at $10,000 per charge, for a total of $50,000.00. Good luck." That was it. I was done. It was the fastest part of the entire process, having finished at 5:10 p.m., the latest I was aware a judge had arraigned someone at the jail.

"I'm not sure what just happened," I told Natalie as I met up with her again. She and Audrey were next to each other discussing their experience with the judge.

"I know, it was fast. It made me sick to hear the charges. Do you think—"

"Come make your phone calls," a jailer interrupted.

"What phone call?" Natalie asked me.

"Why are you asking me? I haven't been on this side either."

We stood there, unsure what to do. The jailer pointed a payphone attached to the bottom area by the intake cage.

"What do we do with it?" Audrey asked. We knew it was a silly question, but in the moment, none of us remembered how to use a payphone, or anything that looked like a payphone.

"Hey, what do we do with this?" I yelled.

"Pick it up and follow the prompts. It's a phone. It doesn't bite." He was a new face and was sarcastic but nice.

"But, Officer... Matthews, if that's what your tag says, who do we call?"

"Well, if you want out, you need to call a bondsman. Here's a list of them. We can't tell you who to use, just here's a list." He slid the list of bondsmen through the bars.

"Has anyone called you about me? My husband was supposed to already have that in the works." My paperwork should be well

179

underway since I told my husband what to do before I left the house.

"No, don't have anything on any of you. Sorry."

"Seriously? This is going to take forever." I couldn't believe nothing had been started in the hour I'd been there.

"You're worried about how long it will take and I'm worried about where to find the money to get out," Natalie said.

Audrey focused on the phone, trying to figure out how to use it. Picking it up, she listened for a dial tone. "So which one do you think we should call?"

I shrugged. "Just pick one. I don't know anything about any of them. Call one and tell them we'll all use the same one."

"Okay. I guess we'll use Big Daddy Bail Bonds." She called and explained the situation. She'd have to put down $1,000.00, ten percent of her $10,000.00 bond.

"That means I have to put down $4,000.00 and you have to put down $5,000.00. Where are we going to get that kind of money?" Natalie panicked.

"Call your sister. She'll help figure it out."

"She doesn't have it, either. What do I do? My kids need picked up from daycare, too. That's a lot of money. My father's dying of cancer and I've spent every dime I have for his medication. I'm probably going to lose my job. I can't believe these guys did this. And a bond? Did they think we'd run away? After all these years working with them and they put a stupid bond on us." She was stressing, and I felt terrible for her. The words Scott Libby said to me in our meeting rang in my ears. *He has a target on your back, Rebekah. Audrey and Natalie are just collaterals.* She was in the mess because of whatever it was I was accused of doing.

"I know, I know," I said, trying to comfort her. "Your sister can help. Give the bondsman your sister's information. She's not going to let you stay in here. We'll make this be okay."

"It's not going to be okay," she said.

Audrey finished with her call and I pushed Natalie to the phone. "Call them. Just give them your sister's number."

I listened while she made the call and explained the need to call her sister. She sounded much better on the phone. She finished and handed me the phone. Each time one of us was done, we had to hang up and call again.

"Hi, this is Rebekah Thonginh. I need to bond out of jail. My husband was supposed to call someone, but it doesn't sound like he has. I'm with Natalie and Audrey, the two you just spoke to."

"Okay, I thought you'd call. My name is Christie. We knew there were three of you and the first one said you all were using us, so we already have the paperwork started. What's your husband's number?" Christie sounded very pleasant, a welcoming sound against harsh jail shouting. I gave her my husband's name and phone number, thankful I could remember his number. I didn't have anyone else's memorized.

"I'll call him and have him come down here. We'll need $5,000.00 to get you out."

"When you call my husband, tell him there's a check sitting on the bar in the kitchen. I told him, but I don't think he understood. I pulled my retirement out after I resigned from the State. It's sitting on the counter. I need him to bring it so I can pay you." I kept reiterating, fearful they wouldn't understand.

"We'll call him. Since you're the last to call, we've got to get the other two's paperwork done first. Then we'll do yours. So, don't worry if it takes a little bit. When you do get out, come directly here and be careful of the cameras. They're all over out there."

The media was still in the parking lot.

I relayed the tip. "You guys might want to hide when you walk out. Cameras are still out there."

"That's what I heard," they both said.

"Guess we can sit down again or wander the halls. No one's paying any attention to us."

For a minute, it felt like we weren't the ones under arrest and trying to spend a fortune to get out of jail. No one seemed to care what we did. We milled around, talking with each other in the open area between the mugshot wall and intake cage. The drunk cage was to our left.

"Audrey Lauren, your bond's posted," Officer Matthews yelled.

"Guess I'll probably talk to you guys tomorrow and we'll figure out what to do," she said as she left. It was the last time I spoke with her for five years.

"I don't even—" Natalie started when a loud voice rang out behind us.

"Why they get to be standing out there? They ain't cuffed or nothin. Why they ain't be in cells?" someone yelled from the drunk cage and banged on the door. It roused the others.

"They inmates? They inmates out there? Hey, that ain't fair. She's in heels, too. What's going on?" More rattling and commotion.

"Be quiet and sit down," Officer Matthews yelled. "You two probably want to come over here away from them." We didn't hesitate. The jailers might not care we were wandering, but the inmates did. The jailers didn't want them getting riled.

"I really have to pee," Natalie announced as we moved to a quiet side. I busted out laughing.

"Okay, I don't know how we do that from this side. I'm holding it, no matter how bad I need to go."

"I can't. Who do I ask?" Natalie was desperate.

I couldn't help but laugh. "I'll ask Officer Matthews. I think they have to escort us to a restroom." I started yelling. "Officer Matthews. She's got to pee." I could have been more discrete, but it was too much fun. Natalie looked mortified.

"I'll get a female, hang on," he said.

A female jailer appeared and escorted Natalie the restroom. Within seconds though, she was back, the female jailer smirking.

"What happened?" I asked.

"I'm not peeing here. She was going to watch. I told her never mind. We went to the restroom, she stood there at the door, and I took one look inside. It was gross. I asked her why she was still standing there. She said she had to stay and watch. She even apologized for having to stay. I told her never mind, I could hold it." She was completely grossed out.

My bladder was tight, ready to explode, but she had just confirmed for me that I could hold it for days if I had to.

"I have to sit down. I can't hold it if I'm standing." I followed her back to the chairs near the intake cage.

"You guys want to eat?" someone asked, rolling a food cart toward us.

"Nope, all good here. Thanks though."

They laughed at us and kept going. If we were here for too long, we'd probably wet the cots and then starve to death.

The anger was wearing off again. I no longer wanted to punch anyone in the face, nor did I want to run away. While we had to hold our bladders, couldn't eat, were about to drop a chunk of money on a bondsman, and were charged with things we never did, I still thought it was amusing. It was that morbid sense of humor coming out.

"Reynolds, your bond's posted," Officer Matthews yelled.

Natalie grabbed her paperwork and darted for the exit door. I wondered how long it would take her to find another bathroom.

I waited for an eternity. The jailers kept working and I thought about the cases. Tired of watching, I closed my eyes and formulated a plan, deciding what I would do as soon as I walked out and what I would do tomorrow.

"Why is she in the hallway and not a cell?" I snapped my eyes opened and saw a woman standing in front of me, glaring. "Why are you here?"

"I'm waiting to make bond."

The woman scoffed, not believing me for a second. She yelled at the intake cage. "Why is this female out of a cell?"

"She's waiting to post bond," said Officer Matthews.

"At almost 6:00 at night?" she asked in disbelief. Maybe she was part of a new shift. How could she not know what I was doing out here? "Why is there a news van outside? Why was the judge here? What's going on around here?"

"Girl, you don't even know…" Someone said as the woman entered the intake cage. They explained the drama of the day as I leaned my head against the wall again, amused by their chatter.

"Ross, your bond's posted," Officer Matthews yelled. I bounded over to him, ready to grab my paperwork and leave.

"Man, thought they'd forgotten about me," I said.

"No, you're just the last one. It takes a while sometimes."

"Do you know if the news vans left?"

"I don't. They were here a minute ago, but I don't know." He slid paperwork through the bars for me to sign. I didn't read anything, just signed. Being in a much better mood and thinking about the media again, I wondered just what kind of mugshot I took. After all, it'd be everywhere.

"Can I see my mugshot?"

Surprised, he shook his head.

"You don't want to see it."

Now I needed to see it.

"I do. I want to see how bad it is. I'd rather know now than see it on TV. Come on, just for a second… Please?"

"Hey, bring me Ross' mugshot." He laughed. "She really wants to see it."

Several officers crowded in, laughing. "We've seen worse, it could be worse."

They slid the picture through the bars. My mugshot made me looked as if I was going to shoot someone in the face. The officers laughed even harder.

"Holy crap. That's horrible." I was appalled.

"No, it's not horrible. Trust us, we've seen worse."

"I don't know about that. This is pretty bad."

They laughed with me and handed me the completed packet of paperwork. "You're all set. Just go through those doors right there." They pointed at the solid lobby doors.

"Thanks, guys. You helped me have a great laugh about this mess."

"Anytime. Be careful out there." They had made the last few minutes of this humiliating nightmare bearable.

As I moved toward the exit, I realized however I walked through the doors would set the stage for everything that followed. I could look happy, look mad, cry and act like this was horrible, which it was. But anyone else who might be watching would also know how I felt. Most of all, it would set the stage in my own mind. I would follow that stage throughout the entire process.

As the doors opened, I saw my first glimpse of the lobby as a criminal. My husband was walking through the glass entry doors, stressed as we made eye contact. He needed to know everything would be okay and nothing was going to get me down. Taking a step forward, I placed one arm behind my back, the other arm in front of me, bent my knees, and with a massive smile, took a bow.

He laughed as we met in the middle of the lobby and wrapped his arm around me. "Well that looked nice, Honey. That was a really nice bow, but you look pissed, even with that smile on your face."

"Well," I chuckled seriously. "They've opened Pandora's box. They started it and I won't stop until I've finished it."

Chapter 26

September 26, 2013

"I need to make an appointment with Peter Schulte," I said as soon as a receptionist answered the phone. I wasn't taking no for an answer. Our case was so big it was spreading across the national news. I had planned to use Mr. Golden if my case became criminal, but this was too big and had nothing to do with what I thought it would. I needed a high-profile attorney to fight a high-profile case. I didn't care if Mr. Schulte was out of town, in trial, or dead. He was going to meet with me.

"Okay, I can schedule an appointment with him for later this week or next week. What's your name?" a woman calmly asked. This was a regular phone call for her, one she took multiple times a day.

"No, I need an appointment today. I'm not waiting until next week. I can't wait. I have to see him today."

"Well, he's out of the office today. I can try to get in touch with him and see if he can do it any sooner. What is your name?"

I wasn't getting anywhere like this. Mr. Schulte probably already knew about the case. He was Fox 4 News' legal analyst. If I told the receptionist the situation, she might handle it differently.

"My name is Rebekah. I'm one of the CPS ladies who were arrested yesterday. The media has it all over the news. I'm sure Mr.

Schulte has seen the story. I need to hire him and I don't want to wait."

"Oh." She couldn't hide her surprise. "Yes, yes, I know who you are. Let me see if I can get in touch with him and I'll call you right back." She hung up and I watched the clock. Part of me was terrified, intrigued, relieved, and paranoid, wondering if Mr. Schulte would tell me he couldn't or didn't want to represent me.

I was in fight mode in a way I'd never been before. I'd never been arrested. None of my family members had ever been arrested. Even when I was an officer, I didn't deal with whatever happened after the arrest. I knew the terminology. I knew someone had to bond out. I knew someone should get an attorney. Mostly, I knew someone had to fight.

My husband wasn't handling it well. After we got home from jail last night, he had disappeared, leaving me alone with our children. When he returned, we fought. He was convinced I had known this would happen and purposely didn't tell him. He said the way I acted and how I casually left with Officer Ballard to the jail after hearing Natalie's name made it seem like we had rehearsed it. I hadn't cried, freaked out, or panicked. I couldn't convince him I had thought about running out the back door or punching someone in the face.

"Who was on the phone?" my husband asked as I entered the living room. He was changing Kragen's diaper.

"I called an attorney in Dallas. I'm waiting for him to call me back."

"Dallas? Attorney? Don't you want to wait and see what happens? This is jumping the gun a little."

"Why would I wait? My first court date is right around the corner and I don't want to go alone. Not to mention, the media is in a frenzy. I'd like someone to control it." I didn't understand what he meant by wait and see.

"How about we find out what's going to happen and then we find an attorney. Maybe a local one." He didn't remember I had already tried to find one in town. There was too much work conflict with the local attorneys, and I needed someone who could take on the media.

"I've already been indicted? This isn't like having a fight with someone and the cops getting called, then getting arrested, going to jail, and then waiting to see if they'd drop the charges or if the DA would throw it out. We're way past that point."

He didn't seem convinced but didn't argue. "So, who's this attorney in Dallas and is he legit?"

Kragen's diaper was changed and he crawled up on Daddy's lap to watch him play a video game.

"I found the attorney online, back in March when I was supposed to interview with the OIG investigator. No one around here knew what OIG was, even if there hadn't been a conflict. According to his website, this guy teaches the Fourth Amendment to other law enforcement personnel, used to work for the Dallas district attorney's office, he's a reserve police officer, and he's Fox 4 News' legal analyst. He's literally been on all sides and he can handle the media." Leaning against the back of the couch, I held my cell phone in my hand, willing it to ring.

"Okay, if you believe everything you read online. But why didn't he go with you to the interview if he's so great?" He was suspicious. I didn't blame him. People can put anything online and make themselves out to be something they weren't.

"Because he was on vacation and I couldn't delay the interview. He can handle this. I just need him to call me back." No sooner had I said it, my phone rang. It was the attorney's office. I stepped back into the bedroom so I could hear better.

"Hi, this is Anita with Pete Schulte's office," the voice said. "Pete can meet with you today at 10:30 or later this afternoon at 2:30. Which would you prefer?"

I had no intention of waiting until 2:30. I wanted the morning appointment, whatever it took to get ready in time and out the door. "We'll be there at 10:30."

"We'll see you then."

For the first time since Officer Ballard showed up at my door, the tension in my shoulders and spine relaxed. I could meet this guy, make sure he wanted to take the case, and he'd get things under control today. As much as I was in fight mode, my anxiety persisted. The thought of driving in downtown Dallas traffic to a place I'd never been took over any thought of going alone. I'd also received multiple calls and texts from concerned friends and family. I never had time to warn anyone before everything was blasted all over TV. Everyone was worried, and I hadn't been able to respond.

"Honey, let's go to Dallas and meet with this attorney." I had to convince my husband, who hated to be rushed. In order to make it on time for the appointment, we would have to rush.

"Okay."

I paused and took a deep breath. "The appointment is in two hours. At 10:30, today."

"Two hours? Today? We couldn't we do it next week?" he asked, frustrated. "You know I hate being rushed like this. You aren't ready, I'm not ready. Who's going to watch the boys?"

"The media is calling Natalie. They've shown up at Audrey's house. I don't want them here, and if they know I have an attorney they'll leave me alone. I need to know I have an attorney on my side, and he can get me in at 10:30. I've already showered. I just have to put on makeup and someone from church will watch the boys."

"We don't even know if this guy knows what he's doing and you want to drop everything and go see him, now?"

My phone beeped, another text. It was from Sarah Ashmore, a friend who used to work with me as a dispatcher and later reserved with me for a local police department. Now she worked full time as a police officer for the city of Murphy.

Hey, I don't know what your attorney situation is, but I know a great attorney in Dallas. He's a police officer, too. I've worked with him before. His name is Pete Schulte.

I couldn't believe her timing.

Wow, thank you! I just made an appointment with him. Our meeting is in two hours.

"I may have found Mr. Schulte online, but Sarah Ashmore's worked with him. She just recommended him, and she didn't even know I was looking. I think we're good. I mean, what are the odds of that?" I showed my husband the text message, hoping he'd relax and just go with it today.

"Okay, okay, fine. You know I hate rushing but let's go."

He jumped in the shower while I called a lady from church. She assured me someone would be over within the hour so we could leave. An hour later, my husband and I were on the road, driving to Dallas, to meet Mr. Schulte.

Chapter 27

September 26, 2013

For a small-town girl, walking into Peter Schulte's office was walking into a different world. His skyrise office was more intimidating than the stereotypical downtown offices on TV. Glass entry doors opened to lobby couches that looked like they were never used. A massive glass wall separated us from the luxury furniture. A cloudy glass divider, when opened, revealed two receptionists working quietly at tidy desks. Mr. Schulte's office was out of our league and far too expensive.

Mr. Schulte worked high-profile cases with well-known, generally wealthy clients. Once, someone had shot at him through his window from the ground, quite a task considering how high up we were. I was the opposite of his usual clientele. We were not rich, not important, and I had only been a lower middle-class state employee.

My husband and I gingerly sat on the couch and waited. I was nervous, scared, and exhausted, but also anxious.

"Why am I here, Honey?" my husband suddenly asked.

"What do you mean? You're my husband. I need moral support." I was surprised by his question.

"You don't ever need moral support. You've always handled everything on your own. I don't know what I can bring to this."

He was right. I generally handled things on my own and I rarely asked for help. But I had to. He was usually gone, working in the Gulf. I couldn't wait around for him to come home. It only complicated things that I had a strong personality, sometimes characterized as an alpha female. It made asking for help even worse.

"You're my husband. You always think I don't need you. Besides, I think it would be easier for you to meet this guy with me instead of me telling you about it later."

"I still don't know how we're going to afford him. I mean, look at this place."

"I know. But we won't know what he costs until we speak to him. He's the only one who even remotely understands what's going on. I want to—"

"You must be Rebekah," Mr. Schulte said, entering the lobby. I recognized him from TV.

"Yes, I'm Rebekah and this is my husband, Ty," I replied, shaking his hand.

"Nice to meet both of you. Let's go back to my office." He led the way down the hall, passing pictures of Dallas Cowboy jerseys hanging on the wall. My husband was a huge fan, so I nudged him as we walked by. He just smiled. For once, he didn't care.

"Right in here. Can I get you something to drink?" Mr. Schulte asked.

"We're fine," I said.

"Well, have a seat. It's nice to meet you finally. I'm sorry it has to be under these circumstances."

"Finally?" I asked.

"Yes, finally. It's a funny story. One of the news stations called and asked if I knew anything about the situation going on in Greenville. That's generally how it goes since I analyze these things for them. I told them I'd find out and not thirty minutes later, you called. I had to call them back and tell them you might end up being a client so I couldn't talk to them anymore. I couldn't believe the timing." He leaned back in his chair. He looked as successful in person as he did on TV. Handsome, around my age, clean cut. He also looked like a cop. He just had that persona about him. He seemed happy and excited, like he enjoyed his job and was genuinely interested in the situation. "So, tell me, you've been charged with five felonies?" He clearly knew the story.

"That's what they say." I handed him the paperwork. "One charge of Tampering with Physical Evidence and four charges of Official Oppression. But I thought Official Oppression was a misdemeanor." I really hoped he could fix whatever was wrong with the charge.

"It usually is, depends how it's worded." He glanced over the paperwork, the wheels in his mind turning. "I think the Official Oppression charges are worded incorrectly. That will be an easy fix. The DA's office will just change the charge and it will be a Class A misdemeanor. They may have already fixed it. So, tell me what happened."

Fearing he didn't have a lot of time and concerned I'd forget something, I took off with the story, speaking ninety miles an hour.

"I worked for CPS. I resigned in July. My coworkers called a report into OIG. In March I had to interview with the investigator. I refused to talk to him. I didn't know what the charges were until I was arrested and handed this paperwork."

"Wait, you interviewed with the OIG investigator?"

"Yes, but I wouldn't speak to him, so then—"

"So wait, hold on. He doesn't have a statement from you?"

"No. He said it was a criminal investigation, so I said I wanted an attorney and refused to talk to him."

"Just like that? You said you wanted an attorney and you didn't say anything else?"

"Yes. He did read me what sounded like the Miranda rights. I told him I wasn't signing his waiver and I wanted an attorney. I told him I didn't want to talk to him." He was making me nervous, like he didn't believe I had walked out.

"Okay. That's pretty good. You can keep your mouth shut better than most officers. Most want to tell their side, whether it's good or bad, because they think it'll help." He leaned back in his chair, waiting for me to explain more.

"My side of the story wouldn't have gotten me anywhere. This guy said criminal case and I said attorney."

"Okay, I believe you. Continue."

I wasn't sure he really believed me. "In July I resigned from my position. By the time I resigned, we all thought whatever criminal case it was was completely over. Marissa, my boss' boss' boss said no one could get an answer from the DA's office about any charges being filed. Natalie, my supervisor was transferred to Dallas and she kept working. She worked right up to yesterday, as a supervisor. They haven't fired her. She's on administrative leave again, getting paid. Audrey, the other one arrested, retired because, well, I don't really know other than the investigation made her mad."

"Natalie's been working the entire time?"

"Yeah, or on leave but still getting paid. But she was working as a supervisor when this happened. Arrested in front of her employees."

"Okay, tell me about the charges."

"Okay, well, first, I didn't tamper with anything." It didn't occur to me at the time that everyone says they didn't do it.

"Continue."

"And they've charged me with these illegal searches. You can see those names, those names right there," I said pointing to the paperwork. "Each are parents' names on different cases. We never searched anything illegally. That case there, that's not even my case. I don't know what they think I did on that one. I helped on it for like two hours. And that case there, that case Dad went to jail for drugs and we had a Writ of Attachment on it. And that case, that was a kid. I think they're saying we took a cell phone. This case is where I had to find a missing baby, so I did search a house." I needed to catch my breath.

"Okay, so that was the illegal search. That makes sense. But Official Oppression is hard to prove."

"No, it wasn't an illegal search. I was there to find a missing baby. And there was another investigator with me and two deputies, and they weren't charged with anything. But they were there, and the officers broke down the door to the house…"

"And that's when you guys did the illegal search?"

"No, it wasn't illegal. We had to go into the house to see if anyone was there and we had to look for the baby."

"Okay, so then it turned into an illegal search."

Why was he saying that? Was he trying to make me admit to something? Was he trying to rile me up and frustrate me? Did he not believe what I was saying?

"No, it wasn't illegal. I had court orders, signed by the district judge that authorized it. They said 'by any means necessary.' I have a copy of them with me." It felt like I was being interrogated.

"You have them with you? Really?"

"Yes, right here." I handed him the orders.

His entire demeanor changed while he read. "Okay… Hmm… Well, okay. I don't think I've ever seen anything quite like this. I'm not even sure if the Family Code allows for these to be worded this way. But whether it does or not, it wouldn't be your fault."

"Well, our CPS attorney said they did. I mean, we couldn't break down the door, the police had to do that, but once it was down, we could go in."

"That's what it says here. The orders clearly explain what you could do and you should be protected by them. These change everything. I'm going to have to do some research, but I'm telling you I've never seen a case, ever, where someone was arrested for following court orders. If you had been a police officer, this never would have happened. Official Oppression is beating up someone, blatantly doing something to someone. It's extremely hard, if not impossible, to prove. This, what you're charged with, isn't Official Oppression." He laid the orders down on his desk, thinking.

"How about the felony?" I was more worried about the felony. How would I prove I hadn't falsified or tampered with something? It felt like it was my word against OIG's since CPS management had already said they didn't see anything wrong with the case.

"I'm not even worried about that case. I'm already aware of it and there's nothing you could have done differently in it. They just want a scapegoat. You don't have to prove you didn't. The State has to prove you did. The burden is on them. So, with that being said, do you feel better after talking to me?"

"Now that you're not interrogating me, I do."

He laughed. "I had to make sure you weren't hiding anything. It wasn't meant to be an interrogation. By the way, how did you hear about me? I have no idea how you found me."

"I googled you. And then this morning, right after making an appointment, Sarah Ashmore sent me a message telling me you were amazing. She said to say hi to you."

He laughed again. "I know Sarah. Tell her hi back. So, you do feel better after talking to me?"

"Yes, I do."

"Good. If you didn't, then I'm not the one for you. If you do though, then I've done my job and we need to talk about the rest of it," he said, pulling out a contract. "If you want me to represent you then this is what it will cost. I usually charge twice as much, but I think you're getting screwed and I want to cut you a break."

"Can we make payments?" The remainder of my retirement check wasn't nearly enough to cover a portion of his fee.

"Sure can. Payments are $2,500.00 a month."

"Okay good. We can do that." I breathed a sigh of relief and grabbed a pen to sign the paperwork when my husband stopped me.

"Don't you think we should talk about this?" he asked.

"Oh sure, you guys need to talk. I can leave the room," Pete said. "I didn't even stop to think about that."

I glanced at Pete and back at my husband. Were these guys crazy?

"We don't need to talk about this," I whispered to my husband in front of Pete. "No one in town can handle this and I'm not waiting around to find another attorney. There's no one better than this guy."

"It's expensive. How are we going to afford it? I mean, $2,500.00 a month payments? That's twice the mortgage on our house and then some."

"We'll pull money out of our ass if we have to. But I'm not going with anyone else. If you insist on me going with a random court appointed attorney and gamble my future, I might as well go to prison now and just be done. There's no telling who'd I'd get."

He didn't say anything else.

"It's settled. Where do I sign?" I asked Pete.

"Okay, then sign here and we'll get started."

Taking a deep breath, I signed the contract. My future was in the hands of Attorney Pete Schulte, a man I'd met thirty minutes ago.

Chapter 28

September 2013

"Rebekah, this is your attorney," Pete said when I answered the phone. I was in the middle of cooking dinner, exhausted after meeting with him earlier in the day. "The press release is out. That should stop reporters from contacting you directly. And stay off Facebook. Don't comment, don't read it, don't focus on it. It'll drive you crazy. Okay?"

"Sure thing, thank you," I responded.

I didn't listen to Pete's advice. Instead, I opened Facebook and read the comments on social media and the news articles.

The media had everything wrong. Stories ran saying Angel had died because I falsified a risk assessment in her case and Natalie and Audrey had signed off on it. It was clear no one knew what a risk assessment was, or how it worked, and explaining it to someone outside of CPS was next to impossible. Whoever was leaking information made up a story so horrendous, we were all convicted via social media within twenty-four hours of our arrest. According to the news, we were the only three people in the world who could have saved Angel's life and had we done a better job, she'd still be alive today. Comments on social media said we should be flogged, put in front of a firing squad, get life in prison, have our kids taken away, and some even threatened to come to our homes and kill us themselves. Anyone who commented in support of us was part of the *great big conspiracy of CPS* and needed the same punishment, causing the supporters to back off.

CPS didn't help calm the situation. They only commented saying they had been made aware of the arrest of one of their current employees by reading it on the news. When asked about Angel's case they only said, "We're not at liberty to release any details of our possible involvement with the family." It confirmed they didn't know about our criminal case, but it also made it sound like they were covering up something.

The DA's office wouldn't comment on camera, but said the charges were in relation to Angel's CPS case but not connected to her murder.

I watched Angel's aunt, Jennifer, speak to the press on camera. "We don't know what this is about. No one's told us anything. We don't have a problem with CPS. Nothing CPS could have done would've prevented Angel's death. Booksire is serving time for sexually assaulting her, and that's what we wanted. Now we've learned our very own uncle murdered our precious Angel and we're waiting for his murder trial. As long as whatever's happening with CPS doesn't affect the murder trial, we'll just have to wait to hear more."

No one seemed to care what Jennifer had to say. No one realized Booksire and Mr. M. were two different people.

No one understood the Official Oppression charges. Sometimes the media ran the story saying the Official Oppression charges stemmed from Angel's case and other times they briefly mentioned them saying we had illegally searched other homes. Mostly, their stories stayed focused on Angel's case. My identity had been stripped from me and everything I'd ever worked for was gone. I knew I'd never done the things I was accused of, but that didn't matter.

The situation sent me spiraling into depression. I couldn't attend the religious ceremony with my brother and his wife with the charges hanging over my head. I didn't want to go anywhere, and I didn't want to do anything. I tried to keep up appearances, but I was falling apart inside. My sister-in-law brought groceries to the house when my husband wasn't home because I refused to leave the house. She took my children on outings to get them out of the house. Friends from church came over to clean my house. The couple of times I tried to go out in public, I had deliberating panic attacks and came back home.

The holidays made the depression worse. More people came around, as they normally do during the holidays, but I stayed in bed, refusing to visit. I couldn't gather the energy to even put up a tree. I tried to force myself to function. I knew my children didn't understand what was wrong and my husband didn't know how to handle it. He'd never seen me like this. I kept telling myself I had to keep going, for my family, but the depression was stronger than willpower.

It wasn't until Julia barged into my house one day and found me lying on the couch, still in the same clothes I'd been wearing for a week, did I find counseling. She had found me a therapist who knew my background. Had I not agreed to go, she would have forced me into her car and taken me herself. She knew therapy would help, and it did. By the time our next court date rolled around, I had the panic attacks under control and could go into public without a complete melt down.

Chapter 29

February 18, 2014

"Just smile, ignore the cameras, and follow my lead," Pete told me before we entered the courthouse." It was our first time in front of the judge since our arrest. Natalie and her attorney, George Milner, were with us. Pete opened the door, allowing me to enter first. As soon as I walked in, the camera lights blinded me.

"Pete, Pete, can we get a statement?" A reporter shoved a mic in front of Pete's face.

"No comment right now. I will make a statement after the hearing," he casually responded. He was a natural in front of the cameras. "Come on, Rebekah, let's go upstairs to the courtroom. You look nice today."

I knew what he was doing. The cameras were following us, taking in everything he said. His compliment was code to make me smile and chat with him as if going in front of the judge for a pre-trial was something I did every day. I went with it, laughing at his subtle jokes, looking serious at other times. Between therapy, anti-depressants, and Pete's ability to communicate with me, following his lead was easy.

Everything was calm as we closed the courtroom doors behind us. The media wasn't allowed inside. I sat next to Natalie, who hated the media commotion more than I did. She still worked for the State and feared too much media attention would ultimately affect her job.

"State v. Ross, cause number 29269 and the others," Judge Roger Beechum announced from the bench.

Judge Beechum had been the sitting judge in the 354th District Court since before I could remember. We didn't like it when our CPS cases fell in his court. He disliked CPS and sometimes sent children home with their parent, only for us to have to remove them again. The four of us walked from the back of the room to stand before him. The last time I stood in his courtroom, I was an investigator, advocating for a child, trying to keep the child from going home to drug-addicted parents. Now I was a defendant, defending my actions after the fact.

"Where's the State?" Judge Beechum asked his bailiff. We all looked around; there wasn't a prosecutor in the room. The bailiff took off out the door, on the hunt for the missing prosecutor. He returned seconds later, followed by Scott Libby.

My body stiffened. Why was he here?

"Sorry, Your Honor," Libby chuckled uncomfortably. "I thought I had more time."

His laugh echoed in my mind. He wasn't supposed to be here.

"Is the State ready?" Judge Beechum asked, eyeing the tardiness of his prosecutor.

"Yes, we're ready," Libby said.

"I see the Defendant has filed a motion for continuance. Is there any objection from the State?" Beechum asked.

"No, Your Honor. I believe the defense needs more time to review the discovery. I know I do. I was just assigned the case," Libby said.

I really wasn't imagining it. He wasn't here by mistake or to fill in for someone else. Scott Libby was prosecuting my case. The same Scott Libby who had told me he'd never seen anything hinky in any of my cases, was prosecuting me. The same one who had told me this was happening because I made the OIG investigator mad, was prosecuting me. What kind of messed up—Pete's hand grasped and released my arm snapping me out of my trance.

"Your Honor," Pete began. "We don't need more time to review discovery. We haven't received it at all."

"I believe, um, he's correct. I do recall, I do believe it's ready for him. He can get it today before he leaves. It's quite lengthy. The State has no objection to the, um, continuance, no objection." It was like Libby forgot how to speak.

"Okay, I'll grant the motion for continuance. We'll reset the trial date," Judge Beechum announced as he slammed the gavel down. We walked back down the isle of benches to the exit. I was about to burst at the seams, wanting to know how Libby was assigned the case. But as soon as the doors opened, the cameras were waiting.

"Pete, Pete, can we get a statement now?" the reporter asked again.

"Of course, of course," Pete played to the media. I stood next to him, not saying a word, a sweet smile plastered on my face. No one could tell I wanted to shove a dagger into Libby's throat. Pete adjusted his suit jacket and cleared his voice. "My client, Rebekah, is innocent of these charges. We look forward to proving her innocence in court."

It was short and quick. Just enough for a sound bite. The media was satisfied, and the cameras turned off. I could breathe again.

"Hey, Pete." It was Robbie Locker, the district attorney. He had a massive brown folder in his hands as he approached. "Here's the discovery." Pete reached out to take it. "Find a way to make this go away, quickly," he whispered.

Pete nodded, saying nothing.

I wasn't sure if I heard what I thought I had heard, but Pete gestured for me to not saying anything and just go outside. Natalie and I walked side by side, following the two attorneys and waiting impatiently for someone to explain.

"Pete, what was that about?" I asked once we were out of the media's presence, my patience having reached its limits.

"The DA doesn't want to prosecute this case," he said. "But someone around here is determined to do whatever it takes to make sure you and Natalie are convicted and never work for the State again. They want to nail you guys."

"What? Why?" Natalie asked, shock jolting her.

"I don't know. We'll know more when we go through this folder."

The folder contained every statement, interview, recording, and case the State thought they had against us. We knew we hadn't done anything wrong. Evidently, someone else thought otherwise and for whatever the reason, they wouldn't rest until they got what they wanted.

I would spend the next few months driving Pete insane with emails and questions, reviewing over 2000 pages of documents, thirteen DVDs with my coworkers' recorded interviews, others with cases, and eight sworn affidavits. The discovery told me Polly Patterson made the report to OIG and Alison Hayes called in the second report. I heard Investigator Carlos coached a few of them to write in their statement that they feared I'd retaliate and feared for their lives. I just rolled my eyes. Maybe OIG, or someone in the DA's office thought the amount of *evidence* would intimidate me or convince me they had something. It didn't. Instead, I memorized it and made note of what each person involved had said or done to cause this case to come to fruition. The urge to fight grew stronger with every passing day as we waited for something to happen and our next court date to approach.

Chapter 30

August 2014

"He's been fired *for cause*," Pete said over the phone. "Juan Carlos, he's been fired. The DA's office just found out. If the DA's office wants this to go away, it's being handed to them. I'll let you know as soon as I know more." He hung up before I could say or ask anything.

I was ecstatic. Not because I wished termination on someone but because the termination meant the State just lost any credibility with their investigator. Our next court hearing was in four days and the State just had a brick wall land on their heads. I called Natalie.

"He's been fired," I screeched.

"Who?"

"Carlos. The OIG investigator. He's been fired *for cause*. I can't believe it. You know what this means, right?"

"That he screwed up and someone finally figured it out?" She squealed.

"Well, probably," I replied, a bit thrown off by her explanation. "But that's not what I mean. The State doesn't have their key witness anymore. His credibility is shot. And there's no way for them to introduce his investigative report into evidence. Without that, what's their case? They have nothing on Angel's case anymore. Nothing."

"They don't have anything on any of the cases. We didn't do anything wrong," she said. "I don't get it." I must have caught her when she was distracted. She wasn't grasping what I was trying to say.

"I know that. But on the other cases, there are affidavits with one of our coworkers trying to say they saw us do this or that. Everyone is guessing about Angel's case and the OIG investigator was the only one who tried to explain how we falsified something. And he used Ester as his *expert* and she's been canned, too. There's no one left."

She was too focused on the obvious. "But we didn't falsify anything."

"I know that. But we can say that until we are blue in the face. Investigator Carlos thinks we did. He used Ester as his mini-me to examine the case and since she was fired last year and now Carlos has been fired, there's no one left with any credibility. Get it?"

"So, what's next?" she asked.

"I don't know. Pete's getting more information. I can't imagine how the State can keep going with this. Pete may or may not call me before court. I'll let you know."

That's usually how it happened. Pete gave me an update, a few lines in an email or a quick phone call, and then nothing else until I saw him in court. I knew he was busy gathering information, learning more, doing whatever he had to, but the wait to know more was torture.

Four days later we were in court, standing in front of the judge. Pete filed a motion to quash the indictments, arguing they were defective, or in other words, they should be thrown out. Natalie's and Audrey's attorneys had done the same. Throughout all of this, none of us knew exactly what it was we were alleged to have falsified. Angel's case was over 500 pages long. The risk assessment took up five of those pages. I had read every single page, memorizing most of them. We had a right to know exactly what we were being accused of so we could prepare our case, but we didn't have any idea.

The judge didn't need to rule on the motions because Libby had a motion of his own.

"Your Honor," Libby stumbled on his words. "We, we aren't sure how, we just learned this information when we subpoenaed our witness for trial… No one, no one, um, we had to find out ourselves. I called and was told… Our witness isn't with the State anymore," Libby paused. "We don't know how the State will proceed after this point… We just don't know. We, and um, need some time to figure it out."

How much more time did he need? Our lives were on hold while he fumbled through this.

"Your Honor, the defense is ready to proceed with the case. We're reaching a year since my client was indicted and we're ready," Pete countered.

Judge Beechum thought for a moment. "Maybe the State and defense would like to meet, off the record, and discuss what they'd like to do?"

He wasn't suggesting, he was giving an order.

Pete, George, and Libby disappeared again, leaving me to sit in the back waiting to hear about my case. The lack of control over it drove me crazy. I was used to being in charge, making things happen, and now I had to trust someone else. I didn't wait long before they returned. Pete brushed by me, laying down something next to me.

"Watch my stuff. Don't let anyone take it," he said before turning around and quickly running out the door. Instinctively, I picked up his things, as if someone would rush in and grab it, and realized what I was holding. It was Investigator Juan Carlos' termination letter. Without thinking, I read it. He was fired for insubordination back in July. The letter in my hand was from Human Resources to him, explaining his termination was upheld and he was fired for cause, specifically for insubordination. I was stunned. He had done something blatantly wrong for anyone in the Health and Human Services Department to go that far. I remembered how he treated Natalie and Audrey, and then me, and the rumors I had heard about him threatening and coercing others. Maybe his behavior had caused the termination, or maybe it was something else. Why hadn't the State found out sooner? I had a lot of questions.

Pete and George briskly returned, Pete taking the folder from my hand and gesturing for me to sit still. He, George, and Libby went back in front of the judge, discussed something I couldn't hear, and then came back. Pete didn't have the letter anymore.

"Okay, we're done. Let's go," he said.

"Wait, what?? What happened?"

"We'll talk outside," he explained.

I followed, frustrated at the lack of knowing anything. Once we were away from anyone who could report back to the DA's office, Pete explained more.

"We're going to give them some time to figure out what their next move will be. Our next court hearing will be on September 24. We'll know more then. You just have to trust me."

I wasn't happy. I didn't understand why we would agree to anything or why the State got more time to figure out the mess they had gotten themselves into. But I trusted Pete and if he said it had to be this way, then I'd go with it, hating every second of it.

Four weeks later we went back to court, only to not have a hearing.

"The State's backtracking. They want to go forward with just one case for now and see how it goes," Pete told me after he met with Libby.

"Why aren't we pushing them to dismiss it? This doesn't make any sense." My head felt like would explode with frustration.

"They'll end up dismissing the felony. It's going to happen. They want to see how the murder case goes and make sure CPS isn't brought into it at all so there isn't any *public outcry*. But they'll dismiss it. And I think if they lose on whichever of the oppression cases they pick, they'll dismiss the remaining cases also."

I rolled my eyes. For the last year, we had been going to court on all five cases, together, grouping them like they had anything to do with each other. We had insisted the entire time for separate jury trials, forcing the State to prepare for each case and present each case individually. Now it sounded like the State wanted the same thing, except there was a chance they would only try one case.

"We didn't have anything to do with Angel's murder. The man on trial for murdering her, the uncle, wasn't even involved in my case. He didn't live in the home. My case was about Booksire, the guy who sexually assaulted her. And he's in prison. He's been in prison. He went to prison during my investigation. This is stupid."

"You don't have to rehash it to me. I know. Remember, I'm on your side. I know this already. The media is part of the issue. The DA's office wants the murder trial over so there's not near the backlash at dismissing the felony on you."

"Robbie should grow some damn balls and put a stop to this circus. He doesn't seem like he wants to push this case, but he's not standing up to whoever it is calling the shots." I was infuriated.

"Calm down. There are politics involved, but you know Robbie's a good guy. He's stuck in the middle here. Libby's going to look at the cases and tell us next week which one they'll take to trial first. We'll know more next week." Pete was trying to play nice, and I knew he was right, but I was growing more frustrated at the wait.

"So, what you're really saying is it will be months before we know anything. That's just awesome. Just awesome," I smarted. "It's never just a week."

"We'll see, we'll see." It was Pete's feeble attempt to calm me down.

I knew we didn't have a choice but to continue to wait, yet it still irritated me. Our criminal justice system was slower than I had ever imagined. Pete told me over and over time was on our side. He was right. The more time that passed, the more that things fell apart for the State.

Remaining in limbo was frustrating. I had to call Natalie to vent. We had the same information but venting to each other helped us cope. All we could do for now was wait for next week. But next week turned into the week after, which turned into the month after. And the delays continued.

Chapter 31

January 2015

"Your prosecutor can't be your professor," Professor May Fitz said during our January advisory conference. I had returned to school the fall of 2014 to earn a second bachelors in Paralegal Studies at Texas A&M University–Commerce. I wanted to learn everything I could about the judicial system without having to attend law school, which was too expensive while I was paying attorney fees. I planned to soak up everything taught, read every textbook, and ask my professors 101 questions until I knew everything. Texas A&M University–Commerce was twenty minutes from my house and was the only one in Texas that offered a Paralegal Studies degree accredited by the American Bar Association, the same association that accredits law schools. I knew I had to change careers, and a degree accredited by the ABA would help me stand out.

I had never anticipated my professors would be my prosecutors.

"The rules don't allow it. It has to be a conflict of interest." She was frazzled. If we had been sitting outside, she would have picked up the pack of cigarettes sitting next to her and smoked them all back to back. May Fitz had taught some of my classes during the fall semester and knew I was under indictment. Being under indictment didn't stop me from earning my degree but being taught by my prosecutors was throwing a wrench into things.

"It's not a conflict. I looked it up and searched everything I could find in the code of conduct or the ABA guidelines. Nothing says a professor can't also be a student's prosecutor," I rebutted.

"But, it's a conflict. It has to be. Nothing like this has ever happened before. Ever. Who has their prosecutor as their professor while the case is still pending?" She wasn't really asking me. She was talking out loud to herself.

"Well, who gets arrested for doing their job? And who gets tried by the same DA's office who prosecuted the cases they want to now put me in jail for? There's a first time for everything." I couldn't help but laugh.

"How can you laugh about this? It's not funny."

"It is funny. The whole situation is just messed up. I mean, of every strange thing that could happen… You can't make this stuff up."

Professor Fitz wasn't amused. "You have to drop out. You just have to."

I shook my head. Dropping out was the last thing I would do. The classes were offered on a rotating schedule. If I waited, I would have to wait for another year and a half before the class came around again. That meant I wouldn't graduate until 2018, and I refused to wait.

"Nope, not happening. I'm taking his class, both of them, and whatever the next one is and the rest of them. I'm not giving up."

"The ABA will probably make you quit. It's against the rules." She was beside herself, shaking her head, upset and flustered at the same time.

"We aren't breaking any rules. There aren't any to break."

"Only because this hasn't happened before."

"Exactly. It hasn't happened before. I'm a first. And now I'm being taught criminal law by my prosecutor while my case is pending. I think we should just live it up and go with it." I wasn't backing down.

"What if you get a bad grade? You could file a grievance and contest the grade. And then the argument is, 'he gave me a bad grade because he's prosecuting me and he wasn't fair,' and I don't want to deal with that. The school doesn't want to deal with it. I have to speak to your attorney. I need to know he's okay with this. And then I have to speak to Robbie. I can't imagine either of them are okay with this." She turned to her computer and started typing. I assumed it was an email to Robbie.

"Hold up." I raised an eyebrow. "What do you mean 'if I get a bad grade'? I have no intention of getting a bad grade. He won't have any reason to give me one. That's certainly not an issue." I would do whatever it took to pass his class with an A and not because I begged for the grade like other students. I would pass his class and I would make the highest grade in the class. I had a new motivation for finishing school. I had a point to prove. "What if you supervised the class? Double check the tests and make sure you agree with the grades. Look over the papers. Be the extra set of eyes. Make sure it doesn't come to needing to file a grievance or something."

She stopped typing, thinking. "You're right. I could do that. It would stop anything from happening before it happened. I still want permission from your attorney. I mean, you'll be in there with the prosecutor. What if you say something he can use against you?"

"What if I don't? I think this is being over thought. I'm taking the classes. Pete will email you a letter with permission. I don't think Robbie will argue. Besides, Robbie oversees Scott Libby and Libby is the one handling the direct prosecution. Libby's not teaching any classes, and never has," I said, ending the argument.

I understood where Professor Fitz was coming from. This was highly unusual, and she wanted to protect the program's integrity. I wasn't going to do anything to jeopardize it, and I didn't believe

Robbie would either. We could all act professional, Robbie and Libby doing their job to uphold their definition of the law and prosecute me and me doing my job to uphold my freedom and fight them.

"Rebekah," Professor Fitz said as I was leaving. "Do you think anything stranger could possibly happen?"

"Sure," I responded. "I could get convicted."

I could hear her laughing as I left. I checked my email on my phone as I walked to my car. I was anxious to see if Pete had any news on which case the State wanted first. My heart skipped a beat when I saw his email.

They're taking 29269 to trial.

I re-read the one-line email three times. There was no mistake. The case I was most fearful of, the one that would have implications that would reach the entire state, affecting investigators and children alike, was going to trial. Daisy's case. I had court orders, signed by a judge, allowing me to search for Daisy. I could not imagine the number of children that would be left at risk or the number of investigators that would leave in droves if I lost the case. This wasn't about me anymore. It was about protecting everyone.

Chapter 32

February 2015

"We're prepared to go forward with only one of Ms. Ross' cases," Libby announced at our pretrial hearing. "We're not going forward on any of Ms. Reynolds' cases at this time."

Our jury trial was two weeks away. After Natalie refused the deal the State had offered—testify against me and they would dismiss all of her charges—they decided to sever our cases and try me alone, at least for now.

"Okay, that's fine. We just need to get these cases moving." Judge Beechum seemed relieved. Our cases had congested his docket for eighteen months. "What are the motions we need to hear today?"

"The Defendant has subpoenaed Polly Patterson and Karen Bacon," Libby said. "The State has filed a motion to quash those subpoenas."

I ground my teeth. He wanted our subpoenas rejected so Polly and Karen couldn't testify or be involved.

"Your Honor," Pete interrupted. "Ms. Polly Patterson handled the underlying CPS case this entire alleged illegal search is about, and Ms. Karen Bacon taught a Fourth Amendment class, nine months after this alleged illegal search. They're witnesses in my

215

case and it's crucial they testify." We knew when we served the subpoenas the State would fight them.

"I filed the motion, so I get to go first," Libby mumbled.

"Of course you do," Pete said, giving Libby a questioning glance. "I wasn't trying to take over."

Libby was acting odd, almost like he was unsure of himself. He gestured toward an older gentleman with a bald head. "Also, Your Honor, for the record, this is Dick Wooten. I'll let him introduce himself."

I'd heard his name before, but I hadn't worked with him. He was a regional attorney of some sort and worked closely with Polly, but I wasn't sure what he did for CPS.

"Thank you. Yes, Your Honor, I'm the attorney for Child Protective Services. I'm here today… I was going to file the same motion, but Mr. Libby's already filed it, so I guess we're both here to make the same argument."

It was peculiar for CPS to send an attorney to prevent us from questioning Polly. They had been quiet about our case, even allowing Natalie to remain on paid leave. Sending in an attorney didn't seem to fit. If CPS thought I'd done something wrong, then they should want Ms. Patterson to testify. She knew the details: everything I'd done and how I did them.

"He's correct, Your Honor. Ms. Patterson's sole responsibility is to represent CPS in court. But, any, any facts she learned while working as the CPS attorney is private, even confidential. Her testimony is irrelevant to the Defendant's case. And Ms. Bacon, she represents the State. She's obviously one of our assistant district attorneys. Our office drafted the indictments against Ms. Ross. So, any information Ms. Bacon has would also be confidential as it would be information she obtained while assisting in the prosecution," Libby said, nodding toward Mr. Wooten. It looked like they were tag teaming.

"The only thing I'd add," Mr. Wooten stammered. "Is to, is, is that any information Ms. Patterson gathered... I, Ms. Patterson never discussed the facts of the case, the underlying CPS case, the case that brought these charges. She never specifically talked to, to the Defendant about the facts of that CPS case. So, any information she knows would be confidential as CPS cases are confidential."

Stunned, I stared at the stammering attorney. Whether he was outright lying or really thought Polly had never spoken to me, it was an absurd argument. She and I had discussed the case in detail, and she'd read my detailed, eight-page affidavit and approved it before allowing me to continue removing Daisy. She told me the case was solid and I'd given it to them *signed, sealed, and delivered.*

"Judge, they're witnesses. They're witnesses to facts regarding this case," Pete countered. "Nothing we need them to testify about is confidential. For example, it is undisputed that my client, along with law enforcement, went to a house to find a missing baby. It's undisputed she had court orders signed by Judge Titan. The jury's entitled to know exactly how she obtained the court orders. Ms. Patterson drafted them. Only Ms. Patterson can testify as to what Ms. Patterson did. It would be hearsay for anyone else to try and testify as to what Ms. Patterson did.

"As to Ms. Bacon, we need to know why she provided, to every single worker in Hunt County, a Fourth Amendment training nine months *after* this alleged illegal search. Was she asked to provide it because no one with Hunt County CPS understood proper search and seizure? If so, then no one, including my client, could have *known* if something was wrong with the search until *after* the training. And that's an essential element of Official Oppression.

"I think Mr. Libby's afraid his office will be disqualified if Ms. Bacon's allowed to testify since his office drafted the indictments. That's not our problem. The State allowed these charges to be brought against my client and now we have a constitutional right to defend ourselves." Pete's argument didn't seem to me to leave any room for misunderstanding or for the State to continue arguing against us.

"Anything else?" Judge Beechum asked, peering over his glasses at Libby.

"No, Your Honor. Well, I would say that… I don't believe we're disqualified simply because we drafted the indictments and we certainly don't intend to recuse ourselves. We simply believe that why a particular petition and order was drafted, why they ordered a search of that home, is confidential information." Libby looked uncomfortable with his argument, not keeping eye contact with the judge and fiddling with the folder in his hands.

If this had been any other case, especially with a defendant requesting testimony about how a warrant used to search their home was obtained, the State would have gladly allowed the testimony. Without the testimony, the warrant or the search could be thrown out and all the evidence suppressed. The State would lose their case because they couldn't use any of the evidence from the search against the Defendant. In my case, I was the Defendant who'd not only conducted the search but was also asking for the State to produce the testimony that explained how the authorizing court order was obtained. This time, the State was trying to prevent everyone from knowing what happened. It sounded like the State was covering up something.

A laugh escaped Pete. He must have thought the same thing.

"Is there something you want to say, Mr. Schulte?" Judge Beechum asked, calling him out.

"I apologize, Your Honor," Pete said, clearing his throat. He wasn't sorry. "I already suspected it, but I believe Mr. Libby's just realized it as well. The motion he's drafted to try and prevent this testimony is actually an admission as to what's happened. There wasn't an investigation into my client, or anyone else, until eighteen months after this alleged illegal search. His motion admits Ms.

Bacon didn't provide the Fourth Amendment training until nearly ten months after the search. His motion also admits Ms. Patterson, the one with the sole responsibility to represent Hunt County CPS, routinely spoke to CPS employees in preparation of court fillings, court appearances, and any other number of legal matters because he wants to keep these conversations confidential. Ms. Patterson had to know exactly what occurred in this case, in all the cases. If Ms. Patterson and Ms. Bacon knew CPS workers were breaking the law, they had a duty to report it and they didn't. So, either their testimony will show they're trying to cover up their role if my client broke the law and they failed to report it, or their testimony will show they've known all along my client never did anything wrong, which makes me question the State's motive in trying to prevent their testimony. They can't have it both ways. That's why their testimony is so important."

The room was silent as everyone realized the ramifications of Pete's argument. Natalie and I had asked each other the same question, time and time again. Pete had brought it up in the very beginning. How did I obtain an order to search, conduct the search, remove the baby, and the case go through the entire CPS system, ending with the termination of Daisy's parents and her adoption, if I'd done something wrong? And it wasn't just CPS. The case had gone through the criminal court, too. The DA's office had secured child endangerment convictions on both of Daisy's parents. They said the parents committed the crime on December 16, 2011, the same day they were now saying I'd conducted an illegal search. Both of Daisy's parents had attorneys who represented them for their CPS case and for their criminal case. Their attorneys would have brought up the illegal search and not allowed a conviction. Any of them could have used my affidavit as proof. I'd detailed everything I'd done in that house, believing the court orders gave me authority to do so, and then sworn to it under oath.

"Your Honor," Libby and Mr. Wooten said in unison. Libby stopped and gestured to Mr. Wooten, allowing him to take over.

"Your Honor... I, I wrote this down. Hold on, let me see... Yes, here it is." Mr. Wooten searched through the yellow legal pad he held in his hands. "She knew... Ms. Patter, Ms. Patterson knew the search was illegal. If the Court, if the Court is..."

"Objection." Pete's voice boomed, commanding attention. Mr. Wooten didn't say another word, his mouth gaped open. "Objection, I never said it was illegal. I object to him being in the room. He has no reason to be here. He needs to leave."

I rather wanted to hear Mr. Wooten continue if his argument started with, "Ms. Patterson knew..." but I understood Pete's reason. We didn't need Mr. Wooten trying to insert hearsay for fact, and anything he said that Ms. Patterson said was hearsay. Polly had to admit it herself.

"Sustained. You may leave the room, Mr. Wooten," Judge Beechum ruled, not appearing at all startled by the loudness of Pete's objection. "Mr. Schulte, are you saying there's no other witnesses or procedures you can use to establish how the petition and order were obtained?"

"That's correct, Your Honor. I wouldn't subpoena attorneys if I didn't have to. I know it's rare and not looked on favorably. But this case is unique. We have a former State employee defending charges the State brought against her about court orders the State drafted and gave her, that were signed by a State district judge, that authorized a search the State knew about but that the State now wants to say was illegal. There's no getting around what's eventually going to come out at trial, and their testimony is the only way to properly admit it into evidence. I'm not allowing hearsay."

"Okay," Judge Beechum growled while he rubbed his forehead. He looked physically pained over the complicity of the situation. "I'm inclined to grant the State's motion to prevent the testimony but only if the State is willing to admit to the facts behind the court orders. Is the State willing to stipulate, to admit, to the facts?"

Libby was still trying to gather his composure, clearly startled by the objection. "Okay. Well, I'll, I think I, I formulated a response. Um, the, the State doesn't have a problem stipulating, admitting, to the facts."

Pete interrupted. "Can I clarify? The State's admitting that Ms. Patterson drafted the petition and order for the court orders, and that the orders were presented to Judge Titan, who signed them, and that based on those court orders, my client and law enforcement went to the house?"

Libby silently nodded.

Pete continued, "And the State is admitting that Ms. Bacon taught the Fourth Amendment class nine, or nearly ten months, after the case in question, and they'll admit why she taught it? I just want to make sure we're all clear, for the record."

Libby nodded, mumbling under his breath.

"Speak up, the court reporter can't hear you," Judge Beechum ordered.

"Yes, yes, Your Honor, we will." Libby said, louder. Even though he'd essentially won his argument, as the stipulation meant the judge was denying our request for these two witnesses, he didn't look happy. I wondered if the stipulation meant he'd have to change his trial strategy.

"Okay, what's next?" Judge Beechum asked.

"When Mr. Carlos presented the case to the grand jury, was there any testimony? If so, I'd like my motion to be granted and the grand jury testimony turned over," Pete said.

"I checked, there isn't any testimony," Libby said.

"That's what I thought," Pete said. Libby had confirmed our suspicions. It was OIG, specifically Investigator Carlos, who'd presented the case to the grand jury. It helped us understand the driving force and the politics behind the case. The grand jury, which consisted of twelve people, were the ones who determined whether there was enough evidence to bring charges against someone. Only nine of the twelve members had to believe there was enough evidence, and they based their decision on what the officer or the prosecutor said. In my case, they would have listened to Investigator Carlos' presentation and watched his official-looking Power Point with "Office of Inspector General" written all over it. I'd seen his presentation, and it looked like it came direct from a government agency. "The last thing I want to address, Your Honor, and I base this off of conversations I've had with the State, but I think once we try this particular case, the other cases will get dismissed. Can we confirm that?"

"That's what's been said." Libby nodded.

"I guess I get to be the… The guinea pig. You know, trying a case like this one, one that's never been done before."

The pressure was on for Pete. Though he was my attorney and trying my case, what wasn't said during the hearing was what happened if he lost my case and I was convicted. Natalie's future also depended on Pete's ability to win. If I was convicted, the State would take one of her cases to trial. If I was acquitted, all her cases would be dismissed. She and George would have to wait to know how'd they proceed. The only case with a mostly certain future was Angel's. The DA said they would dismiss hers eventually; we just didn't know when.

Pete and I prepared for trial over the next two weeks. I knew the court was gearing up for trial when the clerk mailed the jury summons. The judges didn't like to have anything interfere with the trial proceeding after the summons were sent.

My mom traveled from Arizona to join the rest of my family in show of support. We spent the day buying a new outfit, getting our nails done, and enjoying time together. I wasn't nervous or scared. I didn't care if I went to jail for a year, the most the judge could give me. We were ready and didn't think anything could stop us from moving forward.

I'd forgotten about one minor issue. Texas weather is unpredictable.

Chapter 33

February 2015

"An ice storm. An ice storm shut down my damn trial. Seriously, of all the things in the world, it had to ice. Why today of all days?" I yelled, venting, frustrated at the lack of control I had over the weather and the entire situation. We knew the weathermen had warned us it could ice, but Texas weather changes so often and so quickly we were sure it would pass over us. I tried to will the ice to not fall. I begged the temperature to warm. I threatened to punch Mother Nature when Pete called to say we were officially rescheduled.

"Calm down, Rebekah," my mom kept saying, over and over while I paced the floor. "You're going to give yourself a stroke. Your stress is stressing me out. It's late. It's really late."

"God thinks he's being funny. I've been waiting for three years for this to resolve itself."

"Have some faith. There's a plan for you, you just don't know what it is yet."

Though I knew she was right, I didn't want to believe her. Instead, I started telling her to stop living in a bubble when my phone rang.

"Did you see that? Did you see Carlos in that interview? On the news?" Pete was infuriated, his voice loud and stern when I answered. "Today, of all days, he goes on national TV and talks about an open investigation, the investigation he's the lead on, and releases the confidential OIG investigative report. I've never seen anything like it. The reporter reached out to me to comment on Carlos' accusations, but I didn't know *that* was the story."

"What happened? I haven't seen it. I wasn't even paying attention." I started scrambling for the TV, realizing we only streamed and didn't have live coverage. While talking, text messages started flooding my phone from friends who had watched. They were saying the report contained Natalie's social security number, her address, her driver's license, and her weight and height. "Pete, what happened? Tell me."

"I'm filing a complaint. He can't do that. The only reason he did that was to try and influence the jury. He didn't know the trial would be rescheduled. He had his face blacked out on camera. George and I are already in contact with the station, they're taking down the video." He hung up, leaving me wondering what had just blown up.

I needed to see the news report and only knew one person that would record it, even if it was just because she forgot to turn it off.

"Julia," I started.

"What's up, chickadee?" she asked cheerfully despite it being past 10:00 p.m. She sounded wide awake. "Why aren't you spending time with your mom? She came all the way here to see you."

"Please tell me you recorded the news tonight. I need to know you recorded the news. I need to see it."

"Huh? I don't know. I wasn't paying attention. Why?"

"Julia, go look, please."

"Okay, okay, I'm looking, relax. What station? Wait, I think I see something. Oh look, it's that Juan guy. What's going on... OH HELL NO. NO HE DIDN'T. Rebekah, did you see this?"

"No. I didn't see the damn thing. I just heard about it. I have to see it. And I need a copy of it."

"I don't know how to do that. Shit, what do we do? I don't know… Look, look, it has all of Natalie's information all over it. Oh my gosh… Oh my gosh…Everyone knows where she lives. They can steal her identity. Is she okay?"

"I heard. Can you just record the story with your phone? Just hold your phone to it and record it."

"Yeah, I can do that. Easy. Hang on." She hung up and moments later, I was watching the recording.

Investigator Carlos' face was blacked out, telling the reporter he needed his identity concealed because he was applying for an undercover position. Why would anyone announce on national television they're applying for an undercover position? That wouldn't keep them very undercover, whether or not their identity was blacked out.

"What I found was that nothing was done. I reviewed thousands of pages of documents and nothing was done. She left a vulnerable child at risk," Investigator Carlos told the reporter. He was talking about Angel's case, something he focused on in his lawsuit. "She closed out twenty-nine cases before she left for maternity leave, leaving all of those kids at risk. I had an investigator look over those cases and three of them had to be reopened."

My blood boiled as I listened to lie after lie coming from the silhouetted figure. Nothing had been re-opened. Marissa and I had already discussed those cases. Children weren't left at risk. I'd done my job very well, according to her.

"Investigator Carlos believes Angel would be alive today if her case had been handled differently," the reporter said. "Carlos presented criminally negligent homicide charges to the grand jury, but the grand jury declined to indict the three workers on that charge. Instead, they were indicted on several others."

"This is ludicrous. We can play the *what-if* game all day," Pete countered. It was clear the reporter hadn't told him the full story. "This is a horrible situation. There's nothing given in the information that was reported to CPS and to the police department that there was any indication that an uncle was going to murder this poor girl."

No one seemed to remember the family had been interviewed on national TV months before. They had said they didn't have a problem with CPS and nothing we could have done would have changed anything.

The reporter shifted to explaining the OIG report as she showed the camera page after page, highlighting details. I couldn't believe it. CPS couldn't release the report to us, even when the report was about us, so I knew they wouldn't turn it over to the media. Only Investigator Carlos or someone in the DA's office had access to it.

"Pete, I just saw the report. Carlos can't release that report. It's confidential," I said over the phone.

"What do you mean they can't release it? They'd just go through the public information act and get it."

"Maybe, but even so, that's not the report CPS would release. That report doesn't even match what we have in discovery. That report doesn't even have a supervisor's signature on it and CPS would have redacted all of the names and identifying information, at the very least."

"We don't know that though. I'm filing a complaint for his actions as an investigator to release opening talk about a pending investigation."

"I understand. But he also released confidential government records."

"Get me proof that that's not the report CPS would release. And send me screenshots of the video on the news."

"I'll get it to you in a few minutes." I already knew what kind of report would be released. I'd found one, not too long ago, from an investigation in Austin. I forwarded the report to Pete so he could see the difference. It only took seconds for an email response.

And he wasn't a commissioned officer when he investigated you. I can't believe this. All of us, the other two attorneys as well, thought he was.

Adrenaline rushed through me and I nearly fell off my chair. I'd found dirt on Carlos online earlier, but I couldn't prove any of it. Now I had evidence, and Pete was as livid as I was. He was a commissioned police officer, working as a reserve, and though I wasn't any longer, I'd been a commissioned officer for six years. This was a personal insult.

I suspected as much after reading his lawsuit. I take it you have proof?

It was like texting through email with these short one and two liners.

I'll have more proof soon. I think he impersonated a peace officer when he presented the case to the grand jury. I think things would be different had they known he was just a civilian. Civilians don't have authority to file criminal cases.

His comment reminded me of something I'd seen in my paperwork. Digging through my folder of court documents, I pulled out the typed indictment for Daisy's case and looked at the backside. Written along the right-hand side of the margin was *Officer Juan Carlos: Office of Inspector General.* It didn't say *investigator* like he put on everything else. It said *Officer.*

I scanned the page and sent it and the screen shots to Pete. He'd file the complaint in Austin. All we could do was wait to see what happened. Our next court date wouldn't be until April.

Chapter 34

April 2015

"Honey, I have the motion to dismiss. Do you want me to read it to you?" I asked my husband.

Pete had just sent met the motion he'd file in court, and I was excited to share it. It was nine pages long and I wasn't sure he'd stay focused. Talking about my case bothered him, but my enthusiasm and sense of humor while talking about it often upset him.

"Sure, read it to me." He looked annoyed as he tried to sound supportive.

"As a result of his lawsuit and media interviews, defense counsel has learned Mr. Carlos engaged in egregious and outrageous misconduct." I watched for a reaction from my husband, but he didn't do anything. "Mr. Carlos routinely identified himself as an *investigator* and threatened CPS workers with criminal prosecution if they failed to speak to him. He then delivered an *investigation report* to the DA's office, first to the DA, and subsequently to an assistant DA, making criminal allegations against Ms. Thonginh (Ross) and the other two co-defendants. The motion explains how he impersonated a public servant, committed aggravated perjury, committed a third-degree felony of misuse of official information, and get this, committed Official Oppression by intentionally denying or impeding my right to a fair trial. Isn't that ironic?"

"Honey," he interrupted. "I know you're excited, but get to the point. Does this mean your case is getting dismissed?"

"I have no idea. But it means everything's spelled out. It's a court document now. So, anyone can see it now. Even the media if they looked in the Court's file." He watched as I rambled, looking at me as if I'd lost touch with reality. "Everything that's happened so far has been kept quiet and no one has a clue what really happened. Maybe now the truth can come out."

"But what does this mean for your case?"

"I don't know. You know how this case has gone. Nothing about it makes sense. I mean, I'm going to trial over searching for a drug-addicted baby after getting court orders from a judge. Who does that?"

"I can't listen to this anymore. It's exhausting. It's like you're detached from it, like you're not the one it's about. I just don't understand how you do it. You're in your own little world. You even go to school and the prosecutor is your teacher, and you take the class like that's normal. It's not normal." Frustration was building in his face.

"I guess I'll read the rest to myself." There wasn't any use talking about it. He didn't understand how I could distance myself from the case and enjoy the battle, even though I was the one who'd be slaughtered. The stress of the case had taken its toll on everyone; we just showed it in different ways.

By 10:30 a.m. the next day, Pete had officially filed the motion and within hours the local paper ran the story, plastering it online. Facebook exploded with social opinion. Some were supportive of the case being dismissed while others thought we were trying to cover up something. Angel's family publicly said they hoped the case would finally be dismissed despite it having nothing to do with them. It wasn't Angel's case being tried, but everyone still assumed it was. That night, during class, Robbie was unusually preoccupied. His phone continually buzzed, and I wondered if he was trying to answer questions and comments, too.

The next morning brought an even larger surprise. Pete forwarded me an email from one of my former coworkers.

My name is Lori Wright. I am a former employee of CPS. I resigned due to the dishonest, coercive, and intimidating environment being allowed to flourish in that office and county. However, before I resigned, I signed a statement against Rebekah Thonginh Ross and Natalie Reynolds. I am recanting that statement.

When Investigator Carlos interviewed me, and before he recorded anything, he told me what he knew were "facts" regarding the case. He intimidated, threatened, and coerced me, saying if I did not comply by telling the "truth," his "truth," I would be terminated from my job and go to jail. I believed he had the authority to do everything he threatened, and I believed I had no choice but to follow his orders if I wanted to stay out of jail. I can no longer live with this mistake.

Mr. Schulte, I am completely recanting my statement against both Rebekah Thonginh Ross and Natalie Reynolds. I apologize for my role, my mistake, in this case and hope I can, in some way, make things right.

As I finished reading, Pete called. His voice was as excited as it was surprised "Rebekah. Did you read that? I've already sent it to the DA's office. I tried to call Libby, but he sent me to voice mail. I can't believe she put it in writing."

"I can't either. I mean, I don't know what to say. We knew for sure a few of them had been threatened, but I didn't think anyone would actually come forward and admit it. I mean, I remember listening to Lori's interview with Carlos. He practically wrote her statement for her. I heard him say, 'Write down what I wrote here, in your own handwriting.' What happens now?" I couldn't wrap my mind around the turn of events. This only backed up what we already suspected.

231

"I don't know how they'll be able to proceed after this. They have more than enough to dismiss the cases. Lori came forward because she read the story in the paper last night. It gave her the motivation she needed."

"What if they don't dismiss it? Things haven't gone exactly like the norm."

"Then we'll fight it and we'll go to trial. And they can go to trial with witness tampering accusations. We'll know more tomorrow. Hang in there."

I was excited but hesitant. As much as Pete believed in me, he was still looking at the case from a sane, logical point of view. There hadn't been anything logical about it from the beginning. Even if the DA wanted to drop it, it felt like someone or something would continue to push it forward.

The next morning, with the news station waiting in the lobby, we stood once again before Judge Beechum. Pete was ready to attack, almost daring Libby to try anything except agree to a dismissal.

"Your Honor," Libby began, stumbling through his words. "Your Honor, the State has filed a motion for continuance. The State has, we need time, we've been presented with a statement by a witness that was interviewed by Mr. Carlos back in November 2012. This witness, there are claims, essentially the witness claims... The written statement was coerced and is factually inaccurate. Maybe, even possibly... False. The witness may have been, there are allegations of, it appears Mr. Carlos could have possibly threatened criminal prosecution if the witness, um, if the witness didn't cooperate and, um, provide the statement." He almost couldn't spit out his argument. I'd seen him stumble and stutter in the past, but this was intense. He couldn't form a complete sentence and looked like he'd been up all night, completely disheveled. Judge Beechum curiously watched him struggle. "We need, we need more time, we need to, to determine if other witnesses will claim the same thing... That they were coerced. We need to investigate this. We need... A continuance. We ask for as much time as the Court will give us, to, to check the veracity of these allegations."

That wasn't what I wanted to hear. Pete grabbed my arm, stopping the yell that nearly escaped my mouth.

"Your Honor, we filed our motion to dismiss on the 7th. As is stated in our motion, we had already believed Carlos committed misconduct. The statement from the witness came after we had filed our motion. It confirms what we believed was already true. The State has had ample time to investigate this case. They knew Carlos interviewed with the media in February and before that, in November, and both times made false statements and released confidential information. They were already aware of the mishandling of this case. We do not wish to delay this any further. Rebekah was indicted in 2013 and enough is enough." Pete was insistent.

I waited, holding my breath.

"I'm denying the motion for continuance. Jury trial is set for Monday and we will proceed forward." Judge Beechum didn't want to hear anything else.

"Don't worry about it," Pete whispered as we walked out. I could hardly hold myself together. "He can still change his mind over the weekend. There's no way they can go forward with information like this. Just follow my lead."

A news journalist, Theresa Ennis, was waiting for us as we left the courtroom. She'd been to a few of our court hearings and never appeared to believe anything positive about me. She was the one who'd interviewed Investigator Carlos and ran the story in February. This time though, she looked livid and it wasn't at me.

"I'm ready for a statement. I can't believe the absolute mess this has become." She pushed the microphone in front of Pete and signaled to the camera man to start recording. I stood next to Pete, trying to look confident and happy.

"Pete, what can you tell us? You, and the other attorneys on these cases, have filed a motion to dismiss and the State has filed a last-minute motion for continuance. You've made some serious accusations. What do you think will happen?"

"I don't think they can go forward with these cases. I think they have a duty and an obligation under the law to investigate. Was there witness tampering in these cases? Was there someone committing crimes while investigating these cases? If that's true, none of these cases are valid and they have to be thrown out. They have to dismiss." Pete responded as if he had rehearsed it.

I had the weekend to prepare for trial. My mom hustled back to Texas and my husband rearranged his plans. When the story aired on the evening news, I watched it, feeling somewhat vindicated for the first time since this all began. It was clear during the story that Theresa Ennis was furious she'd been duped by Carlos. She wasn't afraid to say so.

"Defense attorneys filed a motion to dismiss the indictments, alleging misconduct by OIG Investigator, Juan Carlos. Ross is scheduled to go to trial on Monday for an illegal search of a house. When we interviewed Investigator Carlos earlier this year, he asked that his identity be concealed. He gave every impression he was a law officer during the investigation," she said, once again confirming our belief he had impersonated a police officer.

"I put together the investigation really objectively. I didn't present anything that couldn't be proven, and they got indicted." The station replayed a piece of the February interview, using Carlos' words against him.

"Records obtained showed Investigator Carlos was not a commissioned police officer during the time of the investigation. Carlos was fired last year, accused of insubordination. He has since filed a lawsuit, appealing his dismissal. Back to you." The camera changed to the anchorman and the rest of the nightly news. Monday would be interesting.

Chapter 35

April 13, 2015

The courthouse was packed with news reporters and people reporting for jury duty. They played on their phones, chatted amongst themselves, or stood half asleep. Pete brought in his law partner, Jonathan, to assist us, and we squeezed ourselves through the mass of people, past the media, and into the quiet courtroom.

"All rise," the bailiff commanded as Judge Beechum entered the room and sat with a groan. The deep circles under his eyes enlarged as he squinted at his laptop.

"Your Honor, we're asking once again to reconsider the motion for continuance. The State needs time to investigate and determine if there is any veracity to these allegations. Without a proper investigation, this case could get flipped on appeal… If there was a conviction." Libby spoke as if he assumed there'd be a conviction.

Judge Beechum was genuinely irritated. "I'm going to grant the State's motion for continuance. But you have six weeks to get this straightened out and that's it. We're going to trial, one way or the other. I do not like doing this when the citizens of Hunt County have exercised their duty and are waiting in the hallways. Go work out a new trial date. This won't happen again."

"Pete, why?" I angerly asked as we left. "Why is it getting reset? There's plenty to dismiss. Why are they pushing this?"

"Just wait. Follow us to his office," Pete responded. "Stay close and follow right behind us." We navigated our way through the crowded hall. Libby, Pete, and Jonathan, having longer legs, got through the crowd first, entering the DA's offices before I could.

"Stupid bitch," a woman next to me snapped. I turned toward the voice, confused, as she hacked a wad of spit from her mouth, landing it on my cheek. "You're a stupid bitch."

I was too shocked to say anything as I wiped the slime from my face, slinging it to the ground.

"I hope you rot in hell," she shouted.

The words rang in my ears as I realized the woman was one of many we would have chosen from had my trial not been postponed. If she had anything to do with public opinion, I was sure to be in jail.

I squeezed myself into the quiet sanctuary of the DA's office. With the door shut, it felt like being spat on hadn't happened. I sat on the bench in the waiting area and took a deep breath, listening to Pete and Libby's voices in the distance. I figured they had forgotten about me.

"Hey, there you are," Jonathan exclaimed as he came from around the corner.

"Yeah, you guys walk too fast. You left me out there and some lady spat on me, called me a bitch, and told me I could rot in hell."

"What? Really? Where?" Jonathan asked, appalled.

"Out there. Some scraggly haired woman." Jonathan darted toward the door and looked in the hall. But in the few seconds I'd waited on the bench, the bailiff had already dismissed everyone, leaving the hallway empty.

"They're gone already. I wished you'd said something sooner."

"You guys were talking down there. I didn't want to interrupt."

Pete joined us just as I'd finished talking.

"Someone spat on her and called her a bitch," Jonathan said.

"What? Show me who," Pete demanded as he went straight for the door.

"They're already gone."

"Okay. We'll figure it out. Let's go talk to the media. It'll be okay." The reporters were waiting, as if they had all day.

"Pete, we've been told the judge reversed course and granted the motion for continuance. Can you tell us why?"

"The District Attorney's office has asked the Texas Rangers to investigate the alleged illegal actions of the OIG investigator who brought these charges against my client and the others. Though I opposed the motion for continuance, I feel confident the DA's office will take action if it is determined Investigator Carlos broke the law." The reporter turned off her microphone and lowered the camera before saying anything more.

"I'm waiting for Mr. Locker to come out of that room. I'm getting a statement from him, too," she said. "And it looks like I don't have to wait much longer." She briskly walked to the DA, blocking his ability to avoid her.

"Mr. Locker, Mr. Locker, can you comment on the surprising turn of events? Did Investigator Carlos impersonate at peace officer and threaten witnesses during his investigation?" She waited, refusing to leave until Robbie answered.

"We've asked the Rangers to investigate. We have to know exactly what we're dealing with. There are some unknowns here and we're duty bound to investigate." His voice was friendly as he gave his short and to the point statement, letting the reporter know he wouldn't offer more.

"So, what now?" I asked Pete.

"We wait some more and see what comes of the investigation. We're set for a status hearing in May and the jury trial in June."

Chapter 36

September 17, 2015

TRIAL

"We're here on State v. Ross or Thonginh, whatever her name is, in cause... Which one or ones are we trying?" Judge Beechum didn't care enough to try to keep things straight anymore.

"We're trying Cause 29269," Libby said as he shuffled through papers.

My family piled into the back rows, as did some close friends, as we prepared to start. If the case had gone to trial a year ago, the courtroom would have been packed. With so many delays, people were hesitant to take off work for fear it would be rescheduled again.

We'd ditched the idea of a jury trial after Libby offered to dismiss all my other cases if I'd agree to a bench trial. Since we never knew the outcome of the investigation against Carlos and our case was still going to trial, we thought it would be better for a judge to determine the law about search and seizure rather than a jury.

"If the State's ready, let's bring in the witnesses so we can swear them in," Judge Beechum ordered.

One by one, the witnesses for the State, my former coworkers, entered the courtroom. I chuckled as they swore on the Bible to tell the truth and nothing but the truth. It should have burned beneath their hands.

"Remember, do not discuss the case with each other or anyone else," Judge Beechum warned as they left the room. "Do you have any opening statements, Mr. Libby?"

Libby stood at the prosecutor's table, just to the right of me. He looked calm and collected, almost bored. His posture reminded me of how he stood when he taught class. This semester he was my professor for Business Law, something neither of us had anticipated as he'd never taught before. Tonight, if I wasn't in jail, we'd go from court to classroom, defendant to student, prosecutor to professor.

"I do. The State believes the facts will show that Ms. Thonginh Ross, while working as a CPS investigator, exceeded the scope of an Order in Aid of Investigation when she tried to locate a newborn child. She entered a residence, with another investigator, and proceeded to search the home, not just in places where the child might be, but elsewhere, going beyond the scope of what the order allowed. She knew from her training the orders didn't allow that. She violated the law of this State and of the United States Constitution."

"Mr. Schulte, you're next."

Pete rose from his chair, confident and determined. He was ready for a fight. Jonathan sat to my left, prepared to stop me from making a fool of myself, if it came to that. Mostly, he would relay messages to Pete so Pete didn't get distracted.

"When Rebekah was assigned an investigation, there were allegations a five-day-old baby had been born at home, without medical care, addicted to drugs, and no one knew if she was alive or dead. The Court will find Rebekah had court orders signed by Judge Titan, giving her, and law enforcement, authority to go into the residences, by any means necessary. When they did so, she and law enforcement saw a bed with blood all over it, leading them to believe there could be a dead child, leading them to exigent circumstance, which allowed them to keep looking. There was no intent to conduct an illegal search, and that's what the State has to prove. This isn't the type of crime where she could accidently conduct an illegal search and still be found guilty. She had to intentionally, knowingly do it. We don't charge police officers with Official Oppression for a search they conducted when it is later found to have been in violation of a warrant. But that's exactly what's been done to Rebekah." Pete sat down when he was finished and whispered near my ear, "That was pretty good, right?"

"Of course," I laughed. "But let's see how well you do for the rest." The joking helped me relax as Libby called Justine to the stand.

Justine positioned herself in the witness chair. Her perfectly manicured face and styled hair were exactly how I remembered them from three years ago.

"On December 16, 2011, did you go to a residence to search for a newborn baby with Ms. Thonginh?" Libby asked.

"Yes, I did."

"Can you take us through what happened when you arrived at the residence? After you and Rebekah got to the house?"

"The officers broke down the door and went in. Then Rebekah followed. I was outside talking to another deputy and then I went in. The home looked like it'd been abandoned, like everyone had left in a hurry. Trash was piled in different areas and it was pretty cleaned out."

The same anger from when I was searching for the baby warmed my insides. I hated that a CPS worker had warned them to flee, putting the baby at more risk. The family never did tell me the CPS worker's name, but after searching through thousands of records, I'd figured it out. Natalie had questioned the worker over

241

the phone with the supervisor on the other line. The worker had admitted he knew about the drug use, assumed Daisy was addicted, and helped them run anyway. He had been annoyed that he had been dragged into the situation but not sorry, or even concerned, about Daisy's welfare. His supervisor had apologized to Natalie, profusely, having no idea what her worker had done. Sometimes I wondered if I'd never have gone to trial if the worker hadn't interfered with my investigation.

Justine and Libby described that infamous day, Justine offering basic, specific answers that sounded rehearsed. She told Libby she took pictures, walked through the house, looked at a journal, and saw blood on the mattress. She confirmed she did think I was looking for Daisy, at least during the search of the bedroom.

"What did the Defendant do that made you think she wasn't looking for a baby and that maybe she was looking for something else?" Libby asked.

"When we went into the kitchen, Rebekah instructed the deputy that was helping us to grab a crock pot or a pot down, it was either up on the shelf or up on the fridge. She wanted to search for evidence of drugs."

"Did you believe that searching a crock pot was authorized by the court orders?"

"No, sir. When…. When the crock pot was brought down so Rebekah could search it, I said there's not going to be a baby in there and that we needed to go find the baby."

My blood started to boil. Justine was blatantly lying. She'd wanted to go eat breakfast. Pete kept me from losing it by giving me the *we've got this* nod and pulled out the photos we planned to use.

"What else happened in the kitchen? Were there any drawers or cabinets that, that were opened by the Defendant or anybody else?"

242

"Yes, sir. I don't recall if Rebekah opened drawers or if she just instructed the deputy to do so. They were working together."

Again, I couldn't believe what she was making up. They had my removal affidavit. At least, I was told that's what they would use against me. Libby had originally planned to argue I couldn't even enter the house, much less toss a bedroom and flip a mattress. My affidavit was supposed to be used as a sort of sworn confession. But nothing in my affidavit said anything about searching a kitchen or a crock pot.

"Did you believe searching through drawers and cupboards were authorized by the court orders?"

"No, sir. I believed she was looking for evidence of drug use."

"Did you believe, based on the training and experience you all received, that a reasonable person would think the court order allowed the Defendant to search a crock pot and a kitchen?"

"No, sir."

"Pass the witness."

"Rebekah," Pete whispered as he stood, ready to cross examine Justine. "Show me where the blood is. Point to it."

"What? Okay, there it is," I said as I pointed to the blatant blood splatters in the picture he held out. I was seething. "You know that didn't happen, right? She's lying."

"I know. But they've accused you of it and now we have to justify it. We can't just say you didn't do it. That won't matter."

"But I didn't."

"It doesn't matter. Sit back and be quiet." Jonathan put his hand on my arm as Pete approached Justine. It was an attempt to remind me to relax, but I was infuriated. It was one thing to argue about searching the residence in general, but to make up something and lie about a crock pot just seemed beneath everyone.

"Justine," Pete began. "My name is Pete Schulte and I represent Rebekah. Now, let's talk about this crock pot."

Chapter 37

September 17, 2015

My trial was turning into a legal argument over a crock pot. A crock pot that never existed.

"Did you take pictures of this crock pot?" Pete asked.

"No. I wasn't concerned at the time about getting Rebekah in trouble."

"Wasn't concerned about getting her in trouble? Okay. Well, did you take these pictures?" Pete showed her the pictures of the bloody walls and mattress. The color in Justine's face drained.

"Yes, I did," she confirmed.

They were pictures she'd taken during the search. For some reason, those, and sixteen other pictures, mysteriously weren't included in our discovery. The DA's office knew they existed. I'd put them on three separate DVDs back in 2011 and had given a copy to the DA's office and one to the police department. The other was in the CPS file. We didn't tell Libby the pictures were missing and chose not to question anyone about withholding evidence. Instead, we found the missing pictures and used them to our advantage.

"Hold on, before we do that, can I clarify something with my witness? I think there's some confusion," Libby interrupted.

"Go ahead," Judge Beechum allowed.

"Are you sure these pictures are ones you took of this particular incident and not…"

"They are."

"But they could be from another…"

"They're from the same incident."

I inhaled, relieved she could tell the truth about something.

"Okay then, no objection." Libby looked distraught as he sat down. Was he trying to figure out a new strategy or had someone lied to him, too?

"Do these pictures bring back memories?" Pete asked.

Justine nodded.

"Okay, good. So, you're worried about a crock pot, about Rebekah searching a crock pot for drugs instead of a baby, right? That's what you said? Tell me, with your training and experience, and with all this blood, a missing baby, drug allegations, and the parents' CPS history, you're saying you didn't think a reasonable person could have believed something bad had happened to the baby and maybe the baby's body was shoved somewhere, like in a crock pot?"

"No. I mean, I didn't think anything had happened. It wasn't my case. Rebekah worked it. She'd gone to the home before that day. She'd done a lot of extensive investigation before I was involved. She'd already found the drug stuff. She did all that."

"Okay, so she did her job. Is that what you're saying?"

"Yes."

"Isn't that what you're supposed to do?"

"Well, yes, but not search for drugs."

"Okay then, do you think that at that point, back in December of 2011, you'd received adequate training to cover every aspect of the Fourth Amendment and search and seizure?"

"Yes. I do."

"Then wouldn't this adequate training teach you that maybe, after seeing all of this, something could have happened to the baby? And, having court orders, that say by any means necessary, maybe you needed to do whatever it took to find this baby?"

"No. No, it doesn't."

"Then why get the court orders? Why reach out to Polly Patterson and write an affidavit and have her present the petition and the order to a district judge so he can sign them? Why do they say you are to observe the premises and immediate surroundings where the abuse or neglect may have occurred, by any means necessary, if you can't do what they say?"

"I don't know."

"But you said you had adequate training. Rebekah's sitting over there charged with a crime, being accused of searching too hard to find a missing baby, a drug-addicted baby, with court orders, and all you can say is you don't know?"

"I... I don't know. I don't know. I'd never worked a case like this before. I never had court orders that said by any means necessary. I never had a case where a baby was born at home. I don't know." She wasn't upset or even rattled. She was calmly sticking to, "I don't know."

"Okay. You were promoted as a supervisor after this, somewhere around the end of 2013, right?"

Justine nodded.

"Let me ask you, based on your adequate training, if you had left the house, without looking everywhere a tiny baby could fit, which could be a crock pot or a drawer, and then the next thing you find out, after you've left, is that the baby had died in the house, and was in one of those locations you didn't search, would you have been in violation of CPS policy for not doing your job? For not obeying the court orders? For not doing whatever it took, by any means necessary, to find the baby and instead, walking away from a capital murder scene?" Pete's voice was loud, almost frustrated. He was an expert in the Fourth Amendment. He knew what questions to ask, where to get specifics. Her answers must have baffled him as much as they baffled me.

"No, sir."

Gasps echoed around the courtroom from the audience. I glanced behind me, wondering if everyone felt the same shock I did.

Sarah Ashmore, who sat behind me, had dropped her jaw in disbelief. She was attending to see what had actually happened, and I knew she disagreed with Justine's answer. No detective would have interpreted the situation that way.

My mom and brother were whispering to each other, Mom's face contorted with irritation. Another friend, Megan, was shaking her head and patting my husband's back. He looked like he wanted to fly out of the chair and hit someone.

The reporters were scribbling notes, no emotion on their faces. I groaned inside. This type of answer was why CPS had such bad press and why CPS had so many child deaths.

"Pass the witness."

Pete sat down and poured a glass of water. "You've got to be kidding me."

"Tell me about it. I'm still trying to calm down."

Libby called Kenderick to the stand. I hadn't expected him to testify and didn't know what he'd say. He'd never given a statement to OIG, so I hadn't thought he was involved. As much as he was lazy, he never lied. At least, not until he was under oath, testifying against me.

"You said there was an RV travel trailer, right?" Libby asked.

"Right. I remember it was out in the county. Rebekah apparently had information that these people kept drugs in a... I think it was a crock pot or something in the kitchen cabinets. She wanted me to search the kitchen cabinets and specifically look in that area. Of course, I told her no, because that was beyond the scope of our job."

I choked on a breath mint. Kenderick couldn't have been more specific, more direct, or more blatant. He and the others had discussed exactly what to say. There was nothing I could do about it except see if Pete's cross examination could turn it around.

"So, Mr. Stinson, you said earlier that you got the impression, on a number of occasions, that Ms. Ross was all about violating people's civil rights. Who'd you report that to?" Pete asked, ready to find the truth.

"No one."

"So, I'm confused. You thought she was trying to violate people's civil rights, but you kept it to yourself? It's okay to tell the truth."

"I don't recall telling anyone."

"So, you didn't report it until today as you were testifying. Fair enough. Do you remember when this crock pot incident was? Or where?"

"No, I don't."

"Right. Let's move on. You remember the case we're here about today? The case you assisted Ms. Ross on to find the missing baby?"

"Yes."

"Is it fair to say this was a rare case?"

"Yes, it's fair, it's fair." It was the only part of his testimony that was truthful. That's all Pete wanted out of him. Nothing else mattered because Kenderick wasn't telling the truth, and we didn't want to give him more opportunities to spin lies.

Brittany Baldwin's testimony was next. I'd met her in 2008 when I'd first started at the CPS academy. She'd only been a trainer for a week. Now she was the training director and responsible for training new workers in nineteen different counties.

Libby focused his examination on the training curriculum. It was how he'd prove I *knowingly and intentionally* conducted an illegal search. Brittany read over my transcripts, recited the title of the

248

classes, and explained, in general, how the academy functioned. Pete's focus wasn't on my training but to show how much Brittany didn't know. Her lack of knowledge would prove the disparity in the training.

"Ms. Baldwin, are you familiar with the procedures for obtaining an Order in Aid of Investigation?"

"I could guess. But no, I'm not sure."

"Okay. I handed you the petition, the affidavit, and the order. Would you agree with me, after you've read it, that it allows CPS and law enforcement to enter the residence by any means necessary?"

"I think so. I mean, I don't know."

"Okay, would CPS and law enforcement be allowed to search for the child? Is that what the orders allow?"

"I mean, I'm not sure, I'm not sure."

"What if there was blood in a room, all over the place? Does that look like a lot?" Pete pointed to the picture of the mattress and blood splatter.

"That is concerning."

"Would it lead to exigent circumstances that would justify a search for a missing baby? That, with all the allegations you read in the affidavit, would exigent circumstances fit?"

"I don't know. I mean, I'd need more facts."

"Let me ask you this question. I'm only basing it off your experience as a training manager. If they had gone to the house, saw the blood, and knew what they knew about the allegations, and they just left and later they found out that the baby had died and was sitting in one of the places that you're not sure if the orders allowed her to look, would that be a violation of any CPS policies?"

"Not that I'm aware of."

Groans rumbled around me. She was the second person to say it was okay to just walk away and not look for the baby. Her testimony lasted for nearly an hour. I was embarrassed for CPS and concerned for future workers. If Brittany couldn't give a straight answer, or even know the answers, how did she expect workers to be adequately trained? She wouldn't have any idea if the instructors under her were doing their job because she didn't know the difference.

Rachel, Justine's supervisor, gave testimony that was nearly identical to Justine's in regard to the crock pot accusation. However, where Justine thought the orders allowed us to enter the residence and Brittany didn't know what they allowed, Rachel was adamant that no matter what the situation was, the court orders never allowed CPS to enter the home. Pete summed it up when he asked her his last question.

"So knowing we have court orders that say by *any means necessary*, and a six-day-old, tiny five pound baby that you admit could possibly be dead because of the amount of blood all over the room, and that you admit was so tiny she could fit in a drawer, a cupboard, or a crock pot, with all of that you're telling this court you wouldn't try to figure out if the baby or the baby's body was in that house, and you're telling this court that in this exact situation, knowing everything you know, having the court orders signed by a judge, you would have told law enforcement, 'Thanks for being here at 6:00 a.m., nobody's home, we're going to come back later'?"

Rachel's one-line answer sent chills down the spines of everyone in the room.

"Yes, that's exactly what I would have done. I would have walked away."

Teri Jones was the last of my coworkers to testify. Her testimony didn't have anything to do with the trial and Pete tried everything he could to keep it out, telling the judge it wouldn't do anything but cause bias.

Judge Beechum didn't care. He overruled the objection and said, "It's a trial before the Court. I'm going to be liberal in what I allow in."

Teri came up with a story about an apartment she claimed I had searched. I didn't have any idea what she was talking about and she couldn't provide any details except that I'd searched kitchen cabinets and opened kitchen drawers. Part of me wondered if she'd forgotten to mention a crock pot. Her story was just as perfect as the others.

Though the State swore in three more witnesses, they only called one more. It was Daisy's mother, C.J., and the only one who told the truth. C.J. was subpoenaed to testify even though she didn't want to. In February, when our case was rescheduled due to ice, C.J. had told someone about being subpoenaed, asking them what would happen if she didn't show up. She'd told them she didn't want to want to testify and didn't understand why I'd been charged. As far as she was concerned, this part of her life was behind her. I'd never understand why the State was pushing the case so hard when the alleged victim didn't want it and didn't think I'd done anything wrong.

Libby covered C.J.'s history, ensuring it was in the open to avoid the appearance of covering up anything.

"Why didn't you have prenatal care?"

"Well, I had an open CPS case with my son. I wanted to kind of close that. I didn't want to interfere in keeping him in foster care longer, plus I was in a really bad spot in my life. I wasn't doing good things, and I was in a terrible relationship. It was very abusive. I was trying to run off, and I was trying to get better, but nothing ever got better."

"Nothing ever got better?"

"No."

"Were you, while you were pregnant, were you taking any illegal substances?"

"Yes."

"What were you taking?"

"Regrettably a little bit of everything. I just didn't want to stop." C.J. had signed a drug acknowledgement confession for me, the day I removed her daughter. We'd spoken for nearly two hours at the office while she told me what she'd been doing and where she'd been hiding during her pregnancy. She'd admitted to using methamphetamines, cocaine, marijuana, K2, alcohol, and cigarettes during her pregnancy.

"All right. Now were you concerned at all that CPS would be coming to look for you and your baby?"

"I was expecting it and I was ready for everything to be over, so, yes."

"What? Ready for what?"

"For everything to be over. I wanted a better life for her and for myself."

"Oh." Libby paused before changing his questions. "Well, let me ask you this. This might sound odd. But did you give anybody from CPS written or express permission to go searching through your cabinets and drawers in your kitchen before you left the house?"

"Well, no," C.J. said.

"Pass the witness."

Pete took over, intending to bring out the truth with his cross examination. "C.J., can you describe the birth?"

"Sure, my husband was there. My water broke right in his face and he ran out of the room. I delivered my baby by myself. There was so much blood. It was bad. When I went to the bathroom to clean up, my husband tried to clean the bedroom. He wanted to hide the blood."

"Hide it in case CPS came? You testified before you assumed CPS would come after you. Was your husband trying to hide evidence of the birth so no one would know what happened to your baby?"

"Yes. He did that. He was the one who wanted to run. Blood was everywhere. It had sprayed the whole room."

"Really, okay. So, are you saying that anyone walking into the room and walking around the corner would have seen the blood?"

"Oh yes, certainly, no doubt."

"I see. Where is your daughter now? Is she back with you?"

"Oh no. She's in her adoptive home. I just wanted what was best for her. That's all I ever wanted. She's doing really well."

"That's good. I can tell you care about her. Could you show the Judge how big she was?"

"Oh, my goodness. She was really itty-bitty. Maybe about five pounds. I never got her weighed. I just delivered her and tied her cord off with a shoestring." She started to cry.

"I can tell you care. I'm sorry you're having to go through this. Can you tell me when it was you finally found out law enforcement or CPS had actually gone into your house and looked for the baby?"

"I found out through Scott Libby when I was being subpoenaed for this thing."

"So, you had no idea until after these charges were brought forward that this was even going on; is that right?"

"Yeah. I'd already done my time and everything. I thought this was all over and behind me."

"C.J., did you feel like your rights had been violated when they were looking for your child? When they were doing this emergency search for your baby, did you think that anything had happened that wasn't necessary or a regular thing for them to do?"

"Well, no. I didn't think it would be illegal. I figured that, that would be something they legally could do. That's what I would think."

"Fair enough. I think most people would agree with you on that."

"C.J., one more question. I'm sorry. I don't mean to upset you."

"I know. I know." She was quietly sobbing, tears dripping from her face.

"If someone didn't know that you had given birth or whatever happened, could there have been a reasonable belief that something bad had happened to your daughter?"

C.J. looked up at Pete, wiping her eyes. "Yes. Oh yes. There was so much blood… It looked like, looked like somebody tried to kill somebody."

"Looked like someone tried to kill somebody," Pete repeated. "Fair enough. Pass the witness."

Pete returned to his seat. "Did you hear that? You didn't even come close to Official Oppression. Wow."

"I told you so," I said.

We didn't call any witnesses. Other than Justine, who didn't appear to really know the facts, there weren't any witnesses who could testify in behalf of me. The witnesses the State used had testified of instances of alleged illegal searches that no one else had seen or heard about. It left me unable to refute their accusations. We didn't want to use Deputy Ridley. He'd told Libby he suddenly couldn't recall the day in question. We didn't argue with him.

Unlike many defendants who can't wait to get on the stand and tell their side, I didn't have any intention of testifying. I'd stayed quiet through the entire process, utilizing my Fifth Amendment right to remain silent, leaving nothing to be used against me. If I testified, I'd open the door for the State to ask me anything they wanted. If I didn't testify, there would be no testimony. It was a better strategy than offering a testimony that sounded like I was justifying, overly explaining, or denying allegations.

Libby chose to present his closing arguments after Pete, so Pete had to go first.

"Your Honor," Pete said as he began his final argument for my case. "I won't bore you with what I'd tell a jury. You're aware of the law. What I will say is that the State has to reach a burden of proof, the proof of beyond a reasonable doubt, and they just can't get there. They cannot show that Rebekah intentionally and knowingly subjected C.J. to an illegal search.

"This is not Official Oppression. Official Oppression is knowing you've done something wrong. It's a police officer arresting someone, putting them on the ground, and then going up to them and kicking them in face. That's clear Official Oppression. We hope you agree with us, that the State has not met their burden, and find Rebekah not guilty." Pete sat back down and listened to Libby's closing argument.

"If it pleases the Court. The Defense wants to continue to talk about what a reasonable person would have thought if they had walked into that house. Well, too bad what a reasonable person would do because the testimony is the Defendant didn't believe that a baby had died in that house because that's what Justine told you. She said they had discussed the fact that the baby was born there and was no longer there. They had not discussed at any time that the baby had probably died—"

"Objection," Pete interrupted Libby in the middle of his argument. It was something attorneys rarely did to each other, and only did in extreme cases. Attorneys couldn't interject facts that weren't said in the testimony. Libby's closing arguments were so far from what happened in trial, we wondered if he'd written them the night before and didn't change them after hearing the actual testimony. "I'm going to object at the mischaracterizing of the evidence. Nothing like that came from Rebekah. That is a complete incorrect synopsis."

"Continue, Mr. Libby," Judge Beechum said.

"Okay," Libby said, trying to regain his composure. "The Court's going to remember whatever the testimony was, but I believe the testimony is, is that there was never a discussion between them or law enforcement that this baby had probably died. The issue is: does the Defendant allow her desire to find narcotics override her job responsibilities and override the people's rights?" Libby continued with his argument, rehashing the testimony, and painting me as a serial searcher whose sole focus was finding drugs.

Judge Beechum didn't need time to think about it. He'd made up his mind long ago.

"All right. If the Defendant will stand," Judge Beechum said. We stood, me, Pete, and Jonathan, and waited. "Ms. Ross, considering all the evidence heard today, the Court finds you guilty as charged."

Chapter 38

September 17, 2015

"I need to appeal. Can you write the appeal?"

Unfortunately, Pete didn't handle the appellate process, and I needed an attorney who specialized in it. As soon as we were outside the courthouse, I called Jessica Edwards. She'd been the CPS prosecutor before Polly, and we'd worked together quite a bit. She knew the CPS system inside and out and had been the one to teach us how to use an Order in Aid.

"When? You weren't convicted. You're joking," she said, pausing as if she was waiting for the rest of my joke.

"I'm not joking, not even a little bit. Like five minutes ago. We just left the courthouse. Judge Beechum said I was a public servant and he expected more of a public servant. He said he couldn't condone my behavior and I had to be held to a higher standard." I stayed matter-of-fact, trying to stay as objective as possible.

"There's no way. What did he say you did wrong? You had court orders."

How was I supposed to explain when I didn't even understand myself? It was confusing and irregular, and anything I said would sound made up.

"I actually don't know. It sounded like they thought I couldn't enter the house, but then everyone said I'd searched the kitchen and a crock pot, which I didn't. The mom on the case didn't think I'd done anything wrong. I really don't have any idea. They kind of made it sound like I should have just walked away and never gone inside the house. They made me sound crazy in there. So, can you write my appeal? I need to know how much you'll charge so I can get the money together." We were strapped after fighting the case for the past two years, but I wasn't going to let that stop me from fighting.

"I can't believe this. He gave you probation, right?" she asked, still in disbelief.

"Yes, it's probation. He sentenced me to a year in jail but suspended it for two years. I have to pay a $2000.00 fine, do 150 hours of community service, and he sanctioned me thirty days in jail. Oh, and I have to pay a $50.00 crime stoppers fee. I'll give Libby a brownie point. He told the judge he didn't think jail time was appropriate for me. I know that's unusual for a prosecutor to do.

"Now you're joking. Jail time? The judge didn't give you jail time. A sanction is day for day. There's no way." Her voice grew louder the more shocked she became.

"He did."

She had all the emotions and responses I should have had. When Judge Beechum convicted me, Pete was infuriated. He'd kept an excellent poker face, not letting anyone know how he felt until we'd left the courtroom. Everyone else was shocked, still in disbelief. The media hadn't even stayed for the entire trial, having left shortly after hearing C.J. say she didn't believe I'd violated her rights. They had told someone as they had left it was obvious it'd be a not guilty. Now they probably wished they had stayed.

I hadn't felt anything. I knew I'd be convicted as soon as I heard Kenderick's testimony. I'd known everyone else would say the same thing. Libby's closing arguments, straying so far from the evidence, sealed any last doubt I'd had. Now it was time to move on to the next step.

"When do you start the jail time?" Jessica asked. "I seriously can't believe this is happening."

"Not until October 8th or something. We come back then to finalize everything. They're supposed to dismiss my other cases, and Pete's worried something will *accidently* go wrong and it won't happen. So, we're keeping the appeal quiet until everything's final."

"Okay, so we can't file the Notice of Appeal until after the 8th. Will you still be able to finish school? Surely they'll work with you on that."

"Yeah. I have class tonight. Libby's class. But that's also why we come back on the 8th. Judge Beechum wants me to give him my school schedule."

"I'll write the appeal. Was Natalie convicted too?"

"She doesn't go to trial until next month, but I assume she will be. After the way it went today, I know she will be."

"This is outrageous. It can't stand. You were following court orders. Even if you did do something wrong, I know you. I'm sure you didn't have any intent to do it, whatever it was," she said.

She didn't believe me either. But it didn't matter. Whether or not she believed me, we both knew the judgement couldn't stand.

We'd made our way to the top of the garage while I was on the phone. Pete loaded his car with files he'd brought to court while my mom and brothers figured out plans for the evening.

"Did you call someone?" Pete asked as he dropped a pile of files in his trunk.

"Yeah, she'll write my appeal. It's covered."

"Who is it? Who's the attorney? Because this is bullshit and it has to be overturned." His voice was venomous.

"Jessica Edwards."

"But who is she? Is she any good?"

"Of course she is. She was the CPS attorney before Polly Patterson. She's the one that taught us how to use an Order in Aid of Investigation. We worked together before she moved out of town, but she's moved back since. She knows this can't stand. It's not just that it's bullshit, she knows the consequences this conviction will have on everyone else."

"Good. I'm glad she's writing it." Pete's shoulders relaxed. He knew I still had someone on my side. The trial had taken as much out of him as it had me.

"Thanks for everything, Pete," I said. He gave me a hug, something he'd done a few times.

"She'll be okay," he told my mom. She wasn't handling me going through the legal process very well, and my conviction made her worse.

"I know. She's a trooper."

"I'm out of here. I'll check on you tomorrow," Pete said as he and Jonathan left for Dallas.

My mom and my brothers still hadn't decided on where to eat dinner. I didn't have much of an appetite.

"I can't go out tonight. I have class in a couple of hours," I said.

"What? You're still going to class? I didn't think you'd still go. I don't know how you have the energy. I'm sure they'd understand if you missed one class. Which one is it tonight?"

"Mom. It's Libby's class tonight. There's no way I'm missing his class."

"You're going to *his* class? How can you even look at him? How can you stand to be in the same room as him?"

"Well, he's my professor. I have to finish the class to finish my degree. And who better to teach me how to help write an appeal than my very own prosecutor? I think it's pretty ironic." I laughed, the first time since the trial had started.

"You really can't make this up. I swear we're in the twilight zone." My mom shook her head as she left the parking lot.

"You aren't going to let this go, are you?" my husband asked as he drove us home.

"Let it go? The fact my case sets a precedence that says it's open season on CPS workers? That workers won't want to try to find a child or try to investigate, even after getting court orders, for fear of going to jail if they misunderstand the orders? Or worse, if the State decides years later they did something wrong? No, I'm not going to let it go. And Jessica won't either."

He didn't understand the consequences. I doubted anyone did.

"It sounds to me like you just want to beat Libby at his own game."

I laughed again. Part of it was true. "Beating Libby's just an added bonus making it fun. But there's a much bigger picture."

Libby's class was two hours long and held at the Commerce campus and televised live to the Rockwall campus. Pete had advised me, just to be safe, to attend the Rockwall campus for two weeks classes before trial. This would be the first time I'd attend in person.

I rushed to class, afraid I'd be late. Chatter buzzed from the classroom; it hadn't started yet. When I swung open the door, I saw Libby standing at the podium, reading the textbook.

"Rebekah," most of my classmates called as they saw me in the doorway. We'd attended school together for over a year, all of us following the same schedule of rotating courses. They had been disappointed I had attended this class in Rockwall and were thrilled to have me back.

"Hi, everyone! I'm baaaaaaack," I loudly announced. Libby's head snapped up from the book and he inhaled sharply. "I sure missed you guys," I said as I found a seat in the front row.

"Why are you sitting all the way up there?" Courtney asked. We usually sat together toward the back.

261

"I just wanted to make sure I was close to our professor, you know, in case I couldn't hear him or something. You guys could join me. There's no one else up here." Heads shook as they laughed. Some of them already knew the story.

"Okay, I guess we can get started now." Libby wasn't laughing.

I planted myself in the chair directly in front of him, ready to learn and dissect everything he said. Beads of sweat dripped down his forehead as he lectured. He refused to look at me.

I knew Pete was worried and I wanted him to know I'd made it to class and things were okay. The best way I knew to convince him was to take a simple picture, so I casually snapped a picture of Libby and sent it to Pete in an email.

You go, girl. Glad you made it.

I wouldn't miss it for the world. I'll see you on the 8th.

Chapter 39

October 8, 2015

"Considering the Defendant's academic schedule and with no objection from the State, I'll allow Ms. Ross to serve the jail sanction over the weekends. She'll serve ten weekends starting on the 16th. Let's put it in an actual order so there isn't any confusion," Judge Beechum said at our sentencing hearing, finalizing the punishment he'd handed down. "Ms. Ross, you need to immediately report to probation."

Pete had handed Judge Beechum my school schedule and Libby didn't object to the weekend jail time. It made for a quick hearing. Pete wanted to get through it and return to Dallas. He was still upset about the conviction. After I'd gotten out of class that night, a friend, Amy Ling, who was close to the DA's office, had informed me Rachel had been on administrative leave for policy violations while she testified against me. Rachel's entire unit was being reviewed. She'd been found at fault for something serious, but Amy didn't know what it was. She hadn't realized Rachel had testified against me until after the trial. When I told Pete, he blew a fuse. He asked Libby if he'd disclosed everything, something Libby, as a prosecutor, had to do. This type of information could have strongly influenced the judge to not believe anything Rachel said. But Libby denied he'd heard anything ugly or withheld any information. It probably had been the classic situation when a prosecutor said not to say too much so the prosecutor could deny knowledge about it. We were furious but decided appealing was still a better course of action. If we'd been granted a new trial because of the information we'd learned, I'd be right back where I started, having to go through everything all over again. I didn't want to repeat everything, especially if the judge didn't care or wanted me to be guilty.

I was more nervous walking into the probation office than I had been the entire time in court. I'd been here dozens of times, but now I was the one filling out paperwork and peeing in a cup. The small lobby chairs were squeezed together, trying to provide as much seating as possible in the tiny room. A clipboard sat on the counter in front of a closed receptionist area with a note that read, "Fill this out." I grabbed it and scrambled into the only empty chair.

As I read through the paperwork, the young man next to me dropped his pen. I picked it up and handed it back to him, seeing his face for the first time. It was Mikayla's boyfriend. I had been indicted on her case, and now I was filling out paperwork next to her boyfriend. I knew he didn't know about my criminal case. None of the *alleged victims* did except for C.J. and Angel's family. But I didn't know if he remembered me from CPS. Not really wanting to find out, I shifted so he couldn't see my face.

After an hour of waiting, they called me into the back offices where I'd decide where to complete the community service, how I'd pay my fines, and whatever other restrictions I had. The small office I was directed to was empty, so I waited, wondering if the probation officer would know who I was.

"Thank you for coming in today," a female officer said as she entered. She walked around to the front of the desk and sat down, most of her body hidden by a massive pile of paperwork. She sorted through them, checking to see if they were filled out properly. "Ms. Ross is it? Or is it Thonginh?"

I recognized her from somewhere. "It's either one. They don't seem to know which name is correct, so whatever you want."

"Okay, so, you've been convicted of… Official Oppression. Wait, what?" she said, glancing up from her paperwork. "You're one of them."

It clicked. She'd worked for CPS as a caseworker, handling cases after the investigators removed the children. She'd worked Daisy's case for almost a year, guiding the case through the legal system, setting up services for the parents, and eventually seeking parental termination. I knew she'd resigned and became a probation officer, but I didn't know she'd be the one to go through the paperwork with me.

"I'd be *one of those*," I confirmed.

"Okay, let's get through this." I couldn't tell if she recognized me or not. I knew we hadn't met each other except for a couple of times. Almost everything we'd done together had been over email or the phone.

"This has all been a little crazy. Um, here's the restrictions you'll have." She laid a sheet of paper in front of me with boxes already checked by the computer. "You won't be able to serve on a jury, vote, or possess a gun."

"Hold up. Those are restrictions for a felony conviction. This is a misdemeanor. It was treated like a felony, but it's a misdemeanor. I can keep my guns and the do the rest, too."

"Oh, but it was in district court." She studied the paperwork.

"I know. Don't you love misdemeanors tried in district court?" I asked, facetiously.

"Well, the paperwork is just automatically generated and since it was in the district court, I guess it was just automatically checked. Just keep your guns locked up."

I didn't know what she thought of my case, or of me, or even how much she really knew. If she believed my former coworkers and the rumors they had spread, the last thing I wanted was to act like the person they described. "I'll keep them locked up for children's safety. But could we please get new paperwork. With the way things have gone, things need to be completely accurate. With my luck, this would be used as an excuse to pick me up first and ask questions later."

"Yeah. You're right. I'll be right back."

It didn't take long for her to return with the corrected paperwork, and we finished the rest of the process without any major hiccups. My probation fees were $179.00 a month, I had to complete at least ten hours of community service a week, and I'd report to probation monthly and check in with the possibility of taking a drug test each time that I'd be required to pay for. It would be a long, expensive process, if I had to do it.

I called Jessica as I left the probation office. "It's done. We had the sentencing hearing this morning and I just filled out the paperwork at the probation office. I go to jail next weekend."

"Okay. Get the Notice of Appeal drafted and we'll file it next week," she said.

I didn't know how to draft a Notice of Appeal or what it looked like, but I had access to a form generating program for paralegals at school. I figured I'd might as well test out the program and see how well I could find something I knew nothing about. I spent the weekend researching and stumbled across an appeal bond. It looked like something that could keep me out of jail.

"Jessica, I see this thing called an appeal bond. Does that really stop the jail time while an appeal is pending?" I asked over the phone.

"It's supposed to, but I've never filed one. Do the research and find out how to do it, what the bond needs to be, and how to argue it in case the judge orders a bond you can't afford. I'll find out if

Robbie will agree to it, but he may want the decision to come from Judge Beechum."

She didn't have to say anything else. I utilized another database I had access to through school and researched everything I could find out about appeal bonds. Printing off the opinions handed down from the Courts, something we referred to as case law, I summarized them so Jessica could easily understand what to argue. She'd never dealt with this type of situation as a CPS prosecutor, but I'd summarized enough cases for her while I was an investigator that I knew how to simplify it for her. She was skilled at taking nothing more than those summaries and arguing an entire case.

Judge Beechum couldn't give me a bond higher than he'd given me in the beginning, and I didn't fall into any of the reasons he could use to refuse to grant the bond. By the time Libby's class rolled around the following week, I knew I wouldn't have to go to go jail or continue with probation. But Libby didn't have any idea.

"Have a great weekend," he told a student as she left. I had waited for the two of them to finish their discussion so I could speak to him alone. He tried to leave the room, but I caught him.

"Libby, I need to talk to you about something, please."

"Go ahead." He squirmed, eying the doorway.

"Are we okay?"

The question surprised him. "Um."

I continued, curious how he'd react. "Are we okay? It feels like we need to address the elephant in the room, and I know Professor Fitz wants confirmation, too. Are we okay?"

"Yeah, I mean, if you are, then sure."

"I'm fine. I think we can be professional. This is school. You're my professor. The fact you worked so hard to convict me doesn't matter when we're in the role of professor and student. Is that fair?"

"Yeah, of course. I think we're fine." He stopped fidgeting and relaxed at my backhanded comment.

"Okay. You're sure?"

"I am now. I wasn't at first. When I saw your name on the roster, I told Robbie I didn't want you here and asked him what I could do about it. He said nothing. I guess you and he had a few classes together. Robbie said we don't always get what we want and I had to deal with it. It seems like we're okay though."

"I'm glad to know that. I just wanted it out in the open."

"That's understandable." I picked up my bag and started for the door when he said, "You have a great weekend."

I spun around just in time to see dread wash over his face.

"Really?" I asked. I was highly entertained, mostly by the look on his face. It was only Tuesday, but his class was only once a week.

"I'm sorry. As soon as I said it, I knew how it sounded. I tell everyone have a good weekend. It's just what I say. Then I remembered where you'll be this weekend. I really didn't mean it that way."

"It's okay, Libby. No hard feelings. I'm going to make sure I make the best out of my weekend. See you soon." I couldn't help but laugh.

Jessica and her family were supposed to leave for a family vacation on Thursday. But it was the only day Judge Beechum could hear our bond motion, so she delayed her vacation with the sole purpose of keeping me out of jail.

"Your Honor, we've filed a Notice of Appeal and are requesting an appeal bond pending. Rebekah's never given this Court any indication she wouldn't come to court or fulfil her obligations while she was on bond during her trial. We ask that the Court grant our request for an appeal bond in a reasonable amount the Court sees fit," Jessica argued.

"The State isn't going to waste any of the Court's time in arguing over this. It's clear the Appellant has plenty of case law to back up any argument the State might make. And she's evidently already secured a bondsman, too," Libby said, glancing at the stack of research in my purse and the bondsman standing behind me.

"I guess this stays the probation," Judge Beechum said thoughtfully.

"And the jail sanction, Your Honor," Jessica reminded him.

"And the jail sanction. I guess it stays all of it." Judge Beechum paused, thinking. "Okay, let's do a $10,000.00 bond; that's how much the bond was on her original charge. We need an order abating everything so everyone understands what's going on. You know, this just delays the inevitable." He leaned back in his chair, his eyes studying Jessica and then me. He focused back on Jessica. "Well, I guess it could get overturned. We'll have to wait and see."

Judge Beechum had worked with Jessica for years when she was a felony prosecutor and then when she became a CPS prosecutor. He knew what she was capable of.

With the hovering jail time and steep monthly probation charges no longer occupying my mind, I turned my focus to research. Just as I had done with the trial, I wanted to understand every facet of the Appellate process. I wasn't going to be clueless about something that would determine my future and reinstate protection for the futures of at-risk children and investigators throughout Texas.

Chapter 40

December 16, 2016

"You've got to be kidding me. There really isn't anything you did wrong," Jessica yelled through the phone.

It had been exactly four years, to the day, since I'd searched for Daisy, and two months since filing our notice to appeal. The court reporter had recently finished typing the transcript and Jessica was reading it for the first time.

"I do believe I told you that." I'd been waiting for this moment, the moment where she'd know, just like Pete had known, I wasn't hiding anything.

"I know you told me. And I knew you, from working with you for so long, but I thought there had to be something more. To be indicted, arrested, and convicted had to mean there was something more to it. I thought maybe you'd done something but just didn't realize it. Or maybe you were so caught up in the case that you couldn't see it objectively. I just can't believe this. I really didn't think I'd actually have to write the appeal."

"Wait, what?" I felt numb, blindsided. I'd never expected her to quit.

"No, really. If you want me to be honest, I just wanted the transcript. I had to know what had actually happened in trial. I really thought I'd read it and find out either you lied to me, which

I highly doubted since I'd known you so long, but still, people do some strange things, or the more likely scenario, I'd figure out where you weren't seeing it objectively, being caught up in it and all. I'd point it out, saying, 'See, this is why you were found guilty. You might not understand it, but this is what you did wrong.' I never thought it was this blatant that you didn't do anything wrong. This is the biggest miscarriage of justice I've ever seen."

"You're telling me. I lived through this mess. I'm still living through it. I get to call my bondsman every Tuesday and be reminded I'm still living through it."

"Was Natalie's trial as bad as yours?"

I'd attended Natalie's trial and it was worse than mine when it came to lack of evidence. She went to trial over Ashley's case, and the State argued she had conducted an illegal search and seizure by taking Ashley's phone away and seeing the text messages from the adult male who was sleeping with Ashley. Ashley, an adult by the time of Natalie's trial, was on felony probation for possession of controlled substances. She testified against Natalie, claiming she'd never given her permission to have the phone.

The state claimed Natalie's removal affidavit didn't sound like it was written by a social worker but that it sounded like it was written by a seasoned, trained, experienced police officer. It was as if Libby thought CPS employees shouldn't have the ability to write a well worded, detailed, coherent affidavit. Because Natalie wrote well, the State said it made her look as if she thought Ashley was a suspect and not a victim.

The rest of the testimony from the witnesses, the majority of it from Ester, said even though they didn't actually see me do it, they knew it was me who'd taken the phone, searched it, and refused to give it back. Ester claimed she'd physically jerked the phone out of my hands in an attempt to prevent me from searching it for drug evidence. I'd never touched the phone.

271

By the end of the trial, I had emailed Pete, asking if the State, though they had already dismissed the case against me, could change their mind and re-indict me. The testimony at Natalie's trial condemned me, not her.

George had argued that even if the search had occurred, CPS was Ashley's parent. CPS could consent to a medical surgery, even consent to amputating Ashley's leg, because CPS was the legal guardian. If that was the case, then why couldn't CPS, as the legal guardian of a foster child, remove a phone to prevent a foster child from harming themselves and running away back to the adult male who was raping her.

Judge Beechum convicted Natalie anyway, sentencing her in seven words. "Give her whatever the other one got."

Jessica was speechless. She was glad Natalie also had an excellent appellant attorney. She'd hired attorney Michael Mowla, Board Certified in Criminal Appellate Law. Her conviction couldn't stand any more than mine could.

"And Audrey? What of her case?"

I crinkled my nose. "Her case was dropped as soon as Natalie was convicted."

"Oh."

Once Jessica fully believed me and read the full trial transcript, it was time to work. I'd been researching for months, but now I had to compile the cases together so she could review them and determine the law she'd write into the brief. That was the whole point of an appeal. It wasn't another trial or presenting witnesses again or reviewing discovery. It was reading the court transcript, conducting legal writing and research, and arguing the law. You could only use the court transcript and the exhibits entered into evidence at trial.

Most defendants don't have an active role in the appeal as there isn't anything they can do. But I'd taken the legal courses at A&M and had soaked in everything I could from Libby and my other professors. Research became a passion, if not an addiction, and Jessica had noticed. She hired me as her paralegal, and I took an active role in researching and writing my appeal.

In February, after months of research, Jessica and I camped out at her house for three days straight, compiling the seventy-eight-page brief to submit to the 6th Court of Appeals in Texarkana. Pressing the submit button on the computer was both reliving and nauseating. Though Jessica had made it a point to shower each morning, I had done little to revive myself outside of quick meals and a few hours of sleep. The fate of months of work and seventy-two hours of intense typing rested in the hands of three Justices, and all we could do was wait for their decision on Judge Beechum's verdict.

Chapter 41

September 2015

"What are oral arguments?"

Excited, I'd called Jessica before the sun was up, right around when I thought she woke up each morning. I'd been waking up at 2:30 a.m. every morning, without an alarm, to check my email for anything from the 6th Court of Appeals. That was the time the Court sent their batch of emails and if there was an update or something filed in our case, we'd be included. This morning, I'd received a notice from the Court and had paced eagerly around my home, waiting for time to pass and hoping I didn't wake my children.

Jessica sounded groggy, but she perked up as excitement claimed her, too. "I can't believe this. Well, the Court requests arguments sometimes. It's rare, but it happens. Usually it's when the case is unique, or it presents a question of law that hasn't been decided, or when the ruling on a case would affect a vast amount of people. I guess your case fits under all of that."

"So, you and Libby will argue about my case in front of the judges?"

"Yes. It's been a long time since I've presented arguments. The judges get to ask questions on any case we used, so you'd better start briefing the 200 cases we used in your brief so I can study them and figure out what to say. You need to brief Libby's cases, too. They could ask me about those cases. We wrote a really long brief."

Jessica and I had worked together to address eight points of error, with the first six points explaining the different reasons there wasn't enough evidence for the judge to convict me. Generally, a brief for a misdemeanor case has one or possibly two points of error. We far surpassed a standard brief in the amount of errors presented and word count. The State, specifically Libby, also wrote a brief. Libby's brief wasn't as long, but it had a unique twist. He asked the Court of Appeals to re-define the word "unlawful," saying it would be clear I'd committed an offense if the definition was changed. Jessica and Libby both described my case as a case of first impression, a case that had never happened before, and both sides requested oral arguments. The Court of Appeals granted them.

The Court not only requested the argument, they were coming to Greenville instead of making us drive three hours to Texarkana. Now more local attorneys were likely to attend. Jessica planned to use the opportunity to get the story out so the facts would be known as they really were.

Jessica had already received slack from local colleagues for hiring me, many questioning her sanity to hire someone convicted of violating people's rights and accused of tampering with evidence. Taking an unorthodox approach to prepare the arguments didn't help matters. We spent three days locked inside a hotel room before the oral arguments. It was the only way we could focus and ignore the constantly ringing phone or non-stop office interruptions. We felt like college students cramming for final exams.

"I need more on that case where they had the order to remove. That case from the 5th Circuit," Jessica said.

"Wernecke v. Garcia? I've got it. I highlighted the section…"

"And Gates, give me another copy of Gates."

"Here's that one, it's page…."

"Which one had the story about the officer who smelled marijuana and the CPS worker? I need that. This doesn't make any sense. I don't understand how you were convicted. The argument against you doesn't even make sense."

"I think we need to focus on the kitchen and the crock pot. Libby seemed to focus on that. His brief says the orders gave me authority to enter the residence. He conceded that part."

"True. Let's try that."

I continued to compile cases, keep them organized, and regurgitate the main points. Jessica wrote and hashed out our argument. When Wednesday came, we were ready.

Jessica and her associate attorney, Erik Zimmerman, sat in the front right of the small courtroom with Libby on the left. Natalie and I sat together among the audience; the Justices didn't know we were the Appellants. Natalie's attorney, Michael, sat at the front with Jessica and Erik.

As the three Justices walked into the room, their robes flowed around them. The magic of the moment intimidated me, and I was grateful Jessica was in front with them instead of me.

Jessica went first. Her argument was clear.

"Rebekah had court orders, signed by a judge, allowing her to enter the residence and search for the baby. The State wants to argue she should have left the residence once she knew a child wasn't there. Your Honors, she couldn't have known a child wasn't there until she looked in every place a child might fit. The child was a five-day old infant, tiny, itty-bitty as the mother described, and blood was all over the room. It was so bad it looked like someone had been killed in there. The mother of the child described it like that. Clearly, for someone who didn't know what had happened, that rises to exigent circumstances. If Rebekah had searched through a match box, then we could talk about searching in areas a child wouldn't fit in. But she didn't. She's accused of searching in places that a child would fit."

Libby argued next.

"Your Honors, the law is clear, you cannot search a home without a warrant and Ms. Ross didn't have a warrant. She didn't have exigent circumstances. She didn't have a reasonable belief a child had died in the residence. She knew she couldn't search in any of those areas. Everyone in the Hunt County office knew that. But Ms. Ross seems to think she's above the law, able to do whatever she wants and get away with it."

"Mr. Libby, let me ask you," one of the Justices said. I didn't know which one was which, despite looking them up and reading their backgrounds. "Are you saying she couldn't even enter the house? It seems we have an interesting case here. It's State against State. We've never seen something like this."

"No. I didn't take that stance at trial, so I won't change and take it here. The State concedes she could enter the residence with the orders she had."

"Then are you saying she couldn't search anywhere? How would she know if a child was in the residence or not if she didn't search everywhere?"

"She didn't intend to search for the child. She was searching for drugs. You can't search for something that's not authorized."

"What if the baby's fingers had been chopped off and put in a match box? How would she know if she hadn't searched everywhere?" The Justice's question startled everyone in the room.

Jessica had warned me not to read into the questions the Justices asked. She said it would sound like they were on our side when they questioned Libby and it would sound like they were on Libby's side when they questioned her. It would be extremely difficult to know what they were thinking. It was hard not to get my hopes up, especially after such a violent question that seemed to support my case.

"There wasn't any indication that was the case," Libby stumbled, surprised by the directness of question.

Jessica then spoke for ten more minutes, defending me against Libby's answers and explaining lasting implications as she answered more questions.

"For this conviction to stand, it would have fatal consequences on the entire State, on every CPS worker in the State and on children. If this conviction stands, children will die. Every worker in the State will constantly be looking over their shoulder, afraid to do their job for fear they may do something wrong and get dragged to jail for trying to save a child's life."

"But what authority did she have to search a crock pot?"

"She had court orders, exigent circumstances, and common sense, Your Honor. I have represented CPS and I adopted four crack babies. I know what these parents do their children. I've seen it. My babies didn't weigh three pounds when they were born. If you can fit a five-pound chicken in a crock pot, then a three-pound crack baby fits even better. And that, that is the reason this can't stand."

Jessica sat down, out of breath and nearly emotional, but she had said what she needed to say. Her point was understandable and relatable.

The wait for their opinion was excruciating. With no idea how they swayed, I kept checking my email every morning at 2:30 a.m.

Two months later, the 6th Court of Appeals in Texarkana issued their opinion. They would uphold the trial court's ruling and uphold my conviction. Their argument was all over the place. They bounced back and forth, trying to explain why they were upholding the conviction. As I read, I whittled it down and concluded they would uphold it any way they could.

I wasn't sure how I'd react, if I'd cry or get mad, if they upheld the conviction. Yet once again, I didn't feel anything. Maybe I expected it so I wasn't surprised. I kept reading, and by the time

I'd read through everything, it was 3:30 a.m. I couldn't wait until the rest of Texas woke up. I sent texts to Jessica and my family telling them the news, rolled over, and fell sleep. I'd figure out how to appeal to the Texas Court of Criminal Appeals when I woke up.

Chapter 42

January 2018

"If Rebekah will drop her PDR, I'll agree to take the jail sanction off the table. I just don't have time to write another brief," Libby said to Jessica one day as they passed each other in court.

She wasn't sure if Libby was trying to be funny or if he was serious. "I think we'll take our chances. But, thanks for the offer."

Afterward, Jessica shared Libby's offer with me in her office. We hadn't come this far just to give up. In fact, we'd just won our first victory and Libby knew it.

We'd filed my Petition for Discretionary Review on January 30, 2017, landing on the Texas Court of Criminal Appeal's docket as PD-0001-17, the very first cause number for the new year. Seven weeks later, on April 26, 2017, the TCCA granted our petition. Knowing they only granted about 11% of the petitions they received, I already knew I'd beaten the odds. My case was going before the nine Justices who presided over the highest criminal Court in Texas.

Texas has two Supreme Courts, the Texas Court of Criminal Appeals (TCCA) for criminal cases and the Supreme Court of Texas for civil cases. A defendant doesn't have a right to appeal to the TCCA like they do for their first appeal to the lower Court of Appeals. Appeals to the TCCA are discretionary as the Court chooses whether or not to hear the case. Where a defendant is entitled to a court appointed attorney for their first appeal, if they cannot afford an attorney on their own, they aren't entitled to one to appeal to the TCCA. If they want to continue with the appellate process, they have to file the petition on their own or hire a private attorney. I was fortunate enough to have Jessica, the funds, and the knowledge to assist me in my own appeal. How many others sat in prison, stuck with the whatever decision had been handed down by the Court of Appeals, because they were unable to continue with the process? I knew the majority of opinions the Court of Appeals handed down were solid and correct. But sometimes, in a case like mine, they got it wrong.

When granting the petition, the TCCA specified which point of error they wanted us to address in a brief. We weren't to stray from the topic. We were to explain how the Court of Appeals erred, or what they got wrong, when they had ruled the trial court had sufficient evidence to convict me.

Once again, Jessica and I tackled the task of research and writing. With the help of some colleagues, the brief was proofread and the argument condensed for simplicity. As requested, we narrowed our focus and argued there weren't enough facts to support a conviction beyond a reasonable doubt and the Court of Appeals had incorrectly interpreted the law. I filed the brief on June 12, 2017, followed by the State who filed theirs on August 8, 2017. It would take anywhere from six months to a year before we would hear anything.

The Court of Criminal Appeals released decisions every Wednesday morning. Just as I did with the Court of Appeals, I watched my email for notifications to see if there had been an update. I also checked their website, where they published the list of opinions they handed down. I didn't fully understand how they handled notifications but assumed we'd be notified before the decision was publicly listed, just as we'd been with the Court of

Appeals. Every Wednesday morning for months I'd tell Natalie, who was usually on her way to work, that there wasn't any news. Michael had filed her PDR and then later her brief, and she and I were waiting for an answer together. They had granted our petitions the same day and I suspected the TCCA would hand down their decisions on our cases at the same time, as that appeared to be the pattern.

We'd been in limbo for nearly six years, never able to really plan our lives. We were still on bond, calling in to our bondsman every Tuesday like clockwork. As much as we thought our cases would be overturned, we'd been disappointed many times before.

We'd played the various scenarios to each other. The TCCA could reverse part of the judgement and send the case back to the 6th Court of Appeals, leaving us in a continued limbo while the 6th Court of Appeals reviewed it again, the same Justices determining our unfortunate fate another time. I'd seen a few cases go back and forth like that multiple times. They could affirm part of the conviction and request the lower court to correct another area. They could uphold the conviction all together. They could also acquit, freeing me completely from my conviction. There were multiple possibilities and variations.

The list of decisions the TCCA had made the past kept me on edge. Talking with Natalie helped, but I still waited for every Wednesday. Every email. Every update. Every time I didn't see an update from the TCCA, my resolve crumbled. I started preparing for the worst, even if it was too early to receive a decision. If the TCCA said I was wrong and Judge Beechum had passed correct judgement, then I would be done. I'd go to jail, serve my time, and let the dominos fall. I wasn't sure I could fight it anymore. Texas' justice system seemed intent on destroying the safety of children and those who sought to protect them.

I started rearranging my life. I attended a Walking Dead tour with a friend in February 2018 because I knew the TCCA wouldn't decide by then. I continued to not commit to my teenage son's current and future band performances and rehearsals and to his robotics competitions. They were always on weekends. My life, my family's lives, Natalie's family's lives—everyone was waiting for the crippling blow.

Chapter 43

March 28, 2019

Jessica's receptionist and my sister-in-law, Silvia, sat in front of me, her mouth moving, her lips making noise. I wanted to say something, anything, but the words wouldn't come out. I tried to lift my hand to signal for her to stop talking, but my wrist and fingers were too heavy. My arms shook, my chest spasmed, my head spun. My knuckles turned white as I gripped the desk in front of me, trying to control my body. I needed to calm down, to speak.

Now the desk shook. Hot tears poured from my eyes and snot drained from my nose. Silvia stopped talking. I stared at her panicking eyes, willing my voice to find itself.

This was not how I imagined I'd react. I had always kept my emotions in check when judgements were passed, and when I had failed to do that, I hadn't any emotions in me. This was different, new. I didn't understand why I was so emotional, if not completely losing control.

"What? What is it? You're scaring me," Silvia asked, fear wide in her eyes.

I wanted to tell her. I wanted to show her, but I didn't have any control over myself.

"Rebekah, you're really scaring me. What is it?"

She stood up, hastily walking around the desk to my chair. I turned toward her, gasping for air, trying to spit out words. Only grunts escaped. She reached forward, embracing me in a hug.

"It's okay, it's okay, tell me what's wrong."

She'd never hugged me before. The warmth and comfort gave me my voice.

"Acquittal…" I sobbed. "Acquittal… Look…"

I pointed to the computer screen, tears and snot flowing down my face, onto my shirt, and into my lap. It was Wednesday, just after 9:30 a.m. I hadn't received an email first, notifying us that an opinion had been released, like we'd received from the 6th Court of Appeals. When I didn't have an email, I'd pulled up the Texas Court of Criminal Appeals' website, like I did every Wednesday morning, to look through the list of cases they handed down each week. Today, my case was the first one listed, posted for all to see.

"What?" she gasped. "Really? Where?"

She'd never seen the hand down list and had no idea where my case was. I managed to point to the line I needed her to read.

PD-0001-17 ROSS, REBEKAH THONGINH FROM HUNT COUNTY-06-15-00179-CR REVERSED COA; ACQUITTAL ORDERED OPINION JUDGE RICHARDSON-PUBLISHED

"The court order obtained by Ross allowed her to enlist the help of law enforcement to enter the home and locate the child "by any means necessary." It allowed her to search "the premises" to locate the newborn child and observe "where the alleged abuse or neglect occurred." When Ross and the officers entered the home and went into the bedroom, they discovered a mattress soaked with blood and bodily fluid. There was blood sprayed all over the walls. Even C.J. admitted at trial that the room had so much blood, it looked "like somebody tried to kill somebody."

Given the amount of blood on the mattress and walls, the condition of the home, the information Ross had regarding the history of drug use, the lack of medical care to the child who was evidently just recently born in the home, the prior criminal and CPS history surrounding C.J., and given the fact that there was no indication where the baby might be and whether the baby was alive or dead, it is possible that abuse and neglect took place throughout the entire home. Under these facts, we hold that no rational trier of fact could find the essential elements of the offense of Official Oppression beyond a reasonable doubt, because the State presented insufficient evidence that Ross knew, under these circumstances, that her conduct was unlawful. We reverse the judgment of the Court of Appeals against Ross and render a judgment of acquittal."

Scrolling back to the beginning, I noticed the first line of the front page.

RICHARDSON, J., delivered the opinion for a unanimous Court.

"It's unanimous, Jessica. It's unanimous."

Not only had the Court reversed my conviction for an acquittal, but all nine Justices had unanimously agreed. All they needed was five of the nine, but it was all of them.

"We won. Reversed and rendered. Unanimous." Jessica was telling someone behind her. "Rebekah's appeal. We won."

I hung up while she announced to the entire courthouse we'd won. How long it would take Libby to hear the news?

I wanted to be the one to tell Natalie. Michael would tell her as well, but after everything we'd been through together, it was a moment I wanted to share with her before anyone else. She was at work, so I sent her a message to call me immediately. She called within a second.

"What? What's wrong?" she asked.

"Acquitted." It was all I could get out before I ugly cried again.

"No. Really? How? When?" She started crying, too. "How'd you find out?"

"I pulled up the Court's website, like I do every Wednesday morning. Our cases were right there. I haven't stopped crying."

"Oh my gosh...." We stayed on the phone, crying together, all the emotions we'd felt over the past six years falling away in tears.

"I'm going to email Pete. I'll talk to you in a bit, okay?" I told her.

I read the rest of the opinion before I emailed him. The Court had used Pete's cross examination to point out the multiple different ways there wasn't any evidence to uphold a conviction.

Pete called me after he read my email. "Are you ready to be on TV?"

I called my husband and told him the news. He was thrilled, more than anyone else I shared the news with. I told him I was headed home to change my clothes, and he said he would take me to Dallas where we'd meet Pete and the news crew.

Pete had the biggest smile on his face when I arrived. It wasn't often a defense attorney was mentioned, in a positive manner, in an opinion.

George and Natalie showed up next, and we sat in Pete's office with the news station.

The reporter asked me about Angel's case, throwing me off. This wasn't about Angel's case. Her case was over years ago. For a moment, I couldn't remember anything about her case, but I gave the best answers I could. She asked very little about the specifics of Daisy's case. She wanted to know if we felt vindicated, if there was something we wanted to say. I didn't feel vindicated, but I tried to keep my answers professional and generalized. After listening to Natalie and Pete, I wished I'd said more.

She interviewed Natalie next, asking her more about Angel's case than about Ashley's. Where I had generalized my answers, Natalie didn't hold back. Though she was thrilled about the acquittal, she was upset and angry, furious with the criminal justice system and CPS. She had confiscated a cell phone from a teenage foster child who wanted to use the phone to engage in self-destructive behavior, run away, contact her adult male boyfriend, and buy and sell drugs. Allowing her to have the phone was detrimental to CPS' goal of obtaining a stable environment, drug treatment, and rehabilitation. She planned to retire with CPS and had dedicated thirteen years of her life to the work. Yet rumors and speculation from disgruntled employees had been revered and allowed to grow into an outrageous criminal case, taking precedence over years of dedicated service.

When Pete was interviewed, he explained the impact the Court's opinion had. For the first time, we had an opinion that clarified what the State had to prove in order to convict a public servant of Official Oppression. They had to prove all the elements that constituted Official Oppression: that the person was a public servant and that they intentionally subjected someone to a search while knowing the search was unlawful. Beyond a reasonable doubt. They couldn't convict on only proving a few of the elements.

The TCCA said even with the training materials previously presented, Justine's testimony claiming that I had stated I wanted to search for drugs, and the journal and calendar found in the bedroom, it wasn't enough to prove whether I *knew* if the search was unlawful. The Court also explained that had the training materials the State focused on so strongly addressed the specific situation I faced the morning of December 16, 2011, there still wasn't enough to prove beyond a reasonable doubt that I *knew* the search was unlawful because I had a court order authorizing the search of the house. Pete had explained the same thing in his closing arguments when he described a police officer kicking a cuffed suspect in the face. That action was *knowingly* committed by the officer, a vast difference from someone interpreting and following court orders issued by a judge.

Pete finished by saying I'd taken one for the team.

The station never aired the story. Sometimes it seems the truth isn't exciting enough to share. Or it's too confusing. In the beginning, the news stations had only focused on Angel's story. They had jumped on it without fact checking and were later duped.

Now, years later, the real story was too hard to explain and not nearly as exciting.

The next morning, I was back at work like nothing had happened. I received a call from a judge from another county asking for Jessica. She wasn't in, so I took a message, explaining I was her paralegal.

"Tell Jessica thank you," she said. "Tell her thank you for seeing the appeal all the way through. I can't believe what they put that woman through. I have to teach a case law update class, and I was handed the case and told, 'Read this, you won't believe it.' I can't believe they even brought charges against her. Here in my county, I can't get CPS to get up and do anything. And then we have someone who did, and they prosecute her. She saved a child's life and they prosecuted her. I also need to know what happened to the baby. My office staff won't let me hang up until they find out what happened to that little girl. Is she okay?"

"She is, Your Honor. She's doing very well. I found her in time. She survived the withdrawals, and I placed her with a foster family who eventually adopted her. She's doing wonderfully." I hadn't realized my wording until after I'd said it.

"What do you mean *you*?" the judge asked.

"I mean I'm the one who was convicted for searching for the baby. I'm Ross v. State. I also happen to be Jessica's paralegal."

"Guys, she's on the phone. I'm speaking to the investigator." The speaker picked up several voices. They must have crowded around the judge. "I never would have imagined I'd actually speak to you. You don't stop and realize the person in the brief's a real person. And to think you're the one who answered the phone. I can't believe this…"

We talked for another half hour while she expressed her frustration with the CPS system and the example a case like mine would have set had we not fought our way through, never giving up, and constantly moving forward.

After five years, my case was overturned because I never gave up. I didn't give up when I searched for Daisy, and I didn't give up as I fought for the rights of CPS workers to continue to protect children in danger.

I knew there hadn't been any evidence to convict me and that my conviction would set a precedence that would send CPS and other government agencies down a dangerous path. So I kept fighting, kept paying attorney fees I couldn't afford, kept going to school even when my prosecutors were my own professors. I didn't stop, not until I'd proven what it meant to search with court orders and how to handle the CPS unknown.

The journey isn't over for Child Protective Services. There are still problems, coverups, and subpar workers. But this was the first step in a long journey for them.

For me, my days working for CPS are over, but I haven't given up. I keep fighting, helping parents, children, foster parents, and relatives in stressful, sometimes impossible, legal battles of their own. There's still battles to win and people to save.

A Road of Recovery

Written by C.J.

It is always darkest before dawn.

I've heard it before, but I never quite understood what it meant until I experienced it

for myself.

I know confessing what I'm about to say could be dangerous for me and my family. After all, I was the one who asked for my identity to be revealed. However, I believe so confidently in the power of the message of recovery, that it is evidence of who I am today and who I used to be, that I believe anyone who reads this, who may need help, will see hope and will know I want to help. I am available for those who are desperate and hurting for an answer. My wish is to help them find a solution to the very real, life-threatening disease of addiction. If my experience can benefit even one person, then it has made all the horrifying things worth surviving through.

This is for anyone who reads with an open mind and a willing heart to truly see beauty spring from ashes of chaos. You may begin to see a Divine conspiracy in the making. It felt that way in how events unfolded.

Unfortunately, the facts about my life, contained in this book, are true. It was before I had any idea about recovery and what life was really about. It was before I knew that life, or recovery, was even available for a person like me. I thought I was only hurting myself, but knowing what I know now, I realize my disease was lying to me in the attempt to keep me sick, to keep me participating in the vicious cycle of denial that kept me in the deepest of ruts. My disease told me I wasn't worthy of a good life and if I tried to obtain one, I would surely mess it up and everyone would hate me, so I might as well not even try.

Not trying resulted in harming so many people. When I thought I was only hurting myself, I was hurting people all around me. I may never fully understand the pain I have caused so many people. From complete strangers to the ones I hold very dear.

I have survived hell on earth. Some of which I was a product of, the others I created.

My life before drugs doesn't exist. I was conceived on drugs. Back when I was a baby most mothers didn't get drug tests, so no one knew I was a drug-addicted baby. My mom used to put cocaine in my bottle so I would stop fussing. I remember being beaten to death twice by the time I was five. I remember being fed cocaine and alcohol with my mother and her three male friends, and they would dope me up, dress me up, tie me up, and rape me at the age of two. I remember my mother going through men like she went through cigarettes, and she was a two to three packs a day kind of person. I spent the most of the first few years of my life in the hospital from injuries or very severe illnesses. Sometimes I'd wake up there from long-term comas and my mother had never come to visit me. Half the time she was so doped up she didn't even know I was gone.

With my father being *dead since I was a baby* and having no other immediate family in the area, I moved out when I was thirteen. I suppose the cops call that running away, but anything on my own had to be better than my life with my mother, or so I thought.

At thirteen, I also started attempting suicide. Around fourteen to fifteen, I started cutting. I was so lost in my darkness that I was so numb I wasn't even sure I was alive anymore. I cut to see if I would bleed. If I bled, I was, therefore, alive. A few weeks before my sixteenth birthday, I decided to try drugs to commit suicide. Nothing else I tried had worked, and I figured a massive overdose would do the trick. What I didn't anticipate is that I would become addicted instead of ending my life.

Without the proper help from a traumatic childhood, I was destined to repeat a lot of similar behaviors my mother did to me, even though the last thing I ever wanted to do was be anything like her. I never sexually abused my children or set them up in a situation to be sexually abused or beaten, but I did hurt my children and family nonetheless.

Addicted to drugs, I started to fit in somewhere. I got attention from men. A few years later, I thought the answer to all my problems was a family complete with children, plus having kids was a good way to get a guy to stay with me for life, or so I thought. Until my addiction manifested itself into really hard drugs all the time and I ended up in a few CPS cases and a divorce. Then another relationship immediately after, one I didn't want but was bribed into with drugs and eventually led me to becoming prisoner at Nathan's house.

I'm glad that awful green room wasn't only repulsive to me. That's the room I was held against my will. My friends were told I was dead, and I was raped during a seizure. I finally escaped and then discovered I was pregnant.

I was hopeless and lost. I hated everything about my life but didn't see a way out of it. Eventually I ended up going back to Nathan. I kept repeating the same sick cycle over and over for years, even after I got out of prison and had another baby, this one planned and with a better man.

Even the events in this book weren't enough for me to fully stop. It did slow me down so I could start my true journey of change, but I needed more to fully wake me up and send the fear of death into me. I needed to know I couldn't play with my disease and other people's lives anymore.

Every once in a while, something happens to people like me, the ones that are consumed by the darkness. Sometimes a miracle happens. A spark will ignite and then flow, actions and events that have the potential to release the people held hostage by the addict who is lost in a lifestyle riddled by their destruction.

For me, I had to come to an unspeakable low.

January 3, 2018 changed my life for good. I was back in jail after yet another relapse and failed attempt at recovery. I'd blacked out behind the wheel from drug use, my two-year-old son in the car with me. When I came to, it was too late. The car was already impacted from a high-speed wreck and spinning out of control. I thought I had killed my baby boy. I'd finally arrived at my rock bottom.

I was going to die from addiction or die in prison.

In jail, I decided I couldn't carry on the way I was living any longer. I decided to end the lies I'd tell myself and get the help I deserved and needed. A miracle happened that day. Little did I know it would lead me to cross paths with an old friend.

So, why confess to all these unspeakable things you may wonder? Because I have to be fully honest in order for there to be purpose. From rock bottom I rose up to a new height I'd never been before. I started to realize I wasn't attracted to recovery because I didn't want the life I had as a young person, for it was also riddled with despair and misery. I wanted to recover for an even better life. One with goals and a future I could only dream of in the past. I used the motivation of the wreck and my realization to come clean and improve my life. To work for the better future I always wanted.

I focused on the simple, small stuff and built my way up toward the person I wanted to be.

I have obtained the life I wanted.

I'm still very young into recovery, and if my dream life is already birthing from a little over a year clean, then what more must be in store for this new life! I must not dare keep it to myself. I have to share what I believe my Higher Power wants a dying world to know. There is hope for those who might have been deemed hopeless. I was once the lost cause and I made it through to say, "It is not too late. You can recover."

You can call me crazy, some do. I don't mind. I'm friends with law enforcement who once put me in cuffs. I am friends because I can see now they were just trying to save my life and keep the world a safe place for them and their families.

I don't remember every detail of Rebekah and my interactions with her during those times, my darkest moments, but that memory isn't essential to send the proper message. It is a privilege to call her my friend today. She cared enough about my daughter and me to never give up.

Some people I have known in my life have heard of the situation with Rebekah being called into court, accused of breaking and entering. They tried to get me to lie on the stand, to make her pay for the injustices. I had to have a moment with them and shed some light on reality. I told them that if they heard of an unstable young woman on drugs, who was trying to flee from justice, who had a criminal record of family violence and a mental health record, and they knew she was expecting to give birth to a baby and heard she did so by herself, alone at her house without seeking medical attention to protect herself, and they honestly didn't know if the baby was alive or dead, wouldn't opening someone else's door without their knowledge be the last thing on their mind?

Seriously, if it had been me, I'd probably have done a whole lot more to try and find the baby. It is crazy to me that people got upset that she had to go to such lengths to recover little babies who were in danger. It was my fault she had to find my daughter to begin with. I wasn't going to try to get her in trouble because she was trying to save my daughter's life! Absolutely not! That is insane!

I wasn't fully submerged in the recovery process like I am today when I was called to the stand to testify against her. I don't remember what I said. But I do know this, no matter my past and my wrongs, I always wanted to be a good person. I had a policy. I had to be honest. No matter what, I would tell the truth. Today, I'm so glad I did. I didn't understand the depths of what Rebekah was facing or what weight my testimony could offer, but I'm so glad it could help a woman who was put at war against her own horrifying disease. She came through and fought, by any means necessary, and became victorious. She set an example for all to see, that good does overcome all odds. She became a hero.

I have been blessed enough to get my life together. To gain a fundamental idea of recovery and to live it out daily. During my journey of recovery, I was blessed to cross paths with Rebekah through a friend, and I learned the outcome of that day in September of 2015.

I am so pleased it all worked out even though she had to go through a lot. I'm also so glad to have a positive effect in the situation, because that is what is right. Something I learned in recovery is to see that life is beautiful in all its ugliness. That some good can emerge from darkness. I'm honored to pass on a message to anyone who may or may not be struggling or knows someone who is, there is hope. Don't give up. You never know who you might help save. Just look at us!

I am pleased to be a part of such a wonderful experience. Special thanks to God for setting me on a journey that led me to this point today. A special thanks to my friend who told me about this unique opportunity, and an even more special thanks to Rebekah and her crew for adding my story at the last minute.

I am no longer ashamed of who I was because of who I am today.

The character in the book, C.J., is me.

My name is LA. And I am an addict.

An addict who is grateful to be in recovery.

(Full name I identify with is LA Williams. Also known as LA Hunt and LA Vargas.)

To You

Thank you for reading my story. Revisiting it to share it with you has brought me a chance for reflection and learning, and I hope that I was able to share that experience with you.

For those who are interested in further reading, the TCCA's opinion can be found at https://goo.gl/oueUYZ. Unfortunately, if you want to read the court records, you'll have to go to the Hunt County courthouse (Texas) in person and ask for a copy. If this is your desire, happy reading. It's over 400 pages long.

If you wish to follow me in the future, you can find me on Twitter at https://twitter.com/rthonginh.

About Me

Rebekah Thonginh works as a paralegal for Jessica McDonald and Associates, utilizing her experience from over fifteen years as a public servant to assist the two attorneys, Jessica and Abigail Spain, with cases involving CPS. She's a member of the State Bar of Texas Paralegal Division and enjoys conducting legal research for appeals handled by the firm.

Together, she and her husband have six children, five boys and a girl, ranging in ages twenty-one to six. She's the proud mother of an Eagle Scout and volunteers as a Cub Scout Den leader.

Book Synopsis

CPS investigator Rebekah Thonginh's only goal is to find a missing baby. The drug-addicted parents are in hiding, and no one knows if the baby is dead or alive. Blood covers a mattress and drips down the bedroom walls in their deserted home. Someone was dying, if they weren't dead already.

Determined to find the baby before it's too late, Rebekah relies on her court orders and sets upon a path that leads to her unprecedented arrest and conviction. With the future safety of children and CPS investigators on the line, she appeals until her case is heard in the highest criminal court in Texas.

For the first time, Rebekah Thonginh Ross reveals the details of the sensational cases the national news got wrong and how she fought for justice when all hope was lost.

List of Names

Attorneys

Bacon, Karen

Cuff, Cason

Edwards, Jessica

Golden, Daniel

Libby, Scott

Locker, Robert "Robbie"

London, Jason

Milner, George

Mowla, Michael

Schulte, Peter "Pete"

Wilford, Jack

Zimmerman, Erik

Cases

Amy, Angel, Jennifer, Gary Booksire, & Mr. M

Ashley Krank & James

C.J., Daisy, Nathan, Mary, John, & Tracey Perez

Cosette & Mikayla

Ms. Childs & family

Wanda Williamson & Son

CPS

Amaru, Rachel
Baldwin, Brittany
Franklin, Ester
Hart, Scarlet
Hayes, Alison
Jacobson, Justine
Lauren, Audrey
Laurence, Julia
Moss, Marissa
Patterson, Polly
Reynolds, Natalie
Ross, Rebekah Thonginh
Stinson, Kenderick
Wooten, Dick
Wright, Lori

Judges
Beechum, Roger
Dollar
Fench
Titan

Friends & Family
Ashmore, Sarah
Ling, Amy
Megan

Law Enforcement
Ballard, Officer
Banter, Officer
Black, Detective
Eve, Captain
Fumer, Detective

Hayes, Jett
Hilton, Officer
Johnson, Officer
Matthews, Officer
Minks, Sherriff
Richard, Officer
Watson, Sgt.
Wood, Officer

OIG
Carlos, Juan

Others
Christie, bail bond receptionist
Ennis, Theresa, journalist
Fawn, Kris, forensic interviewer
Fitz, May, professor

www.ingramcontent.com/pod-product-compliance
Lightning Source LLC
Chambersburg PA
CBHW022330280326
41934CB00006B/589